People in Crisis:

Strategic Therapeutic Interventions

People in Crisis:

Strategic Therapeutic Interventions

DIANA SULLIVAN EVERSTINE, Ph.D.
Director, Emergency Treatment Center
Mental Research Institute
Palo Alto, California

and

LOUIS EVERSTINE, Ph.D., M.P.H.
Director of Research and Evaluation
Emergency Treatment Center
Mental Research Institute
Palo Alto, California

 BRUNNER/MAZEL, *Publishers* • NEW YORK

Library of Congress Cataloging in Publication Data

Everstine, Diana Sullivan, 1944–
  People in crisis.

  Includes bibliographies and index.
  1. Family violence. 2. Victims of crime.
3. Suicide. 4. Crisis intervention (Psychiatry)
I. Everstine, Louis, 1933– . II. Title.
[DNLM: 1. Community mental health services.
2. Crisis intervention. WM 401 E93p]
RC569.5.F3E88   1983   616.85'8   82-23969
ISBN 0-87630-286-X

Copyright © 1983 by Diana Sullivan Everstine and Louis Everstine

Published by

BRUNNER/MAZEL, INC.
19 Union Square West
New York, New York 10003

MANUFACTURED IN THE UNITED STATES OF AMERICA

Foreword

When I was about eight years old and began to read the newspaper, I was puzzled and intrigued by the following report: A *Gendarme* (a member of the rural Austrian police force who in those distant days was heavily armed with sabre, pistol, and an army rifle) saw a man jump from a bridge into the Danube with the obvious intent of drowning himself. The officer leveled his rifle at the man and shouted, "Come out immediately or I'll shoot you!" The man swam ashore.

Over 50 years have passed since and the story intrigues me more than ever. I wish the policeman were still around and I could talk to him. Obviously he had not read Karl Menninger, Edwin Shneidman, or Milton Erickson. What obscure, innate understanding of the irrational side of human nature prompted him to take this utterly absurd, but superbly successful action?

Why is it that somebody as responsible and humane as Victor Frankl dares to ask a depressed person, "Why have you not yet committed suicide?" Why does this not push the patient over the brink, providing instead the motivation to take the first step out of his gloom? Why is it that an anorexic girl may stubbornly continue to starve herself while the members of her family implore her to stop her self-destructive behavior, but may begin to eat when Mara Selvini suggests that she should continue making her loyal sacrifice in the interest of the well-being and the survival of her family?

Enough of these rhetorical questions. They relate only to one aspect of this book. But what they do highlight is important: that our traditional training does not prepare us to deal with unusual, life-threatening situations in which immediate action is decisive, while the patient processes of reflective, passive listening, of uncovering, and of

v

consciousness-raising could result in the loss of sanity or even of life. There is, to begin with, an enormous difference between the human tragedies that may be revealed while we sit in the comfortable armchairs of our offices and those that erupt at the scenes of accidents or of violent crimes, or those communicated by an unknown voice on the telephone during the small hours of the morning, talking about the panic that this night will never terminate—about the experience of eternity within a square yard, as Dostoevsky once expressed it.

There is the important factor of territoriality that rarely, if ever, comes into play in the therapist's own office, simply because his office is *his* territory. But the emergencies that are the subject matter of this book and are the daily bread of the Emergency Treatment Center occur in other people's territory. To disregard this can be fatal—witness the number of policemen injured in the line of duty while trying to intervene in the violent interactions of family members in their own homes.

Finally, there is the fact that emergency psychology deals with events for which virtually nobody is prepared by previous experience and adequate emotional anticipation. We all drive cars, but how many of us know what it would be like to come to an emergency stop while traveling at 60 m.p.h.? We all have read accounts of earthquakes and believe we have some idea what the experience must be like—but the real experience of the earth shaking for seemingly interminable minutes or even seconds is, so we are told by those who know, something that cannot be imagined even remotely. How much more is that the case with the unimaginable experience of intense physical pain, the mind-shattering consequences of severe emotional trauma, the terrifying experience of blind rage, of beastly cruelty, and of the numerous other traumata described in this book that are capable of totally destroying the victim's long-held view of the world. To be of any help, the helper needs to know more than the leisurely, gentle techniques of traditional therapy, of the search for causes in the past, and of the appeal to reason. Emergency psychology and the ability to deal adequately with the manifestations of violent interaction are skills for which most of us, regardless of the extent of our clinical experience, are ill-prepared.

This book, written on the basis of many years of practical emergency work, is an important introduction to this difficult area of specialized therapeutic interventions. Depending on the reader's own professional and theoretical framework, he may agree or disagree with some of the authors' views. However, what matters in this connection is not the supposed truth of one doctrine or another regarding the *causes* of violent interaction, but rather the acquisition of skills in dealing with its concrete manifestations here and now.

PAUL WATZLAWICK, PH.D.

Contents

Introduction

About 3:30 in the afternoon a young mother is becoming anxious because her nine-year-old daughter has not yet returned home from school. Finally, she goes out to look for the little girl and finds her walking in a daze and crying. The girl's clothes are torn, and when the horrified mother asks what happened, the child bursts into tears and eventually becomes mute. Later, the mother discovers that her child has been molested.

6:30 p.m. George's mother throws a pot of hot coffee at him and the side of his face is burning. George is a 14-year-old boy whose mother is a divorced alcoholic. Strange men come to live with him and his mother, and none stays very long. There are many fights and his mother gets especially violent when she is drunk. Later tonight George will slip out of the house and run away. His mother will never see him again.

It's late at night and a car slows down on a deserted back street. Some men throw a young woman out of the car and drive away into the darkness. The woman lies there for a moment, stunned, and then slowly struggles to her feet. She has been raped and badly beaten. She stumbles along the street, murmuring something to herself, in a state of shock.

At 2:30 in the morning, a woman in her 30s runs wildly out of a house without knowing where she is going. She has been beaten severely by her husband. In her panic she doesn't realize that her lips are bleeding profusely, her face twisted with the pain of her feelings. Where can she go? What can she do? This is not the first time this has happened, and the friends she once had won't help because they don't want to get involved.

5:00 a.m. Mike has lived alone for too long and life has turned him down too often. He reaches across the bed for a bottle of sleeping pills, and washes the pills down with Southern Comfort. Soon he will go to sleep alone again, and this time he won't awaken.

To whom can people like these turn for help? Whom can they call? If they do make a call for help it is usually to the police, because a police department is the only agency they know of that works with people 24 hours a day and provides a service that is free of charge. Also, the police can respond directly to the scene of an emergency. But in reality what do police have to offer people who need help in emergencies such as these, apart from legal assistance? Police are schooled in halting disturbances, restoring order, hearing complaints, writing reports, and making investigations to identify guilty parties. But what of the emotional and psychological violence that these victims have endured?

What can a police officer do to help the mother and her child cope with the child's having been molested, and how can an officer prevent the ordeal from scarring both for the rest of their lives? What can police do to prevent the battered wife (who usually returns home to face more beatings) from becoming another homicide statistic? The woman who was raped will be left alone with ugly memories of brutality and humiliation, and it will be a long time before she will feel content with herself again. The suicidal Mike, lonely and desperate, may call the police for help, and if he does he will probably be given the telephone number of a hotline or an address of a distant clinic that will open its doors much later in the day. If he is lucky, someone will find him; if he is not, they won't.

People may think that these are among those rare and unusual kinds of events which only happen to others, but unfortunately these events are recorded daily on the dockets of most police departments, and apparently they are occurring with increasing frequency. According to *Uniform Crime Reports*, issued by the FBI, the nationwide incidence of violent crimes has risen each year since 1977. Table 1 shows this trend in graphic terms, representing the length of time that elapses between occurrences of these crimes anywhere in our country. Since the time lapse is declining from year to year, the table indicates that they are being committed more and more often, thus making it more likely that each of us could become a victim. For the same years, it is meaningful to note that (according to FBI reports) the incidence of "property" crimes—i.e., nonviolent offenses such as burglary, larceny, or car theft—has not increased concomitantly from year to year. Thus, while criminal acts in general are not necessarily happening more often, those which involve violent behavior have certainly occurred more frequently in recent years. The reality that leaps compelling from these data is that there are increasing numbers of crime victims in our society, and that their experience with crime has probably been extremely traumatic to them.

This trend occurs at a time of dwindling resources, in which public mental health care systems are being reduced in capacity and accessibility. In most communities, a victim must wait upon the 8 A.M. - 5 P.M. office hours of the majority of mental health professionals. And even if the victim gets to a clinic, success in resolving the problem will not come easily because the person must speak to a stranger at the re-

Table 1

Violent Crime Clock

Violent Offenses	1977	1978	1979	1980
Murder	27 minutes	27 minutes	24 minutes	23 minutes
Rape	8 minutes	8 minutes	7 minutes	6 minutes
Assault*	78 seconds	76 seconds	68 seconds	48 seconds
TOTAL**	31 seconds	30 seconds	27 seconds	24 seconds

*This category is formally called "aggravated assault," defined as "unlawful attack by one person upon another for the purpose of inflicting severe or aggravated bodily injury" (*Uniform Crime Reports*, 1978, p. 20).
**Includes "robbery"—a category that is not reported here—among the crimes referred to as "violent offenses."

ception desk who may not be of the same ethnic background or class, and tell the stranger that he or she had been raped or beaten or had attempted suicide the night before. In addition, at most public clinics, the victim must submit to a financial "evaluation" to determine his or her ability to pay the fee before being permitted to talk with a therapist. Because of the humiliation that a first experience of this sort can cause, few people who have psychological emergencies get the help that they desperately need. Many never return to the clinic to which they have made an exploratory visit.

Another reason why people often do not get the help they need is that many who are experiencing an emergency do not define it as being "mental" or psychological in nature. Moreover, when a referral to a mental health clinic is suggested, only in a minority of cases is contact established. (A study conducted in a Northern California police department revealed that fewer than 15 percent of the people whom the police Family Crisis Intervention Unit had referred to mental health agencies had subsequently made contact with the respective agency.) The fact is that many people are still fearful of mental health systems. They fear the stigma of being labeled as "crazy" or "neurotic," and they fear the social or occupational repercussions that may follow should someone find out about it.

For their part, mental health professionals have done a great deal to mystify themselves and their methods to lay people, especially those who are working-class or poor. Thus, because poor and working-class people generally feel that they understand the role of the police, they call the police instead of mental health professionals when they have an emergency. When they cannot obtain the help they need from the only source that they know and trust, a cycle of violence may be set in motion or prolonged.

This book addresses the current state of the art of providing professional mental health services for psychological emergencies. It presents a new model for the delivery of psychological care to a segment of the population which has not, until now, been served adequately, if at all. The principal function of the book is to propose strategies for intervention that will be useful to mental health professionals who choose to make themselves available for crisis work. In addition, these strategies may prove useful for clinicians who work with specific kinds of clients or cases (such as those referred to below), or when in the course of clinical practice a serious emergency arises.

The book begins with a description of the activities and achievements of the Emergency Treatment Center, a program of mental health care delivery that was established in 1975 by the authors and Dr. Arthur M. Bodin (Chapter 1). There follows a discussion of general principles concerning communication with people who are experiencing or have recently experienced extreme stress (Chapter 2). Next, a detailed description is given of specific techniques for intervening in situations that contain a high potential for violence—including suggestions for integrating the response of the mental health professional with the response of the police (Chapter 3).

Two chapters on family violence are presented, in which general strategies for working with families are discussed. (Chapter 4). Next, the phenomenon of couples who fight is examined (Chapter 5), with the syndrome of wife-battering addressed as a separate issue (Chapter 6).

Two chapters on children and adolescents follow, the first a discussion of the battered child or adolescent (Chapter 7), and the second dealing with children or adolescents who are sexually assaulted (Chapter 8). The subjects of incest and the dynamics of the incestuous family are taken up in Chapter 9.

Chapter 10 contains a general treatment of the subject of persons who have become victims of violent crimes, as well as a specific examination of the dynamics of being held hostage or being kidnapped. Then, a detailed discussion is presented of the characteristics of adult women who have been raped (Chapter 11).

In Chapter 12 a theoretical view of the causes of suicidal behavior is advanced, and methods of attempting to prevent suicide are proposed.

Finally Chapter 13 sets forth guidelines for the psychotherapist in respect to his or her legal duties and ethical responsibilities. The purpose of this section is to raise the consciousness of clinicians to their duties toward both clients and the public at large.

In general this book is intended to describe, examine, comment, and clarify. It has no other viewpoint than observation and analysis, and no other mission than to inform, suggest, and recommend.

Should any leap of faith be requested of the reader, it is simply that practical techniques of emergency psychology may prove useful in nonemergency situations, and that the best of therapeutic methods will be expected of those who intervene upon psychological emergencies.

REFERENCES

U.S. Department of Justice. Crime in the United States: 1977. *Uniform Crime Reports*, Washington, D. C., October 18, 1978.
U.S. Department of Justice. Crime in the United States: 1978. *Uniform Crime Reports*, Washington, D. C., October 24, 1979.
U.S. Department of Justice. Crime in the United States: 1979. *Uniform Crime Reports*, Washington, D. C., September 24, 1980.
U.S. Department of Justice. Crime in the United States: 1980. *Uniform Crime Reports*, Washington, D. C., September 10, 1981.

Acknowledgments

In a sense this book tells the story of the birth of a clinic, the Emergency Treatment Center. As with most institutional births, many were in attendance and a host of others wished the newcomer well. We shall extend our thanks to some of those people here.

There would have been no Center were it not for Dr. Arthur M. Bodin, who was originally its co-director (with Diana Everstine) and has remained a guiding force as its Senior Clinical Psychologist.

From the beginning, the Center was a welcome guest of the Mental Research Institute. Especially helpful among the MRI group was Dr. Paul Watzlawick, who contributed the Foreword to this volume as well as significant support and encouragement throughout the evolution of the work of the Center.

In its brief history, the Emergency Treatment Center has enjoyed many benefactors in the community which it serves. A few of these worthy persons are the Honorable Rebecca Morgan and the Honorable Rodney Diridon, Supervisors of Santa Clara County, and Lillian Silberstein, Director of the County's Victim-Witness Assistance Program.

The staff of our Center has been an expectionally loyal one, persevering even when the vagaries of public funding made its very existence uncertain. Dr. Eileen Valcov has been one of the Center's counselors since the first day, and David Rasch nearly as long. More recently, Dr. Richard Toft joined the staff and has been a creative contributor to the further development of the Center. Dr. Viola Mecke, who has lent her skills as Clinical Consultant, has helped us immeasurably in our work.

A hallmark of the program described in this book is the close association of the Center with local police agencies. We have enjoyed the cooperation of many officers in these departments, and we are especially grateful to Santa Clara County Sheriff Robert Winter, Lt. Rick Houston of the Sheriff's Department, and Sgt. Tom Sing, Sgt. Wes Bolling, and Deputy Jim Greer of the Sheriff's hostage negotiation team.

In other departments, officers who have been particularly helpful include Sgt. Bob Lockwood of Campbell, Officers Bob Stevenson and Russ Biehn of Sunnyvale, Sgt. Peter Graves and Sgt. Joe Weinreb of San Jose, Sgt. Lucy Carlton of Milpitas, Officer Steve Mello of Mountain View, and Officers Tony Hernandez and Stephanie Wheaton of Palo Alto.

The drafts of this book were carefully typed by Theresa Coombs and Claire Gilchrist, whom we thank for their perseverance. Our editors at Brunner/Mazel, Susan Barrows and Ann Alhadeff, helped us enormously by their concern, attention to detail, and patient indulgence. And Richard J. Kohlman gave us much-appreciated editorial support.

Finally, we are grateful to the many teachers who started us on this path, especially Dr. John Perry and Dr. Roy M. Hamlin, who encouraged us by example and gave us confidence by reflection. Our friends cheered us throughout the completion of this project, and we fondly thank Ray and Gerry and David and Lies, who shared with us the gracious hospitality of the family Roux at the Colombe d' Or.

People in Crisis:

Strategic Therapeutic Interventions

1

Emergency
psychology

THE PEOPLE

When the ancient Greeks made myths, their gods were drawn to such human scale that they experienced problems just as ordinary mortals do. If problems are universally distributed, our best reckoning tells us that they have found their way into the "stuff" that makes us human. And if problems are part of phylogeny, we should not be surprised to learn that even our best friends are beset by them. So it goes for the people next door and for a remote Sherpa tribesman. On those terms, this book is meant to pertain to nearly everyone. The purpose of the book is to describe techniques that may be useful for those who attempt to help people in solving their problems. The problems in question are not simple ones, and the recommended methods of helping people to resolve them are complex. This book differs from other books of its type, chiefly in respect to the kinds of problems that are addressed.

THE PROBLEM

Among the ills that flesh is heir to are the physical traumas of paralysis, heart attack, insulin coma, burn syndrome, and epileptic seizure. Without minimizing the terror that these assaults engender or the fear

3

that they inspire, some forms of psychological trauma can be equally horrific. In these chapters we are trying to describe what people who suffer acute psychological trauma feel and how they think. A second aim is to suggest to psychotherapists ways in which they can think and feel toward persons such as these. Above all, we seek to provide therapists with new methods of helping these people.

The problems that are created, inspired, and exacerbated by violence are the worst that can affect mental life. It is hard to imagine the force that rape, for example, can have upon the woman who has suffered that kind of attack. Who say that the physical violation caused her more distress or pain (however defined) than did the thoughts that filled her mind while the attack took place? What is the locus of defilement? Where do humiliation and depersonalization dwell? What place does rage inhabit, or feelings of despair?

These kinds of questions may have occurred to many mental health professionals and, as a result, our profession is trying to find a new perspective on this primitive traumatic event. In effect, while we may not be able to eliminate the crime of rape, we may be able to provide understanding and counsel for its victims. We are convinced that the physical brutality that is felt by a victim of rape is like the fraction of an iceberg that is found above the surface. Rape is not primarily a medical or even a law enforcement problem. Instead, it creates a psychological wound that can threaten the life of the mind.

Yet rape is only one of many psychological emergencies, and for that reason this book will isolate and subject to examination certain other sources of trauma, namely:

- child abuse
- child molestation
- incest
- family violence
- wife-beating
- suicidal behavior
- hospitalizing acutely disturbed persons

Historically, psychotherapists have largely subscribed to the view that these kinds of events are more symptoms than full-fledged disorders. For example, wife-beating was for many years looked upon as a form of marital conflict on the part of a couple whose male partner had a tendency toward acting out his fantasies of dominance, or in which an overly aggressive wife needed to be "put in her place." Until recently, child abuse was dismissed as excessively extra-punitive behavior on the part of a parent who strove to instill discipline in his or her child. The preceding are examples of a therapeutic environment whose ecology is in the beginning stages of change.

In the past, some deep-seated taboos of everyday life have been reflected in the guiding convictions of the mental health community. Notoriously, Freud found hysteria in his women clients during an era when hysteria was culturally determined. Freud and legions of followers gave more credence to incestuous fantasies than to incestual behavior as a reality, throughout many decades when few cultures would admit that incest was a commonplace occurrence. And for how long has the American credo, "Spare the rod and spoil the child," served to excuse parents who react violently toward their children (to the degree that some are maimed or disfigured for life)? For a long time our profession has permitted some of the values of society to repress our better judgment. While in this somnolent state, psychotherapy has to some extent become the victim of its own unanalyzed defenses. Much more of life is lived in the mind than was once believed; when we are hurt, the emotional wound must be attended to. When a trauma occurs in our lives, the psychological impact needs to be measured in some ways, monitored, and sooner or later provided with relief. In short, these tragic facts of life must be dealt with eventually.

In summary, a theme of this book is the treatment of persons who have suffered serious psychological trauma. Some of the problems to be addressed include those which are not the traditional focus of attention in most private practices or outpatient clinics. Such kinds of problems are, for all that, no less emotional or psychological in nature, and thus they dwell appropriately in psychotherapy's domain.

The process of opening new initiatives in a well-established profes-

sion entails not only providing motivation for change, but also recommending means to achieve new objectives, as well as options among
more than one method. Many clinicians will find, in these pages,
techniques of therapy that are very familiar to them and that they may
use in their work already; some of these techniques may strike them
as new. The authors do not claim that the methods of therapy proposed in this book are revealed truth. Instead, we are advocating a
certain cast of mind that may be useful to those who work with *these*
kinds of clients who suffer *these* sorts of problems.

In the next part of this chapter, the process followed by the authors
in founding a treatment center is recounted. The major relevance of
this narrative is not so much to describe the Center as to frame the
concepts of treatment upon which it was based. As these concepts are
discussed, it will become clear to the reader why we specialize in
working with these kinds of clients who have these sorts of problems.

THE CENTER

As a clinical enterprise, crisis intervention has a long past but a short
history. The concept of crisis intervention simply refers to making a
swift response to a human need. The paramedic services of most
American cities can be said to epitomize this model of care, and many
lay persons have come forward to volunteer for training in the art of
cardio-pulmonary resuscitation (CPR), so that they can lend a hand
before paramedics arrive. The reason for this admirable trend is that
an encouraging percentage of stricken lives can be saved by immediate intervention. An emphasis upon the importance of this kind of immediate response will characterize the descriptions to follow.

The Emergency Treatment Center (ETC) is an independent, non-
profit corporation that is affiliated with the Mental Research Institute
of Palo Alto, California. (For specific details of the Center's organiza-
tion, administration, and sources of funding, see Everstine, 1974;
Everstine et al., 1977, 1981.) As its name implies, ETC was established to provide an immediate service in cases of psychological emergency. It is not a clinic in the traditional sense and, as will be seen, it requires neither a building nor elaborate equipment. Since its first case

was accepted in February 1975, the Center has been in operation every hour of every single day.

ETC was created to provide help for emergency situations such as: family fights; suicide threats and attempts; cases in which a child or adolescent has run away or is beyond parental control; cases in which a person is thought to need hospitalization; cases of rape and child molestation; cases involving any form of child abuse, and/or any sort of personal or domestic upheaval for which people may seek help. If the person who is asking for help says that the situation is an emergency, then an emergency it is. (Should medical treatment be needed, ETC will see to it that medical help is dispatched at once.) The telephone number (292-HELP) is widely publicized, both through announcements on television and under *Crisis Intervention* on the inside cover of each telephone book that is distributed within the ETC area of service.

The Center is located in Santa Clara County, California, whose total population is approximately 1.5 million. The ETC service area encompasses roughly half the county's population (approximately 760,000 people).* The demographic composition of Santa Clara County is somewhat unique in its high percentage of children and adolescents. For example, within the ETC service area almost 20 percent of the population is between 10 and 17 years of age (County Census, 1975). One reason for this phenomenon is that large numbers of single parents have settled in the county, the typical such person being a divorced woman of approximately 30 years of age with one or two children.

The seven-day-a-week, 24-hour-a-day program of the Center is coordinated with the work of police agencies in each of the 12 cities located in our service area. Eight of those cities have their own police departments, while four others are served by the County Sheriff's department, with which ETC also works cooperatively. One reason for this close liaison with law enforcement agencies is that the majority of cases that are referred to ETC (i.e., not self-referred) come to us from

---

*Two other, similar agencies serve other regions of Santa Clara County.

the police. In Chapter 3, the procedures by which ETC coordinates its work with police agencies will be described in detail.

The basic rationale for the ETC program is a belief in the importance of reaching out to people in crisis. In effect, this view is a rejection of the traditional concept of a clinic or community mental health center where therapists wait until clients seek them out. We believe that the purpose of a clinic is essentially nullified if its doors are only open 40, 50, or even 60 hours per week. Our culture expects its law enforcement officers to be its guardians of the night (weekends and holidays included), and that is a role which most policemen and policewomen accept with pride. Even so, few officers indulge in the fantasy that they are skilled psychotherapists. But when a counselor is needed and no counselor can be found, the police do the best they can.

The ETC staff is on call at any hour of the day or night and responds directly to the scene of a crisis event. In this way ETC is able to offer service to persons who might otherwise have been unable to find their way to the local "mental health care delivery system," and who in turn may have called the police as a last resort. Since we often hear from them on referral from police, the people who call are often relieved to learn that ETC is not a part of the vast bureaucracy that is "public" mental health. The reason is that there is often a suspicion of the stigma attached to being a "mental patient" or to exhibiting some kind of emotional weakness or defect. The name "Emergency Treatment Center" was especially chosen for the purpose of neutralizing suspicion, avoiding that sort of label, and dispelling that type of fear.

The most important component of the ETC model is that of making an immediate response to a call for help. Moreover, no call for help is ignored, nor is any caller dismissed because he or she failed to insist that the matter was urgent. Each call is taken seriously. No person's need for concern and attention is discounted. Similarly, a police officer's judgment that help of a psychological nature is needed will al-

---

*The phrases "response to the scene" or "responding to the home" are derived from police jargon. They are used here in preference to "visit to the home," because the latter does not accurately describe the event in question. Instead, "response" both conveys the sense of urgency that attends each visit, and connotes the sense of answering a call for assistance.

ways be accepted at face value. At ETC, an emergency is in the eye of the beholder.

The second most important component of the ETC model lies in making a response to the scene at which the crisis is occurring. * Unlike those who conduct hotlines or host radio talk shows, our therapists do not presume to be able to help people resolve their problems in the course of a telephone conversation. We believe that a person who is experiencing an acute crisis, is in extreme emotional pain, has been the victim of a crime, has had the impulse to abuse a child, or is facing death by his or her own hand is entitled to the presence of another human being who is concerned and would help if a way could be found. For that reason our therapists go to the home of the caller, if the caller gives permission for them to do so. Or if the person prefers, the therapist will go somewhere else to meet him or her, for example, to the home of a neighbor or relative. Among the settings that clients have chosen for meeting ETC staff members are the lobby of a hotel, the emergency room of a hospital, a bar, an airport lounge, the parking lot of a motel, a doughnut shop, and a phone booth located in a shopping center. All-night restaurants are a common meeting place, especially for teenagers who have temporarily run away from home, or for wives who have been beaten and are ashamed of their bruises and too afraid to go back.

A third and no less vital component of the ETC model is a concentration of effort on seeing the emergency through to its resolution. It is not enough to respond promptly to wherever a person in crisis may be. What is needed in addition is the efficient application of effective therapy techniques. Those skills may be required at three o'clock in the morning, and most certainly they will have to be applied in a totally unfamiliar setting. Then, too, there will be a crisis going on, or at the very least a momentary truce will have been arranged just prior to the therapist's arrival. Part of the task of a clinician is to separate the current crisis from long-established, pathological patterns existing within the person or couple or family. Yet in an emergency situation, only primary issues of the moment should command the therapist's attention.

Most clinicians relish the rational and empathic process of learning to understand their clients, interpreting their symptoms, offering advice, monitoring progress, and so on. This process admittedly takes time, although our colleagues practicing brief therapy have convinced us that it needn't be interminable (Watzlawick et al., 1974). Further, the intellectual quality of emergency therapy is more akin to the brief therapy model in that it requires spontaneous strategic thinking, rapidly focused upon the problem at hand and no less insightful for being swiftly conceived. By contrast, the delectable but time-consuming process of interpreting a client's intrapsychic processes is not possible in a crisis situation. Because some of these aspects of figuring-out and seeing-through that are characteristic of traditional, long-term psychotherapy are inappropriate to emergency work, there are some clinicians who would not enjoy the ETC experience.

The sort of person who takes pleasure in the ETC approach and does well at it is likely to be a young clinician who has recently completed training in an institutional setting, and who wants to find out what doing therapy in the "real world" is like. This does not mean that the average age of ETC staff members is especially young, because a majority of the staff are established professionals who combine emergency work with traditional private practice; in fact, the oldest member of our group recently celebrated his 60th birthday. But it does mean that the perspective of the emergency therapist, no matter what his or her age, should be somewhat adventuresome. When a therapist receives a call from a police officer in the wee hours of the morning, or the therapist's radio pager begins to beep while driving along a highway, the emotions felt are a mixture of exhilaration and fear. When entering the home of a stranger, a therapist knows that anything can happen.

Emergencies require caring people who have inquiring minds and a minimum of timidity. They also should have received *more comprehensive* and *better* training in therapy techniques than have persons who work in nonemergency settings. This view is reinforced by recent developments in medical care—for example, the fact that hospital emergency room medicine has become a separate entity for which physicians, nurses, and technicians receive specialized, intensive training. Hospital management has demonstrated, by this trend, a wish to staff its "front line" with uniquely trained personnel. * At

ETC we share these sentiments. When a mental health professional intervenes in a situation that may portend a break with reality, physical injury, or even self-inflicted death, that clinician must be a highly skilled therapist indeed.

Finally, the ETC differs from many emergency services in that those who respond to the crisis calls will be the ones who provide continuing therapy after the crisis is past. This component of the ETC model is extremely significant in that it enables our clinicians to take full advantage of the considerable rapport and understanding which have been gained during the emergency response. As a consequence, the Center has found great success in inducing difficult or high-risk clients to follow through with recommended treatment. Simultaneously, a therapist is enabled to view the crisis situation as the beginning of a therapeutic process in which he or she is likely to be centrally involved. This approach helps us avoid the unfortunate tendency of some emergency services to do no more than extinguish "brush fires."

To summarize, the benchmarks of the ETC model are these:

1) Responding immediately, while the emergency is still an emergency.

2) Active and creative, as opposed to passive, responding, i.e., being able to answer the acute needs of the client and the situation, instead of expecting the client to seek out therapy.

3) Providing the best available care, by specially trained therapists, for the express purpose of seeing the emergency through to its resolution, including ongoing treatment when necessary.

These distinguishing characteristics of the Center are innovative only in the way in which their elements are combined. By no means do we

---

*In the mental health field, no evidence of a similar trend exists. In fact, the opposite is taking place, as paraprofessional staff are increasingly employed in psychiatric wards for the purpose of cutting personnel costs. This development notwithstanding, the authors take the view that because hospitalized patients are the most ill they deserve the highest level of care.

claim to have invented the home visit or to have discovered crisis intervention. As will be seen in the chapters to follow, the difference is one of emphasis and the novelty lies in a new conceptual approach.

Some years ago the theorist, Gerald Caplan, identified three categories of *prevention* in respect to mental illness, namely, primary, secondary, and tertiary prevention (1964). Of the three, only secondary prevention is relevant in this context, for it refers to the early identification of mental illness. Early identification is an important preventive measure, because it implies the discovery of pathology before it becomes exacerbated, or symptoms before they are compounded into syndromes, or even difficulties before they escalate into problems. But although Caplan's work in describing levels of prevention was widely read, discussed, and quoted, little has been done in our country to implement his ideas. Few programs at any level have been given more than token funding, or have been sustained long enough to prove whether or not they could reduce the incidence of new cases of illness. There is no nationwide program of mental illness prevention, much less one designed to promote, foster, or enhance mental health.

One day these desirable aims may be fully realized. For the present, the Center's emergency program effectively demonstrates the secondary prevention model in action. By making our services known to the widest possible public, including each economic level and minority group within the community, we seek to reach people who may be at risk of becoming mentally ill. By swiftly meeting their needs, we may be able to accomplish more by prevention than by treatment per se. In addition, the application of brief therapy techniques makes it possible to keep follow-up treatment to a minimum of visits, reducing the treatment costs per case, and avoiding the consequent intrusion upon the life of the client.

The preceding account of the rationale and purpose of the ETC is intended to be conceptual in nature, by way of an introduction to ETC. In general terms, it serves to clarify how ETC comes into contact with persons experiencing acute psychological emergencies and delineates the larger scale objectives of our program. Step-by-step procedures of the emergency response are included in Chapter 3, and treatment methods are presented in subsequent chapters. The following in an account of the principal types of cases that are seen by the Center, as well as other relevant quantitative data concerning the ETC program.

SOME FACTS AND FIGURES

Each year, ETC opens approximately 700 new cases—individual, couple, and family. The initial emergency visits to these clients last, on the average, 3.3 hours. This fact presents a sharp contrast with the average length of the first visit to a therapist who works in a clinic setting, which is not likely to exceed one hour at the most. In reality, the client of a public clinic may be required to spend the first half-hour of an initial visit filling out forms or being interviewed by a clerical worker, in order to find out whether or not he or she is eligible for free treatment by the clinic.

The average length of time that elapses between the first call for help and the arrival of an ETC team at the scene of an emergency is 20 minutes. By means of radio pagers, the staff members on duty are in direct contact at any time with the answering service that responds to calls made to the 292-HELP telephone number. When paged, a therapist calls the answering service, receives the message, and then calls a co-therapist to provide information about the address and estimated time of arrival. This approach takes advantage of available technology to coordinate and accelerate the ETC mobile response.

Follow-up counseling is a key element of the work of the Center. Each year ETC provides, on the average, nearly 1,800 follow-up visits to its clients (in addition to the initial emergency visit). These visits last, on the average, 1.7 hours. When these data are contrasted with the data concerning emergency visits, this fact emerges: Of the total of 4,893 hours of service provided in an average year, 45 percent are hours of emergency counseling at the moment when a crisis is taking place.

Who are the gatekeepers to this emergency program? Above all, the clients refer themselves. Each year, on the average, more than 200 new clients find our telephone number in the Yellow Pages or learn about us in a televised Public Service Announcement, in newspaper articles describing the Center, or in a poster on a school bulletin board. In addition, as referred to above, many new cases which are not self-referred come to us from police agencies—at least 100 such cases per year, on the average. Another large source of new case referrals is the local Juvenile Probation Department; each year, approximately 90 such referrals to ETC are made by probation officers. In addition, about 50 new cases are referred each year by teachers or school counselors. The above-mentioned are merely the chief referral sources from which ETC receives cases. Other cases come from mental health agencies of every kind, the courts, physicians of nearly every specialty, hospitals, hotlines that advertise advice for suicidal persons, parents who may abuse their children, or drug or alcohol abusers, etc.

BEYOND THE MODEL

Providing a service for those who have suffered psychological trauma by no means requires an emergency program such as that of ETC. As will be clear from the perspective of later chapters, certain advantages in therapy are gained by immediate intervention at a moment of crisis (by analogy with the treatment of severe burns, for example, in which rate of recovery is highly correlated with the speed at which therapy is begun). It is equally true that psychological trauma must not be ignored and that its effects will not disappear by themselves. It is also true that a therapist who helps to alleviate trauma when it is most severe will have a better opportunity to help with the *later* stages of conflict resolution. Even so, making an immediate response to the scene of a crisis is simply not feasible for many clinicians. Yet this should not deter any therapist from making a place in his or her caseload for victims of crimes or those who have sought help in an emergency. In addition, caring clinicians can open their doors to those who otherwise have attempted to avoid the mental health system, because of the stigma associated with being a client in that system.

A key to finding the kinds of cases referred to in this book is, above all, a wish to do so—a species of concern. The difficulty lies not so much in finding cases as in finding well-trained clinicians who will take them on. While more and more listening posts are being provided for people who seek help, the helping professions need to be ready to assume their share of the work.

REFERENCES

Caplan, G. *Principles of Preventive Psychiatry*. New York: Basic Books, 1964.

Everstine, D. S. *The Mobile Emergency Team*. Unpublished Doctoral Dissertation, California School of Professional Psychology, 1974.

Everstine, D. S., Bodin, A. M., and Everstine, L. Emergency psychology: A mobile service for police crisis calls. *Family Process*, 16, 3:281-292, 1977.

Everstine, D. S., Everstine, L., and Bodin, A. M. The treatment of psychological emergencies. In J. R. Hays (Ed.), *Violence and the Violent Individual*. New York: SP Medical and Scientific Books, 1981.

Santa Clara County, California. Planning Department: Census, 1975.

Watzlawick, P., Weakland, J. H., and Fisch, R. *Change*. New York: W. W. Norton, 1974.

2

Communication principles for high stress or dangerous situations

This chapter discusses aspects of communication that pertain when dealing with extremely agitated or angry people, as well as communicating with people under acutely stressful conditions. Even though many of these methods are drawn from our experience in hostage negotiation, the communication principles discussed here are applicable to a wide range of problem situations, e.g., working with a violent family or with a person who is threatening to commit suicide. Some of these principles may seem simplistic because it is the clinician's own language that is being discussed, but it is easy *not* to notice how language is used. It is easy to relax and become sloppy, and to fall into language patterns that would probably go unnoticed in everyday life but might cause problems should a therapist become involved in a high stress situation.

To begin with, some basic rules of communication will be reviewed, the first of which is that a person "cannot NOT communicate" (Watzlawick, 1964, p. 2). When one person says "Hello" and the other person says nothing and turns away, the second person has communicated something quite clearly.

The second basic rule is that human communication is a "multilevel phenomenon" (Watzlawick, 1964, p. 3). In fact, an attempt at communication may prove meaningless when it is reduced to one level. When a person speaks in a way that ignores the *context* of the communication, what is said can very likely be meaningless. Should a person say, "I am not the person who is speaking to you," the sentence must sound odd because it doesn't fit within the context in which it was uttered. Thus, communication has content, which is the information that the individual is conveying, and communication can only occur in a specific *context*. For example, when someone is in a store and the salesperson walks up and says, "May I help you?", that remark is seldom prefaced with, "I am a salesperson and my job in this store is to sell you something." That fact is understood and the relationship of employee to prospective customer is already established. In general, disagreement about the *content* of communication may be resolved quite easily. That is, if someone walks up to a person and says, "You're blue," the person can say, "No, I'm not. My sweater is blue, my face is flesh-colored, and my hair is brown"; both can then appeal to a third party to settle the disagreement. And if someone says that the earth revolves around the moon, the hearer can verify or disqualify the assertion. However, in respect to *context*, disagreements can become more complicated and much more emotionally charged, as will be shown in this chapter.

Contextual disagreements arise in respect to how one person in a conversation misperceives the other, or how one has managed to misunderstand what the other said. While we may like to think that we live in a world of reality, *the reality is that we live in a world of personal opinion* (Watzlawick, 1976). Much of what each of us considers to be reality consists of the sum total of our personally arrived-at, and absolutely unique, set of opinions. This fact is vitally important when a therapist is engaged in a crisis situation. In such a situation, it is highly probable that the clinician will be attempting to communicate with a person who does not share his or her reality or perceptions of the world. The other person may inhabit a totally different value system, may come from a totally different socioeconomic background, and may represent a different ethnic group; moreover, he or she may not have been born in this country. The issues of relationship, and how another person thinks that he or she is perceived, may become critical in communicating with people in psychological emergencies and other high stress situations.

One of the clinician's primary tasks is to understand the "world view" of the person in crisis and to communicate with him or her in a way which is consonant with that view. When this world view is examined carefully, the clinician will probably discover a discrepancy between the conception of present reality of the person in crisis and the clinician's own conception. (For a detailed discussion of how world images may be discrepant from reality, see Watzlawick, 1978, Chapter 5.) When contradictions of this type are observed, a clinician has essentially two options: 1) change the reality conditions which pertain to the person, e.g., by attempting to "make deals" or give practical advice or persuade people whom the person in crisis has mentioned as being significant to come to the scene; or 2) work toward changing the world view of the person in crisis. While the latter course of action may seem an impossible task, it is often the first choice of a skilled therapist and the wiser course of action in most instances. By contrast, changing reality conditions may be very difficult indeed; in fact, any rapid change in those conditions may be disbelieved by the person in crisis, in which case it will not have the desired effect. Instead, a clinician usually tries to help the person in crisis to change his or her perceptions of reality in such a way that the person can see alternative, nonviolent means of resolving current problems.

A third basic rule of communication is that "message sent is not necessarily message received" (Watzlawick, 1964, p. 4). Just because one person has said something does not mean that the other person has understood what was said. Often we assume that the people to whom we are speaking share our views, our values, and our feelings, and we assume that certain words have the same connotations for others as for us. It is helpful to imagine a series of events such as the following: One person, a therapist, says something to another, a person in crisis. The therapist assumes that the person understood what was said, i.e., understood both the denotative meaning and the connotations of the words in the message. But actually the person in crisis has, in some way, misunderstood what the clinician said, and the reply is based upon that misunderstanding. Next, the therapist replies to what the person in crisis replied, which was based upon misunderstanding in the first place, and so it goes back and forth.

Another example to which this rule of communication applies is that of a couple who were being seen for counseling. It was not a seriously disturbed relationship, although the two had trouble in communicating because of their very different ethnic backgrounds (she was Scandinavian and he was from a second-generation Latin family). One of their main problems concerned a woman friend of the wife, about whom they had been arguing for at least six months. While the husband hated his wife's friend, the wife felt that she should defend her. The husband's view was that the friend was immature, loud, and inconsiderate of her own husband.

In counseling, one of the first things each was asked to do was to give a detailed description of the woman in question, with this instruction: "I want to make sure that I hear both sides of the story. I want you to take turns in describing the person to me." When they described her, it seemed as though they were both saying similar things about this woman, and for that reason the counselor asked for more details from each, i.e., "Did you mean such-and-such?" After some time had been devoted to this form of translation from one person's English to the other's, they realized that the particular words each had been using were being perceived as inflammatory by the other. Apparently, because of their different cultural backgrounds, the same words had acquired differing connotations (in effect, differing meanings). Thus ended the misunderstanding. When the session was over, the partners had become aware that they shared a mutual dislike for the woman friend. This example shows how misunderstandings can arise when two people forget that the message sent is not necessarily the message received. The tendency to forget that rule is enhanced when a therapist is under marked stress and is trying to communicate with a total stranger, by definition a person who is probably very different from the therapist.

People begin to structure and to set rules for their relationship as soon as they first meet. This is very important in high stress or emergency situations because a clinician will want to be in control of the development of this relationship while therapy is proceeding. The therapist will want to guide this relationship in such a way that the person in crisis will be so comfortable with the relationship that he or she may form an attachment with the therapist. Establishing a strong attachment may make it possible to induce the person in crisis to be a helpful participant in resolving the emergency. What is said (content) by the therapist will be particularly vital, because he/she may not always have the luxury of employing other channels of communication such as the nonverbal, or time to indulge in meta-communication (discussion about the communication itself) in the heat of the moment. In many cases, a therapist will be talking on the telephone with a potentially suicidal person who cannot see facial expressions or the subtle gestures which often accompany speech; for example, the other person will not know when the clinician smiles or looks worried or concerned. Each will "read" the other only by means of sounds conveyed by a telephone.

In point of fact, English is a very difficult medium for the establishment of relationships. Many other languages have a relationship "code" built into them. For example, French has a familiar mode of addressing another person, the "tu" mode, and a formal mode in which the word "vous" is used (both words mean "you"). Many other languages employ the two-mode system, but these mutually exclusive modes do not exist in English. Considerable social information is built into the structure of languages other than English, and many Europeans who visit here think that we are rude because we are seldom sensitive to social factors in the way we speak. To some degree their judgment is correct, since it is very easy to make mistakes in respect to matters of relationship, especially along the dimension of formality versus intimacy. The French expression "tu-toi" means that a close or intimate relationship has been formed between two persons, such as when a man and a woman are getting close romantically. The grammatical structure of language (as opposed to the actual content) is being used, in this instance, to describe certain qualities of an interaction. Because English lacks this distinction, it provides more opportunities to make a mistake, overlook a "boundary," or get too intimate too soon with another person.

Establishing a relationship through language is a very subtle process, but one whose importance cannot be overly emphasized. For example, this process is especially important when attempting to reason with a psychotic person in crisis, because many psychotics are terrified by close relationships and feel extremely threatened when people try to establish closeness early in a relationship. Thus, making this kind of mistake in the relationship aspect of language can serve to rapidly accelerate the other person's level of anxiety. What is required is restraint, sensitivity, and clarity of expression.

Disagreements about the relationship aspect of communication are often painful and difficult to resolve. The reason is that when two people disagree about the relationship aspect of their communication, it may signify that one person's wish to be seen in a certain light is not being fulfilled. In effect, one person may be interpreting the other's behavior as containing the message: "I don't see you as a person worthy of respect or value; I see you as someone with whom I have a right to take liberties." That kind of approach would be especially dangerous when applied to someone who is struggling with inner feelings of impotence or helplessness. One of the reasons why he (or she) is acting out is to force others to see him (or her) in the way he (or she) wishes to see himself (or herself), namely, as a powerful person. If a clinician makes some slip that could lead the person to think that the clinician does not view him as he views himself, the person may become enraged. People such as these, beneath their outward grandiosity, may feel deeply inadequate, and anything a therapist may do to reinforce this feeling of inadequacy can lead to an escalation of violence.

Two basic kinds of human relationships are called "complementary" and "symmetrical." The classic complementary relationship is that of mother and child. In a complementary relationship, one person is dominant or superior and one person is submissive or inferior; one person defines the relationship and the other accepts the definition (this does not have anything to do with strength or weakness per se, and in fact the "weaker" or submissive person may powerfully affect the relationship). A symmetrical relationship exists between two equals or two people who view each other with equality.

The most common disagreement about any relationship occurs when one person defines the relationship as symmetrical and the other person defines it as complementary. One person asks to be treated as an equal and the other responds by treating the person as inferior (or even as superior). If a therapist treats someone as superior and the person is uncomfortable about that (i.e., is afraid of being treated as superior), he or she may become hostile.

A clinician should be quite cautious about how the relationship is worked out with someone in a high-risk situation such as hostage negotiation. Because the clinician should strive to be extremely flexible in the kinds of positions taken, patience is recommended in these circumstances. It is important to listen for clues that will tell how the person in crisis wants or needs to define the relationship. For example, if the therapist is negotiating with a hostage-taker who is a known criminal and who may view him- or herself as a loser, that person may become very uncomfortable if the clinician treats him or her with deference. He or she may be more comfortable if the clinician takes a relatively more superior position when defining the relationship for the purpose of communication.

A common error that people make when they are frightened and are trying to be friendly is speaking to someone whom they don't really know in a manner that is too familiar—for example, by first name or nickname. People's names are very important to them, and they have deeply rooted and highly emotional feelings about their names. When first meeting someone named "Peter," the clinician may not know that his mother, whom he hated, had been responsible for giving him that name, or that he may have resented that name all his life. Because he always wanted to be named "Tony," it may be that his friends call him that; using his name, or a nickname such as "Pete," may be a source of great embarrassment to him.

When asking about the person's name, it is important to find out what he prefers to be called; for example, "Do you like to be called 'Pete' or is there another name that you prefer?" Most people will respond to that kind of question because it is a courtesy that they respect. When in doubt, it is wise to avoid the presumption of an intimacy that does not, or cannot, exist. In many cultures, first names are not used unless the people have known each other for a long time. For example, it shocks most people of Latin extraction when, within minutes after they have been introduced, Americans use their first names when speaking to them.

The same principles apply to establishing a relationship with someone who is being treated in a crisis situation. If a therapist is talking to a person who has a very low sense of self-esteem—someone who is acting out in sudden rage, holding hostages, or suicidal—this person may be wielding power for the first time in his or her life. Thus, referring to such a person by a first name or nickname could challenge his or her illusion of power; worse yet, there may be no awareness of doing this.

A basic first step would be to introduce oneself and to ask the person in crisis what he or she would like to be called. If the person refuses to reply, it is best to give up on that point and simply refer to the person as "you." If the therapist has been talking with someone for a long time and begins to feel awkward, he or she may wish to ask something like this: "I am uncomfortable calling you 'you'; would you mind telling me your first name, or a name that we can use for the time being?" If there is considerable reluctance, the question should not be pursued. The person may be either terribly frightened or psychologically disturbed, and may wish to hide his or her identity for the time being. The best tactic is to "take what is there," trying to understand the person's psychological state in that precise moment and trying to get a "feel" for the person as an individual. This approach is particularly vital when dealing with someone who is psychotic—that is, someone who may be thinking in a very primitive way, with an undercurrent of magical thinking. Even though what the person says and does may be very bizarre, the therapist should not assume that the person is insensitive or stupid; on the contrary, he or she is probably listening most carefully to every word.

There are other aspects of the way in which we communicate that may facilitate or hinder successful negotiation under stress. A common error is to use the royal "we." Even when attempting to be friendly, "we" usually sounds condescending unless the speaker is referring to something that the speaker and the other person are going to do together. What is more important is to focus upon, and try to understand, the other person's world—to be "in his place" for a moment. In this context, Weakland and Jackson's (1958) concept of the "illusion of alternatives" is especially relevant. Erickson has described a situation that occurred when he was a young boy growing up in a family which kept hogs and chickens (Erickson et al., 1976): He noticed that his father would ask him whether he would like to feed the chickens or the hogs first. The son was being given the illusion that he had a choice, when in fact he did not, because he did not have the choice of whether or not to work at all. His father had conveniently omitted the third possible option, which was to refuse to feed both the hogs and the chickens and, in effect, to loaf.

An extension of this concept can be found in the art of political sloganeering. Watzlawick cited the example of a Nazi slogan that was phrased as a question, namely, "National Socialism or Bolshevik chaos?", which omitted alternative choices (1978, p. 68). In order to make use of this concept successfully, it is necessary for the person who would use it to have a clear understanding of the other person's "world view," and to fit the choices (however illusory) carefully to the template provided by that world view.

In order to understand other people's world image fully, it is necessary to listen carefully to their use of language to describe this personal "world." Do they speak in terms of abstract ideas or emotions and feelings? What do they select from their environment to pay attention to or ignore? As a clinician gains knowledge of a person's image of the world, he or she realizes that, out of millions of possible choices, only a few choices will fit within that particular person's world view. The next task is to discover what this person's choices are, and whether or not they were made under the delusion of a free choice among alternatives. (In Chapter 3, this concept will be discussed further, especially as it pertains to actual clinical intervention in crisis situations.)

Early in this process, it is important to get the person to agree with something, i.e., to say "yes," by inducing him or her to answer trivial questions in the affirmative. The therapist should see how frequently he or she can be led to say "yes" or "okay" by means of verbal feelers —e.g., "Will you think about that for a while?" "Does that make sense to you?" or "Can we agree about that?" When the person begins to respond to seemingly trivial requests, the therapist may be getting somewhere. Positive language has much more influence than negative language (Watzlawick, 1978).

Another important nuance of negotiating with a stranger is to focus upon behavior. This strategy can help the therapist avoid doing something that can cause people to become very angry, namely, "mind reading." This presumptuous behavior implies, to the other person, that one knows what the other is thinking or feeling. For example, if a therapist says, "You are afraid, aren't you?", he or she gives the impression of knowing what the other person is feeling. Instead, the clinician may say, "What you said just now makes me think that you are afraid. Are you?" In that way he or she gives the other person psychological "room" to explain or to deny a feeling. In the same way, these two utterances may sound similar but are quite different: "You're hostile" differs from "What you said sounded hostile. Did I say something to make you angry?" The first utterance implies "You are a hostile person" (i.e., "You are bad; there is something in you that is not right"). The second says: "Your words [not something that I am 'reading into' your words] sound angry, and I am trying to understand why you said them." It is a subtle but an important difference.

The therapist should try not to assume intimacy or friendship when he or she doesn't know a person. It is best to avoid making statements like: "You're a nice guy." A therapist may mean well and want to reassure an angry, frightened person by saying that, but the other person may think: "How do you know I'm a nice guy? You don't know me." Among those who may be acting out in a crisis, many do not think of themselves as nice people; many have a low sense of self-esteem. For that reason, the clinicians should avoid giving the impression of judging the other person's character or figuring out his or her intentions. The clinician should also avoid projecting his or her own wishes onto another, but rather focus upon behavior. For example, "What you did for that person was really kind" or "What you said made sense" are credible statements because they have a basis in reality as opposed to personal assumptions or fantasies.

When describing or explaining something (an event or an action or a statement), it is important to keep the presentation simple and avoid words like "always," "never," "any," or "all"—for example, "You *always* say that" or "That's *all* I'm asking you to do." The reason is that "always" seldom happens and "never" is rare, and exaggerated statements of this kind have a patronizing tone to them. It's easy for the therapist to slip into speaking in this manner, particularly when he or she is excited, wants to make a telling point, or is under pressure and not thinking about how he or she sounds.

This also applies to making a request: Keep it very simple and direct. For instance, asking, "Would you mind giving me the gun?" may prompt the person to respond by saying, "That's right, I would mind giving you the gun," which is a logical, and probably an honest, response to the question that was asked. In this case, poor communication has caused a delay in solving the main problem, namely that the clinician wants that gun. The therapist is scarcely concerned about whether or not the person would "mind" handing over the gun. Another condescending way of making a request is the following: "Would you like to open that door?", which implies that the person should 1) open the door and 2) enjoy doing so (like a "good child"). A final example of a well-intentioned question which confuses the issue is: "Why don't you tell me why you are angry?" The person may tell you why he won't tell you rather than saying why he is angry. "Please tell me why you are angry" is simple and direct and does not get the conversation sidetracked onto absurd issues.

When talking with disturbed persons, it is important to avoid some of the demeaning ways in which some parents speak to their children. Many such persons have had poor relationships with their parents, and when a therapist phrases a comment or question in ways that are parental, he or she may provoke the person to become angry or to "project" onto the clinician a role as substitute for his or her parent. Most people do things for specific reasons, and an acutely disturbed person may be no exception. The disturbed person's system of logic may differ considerably from the therapist's, but *there is a system,* and it is the task of a therapist to discover what that system is. When it is discovered, the person's behavior may make much more sense. Most people, even when agitated, will follow a request as long as the request is presented in a polite and reasonable way, e.g., "Please give me the gun." "Please" is a word that many people in authority are afraid of, or one whose usefulness they have forgotten. Many people in crisis feel trapped and don't know what to do. If a clinician can propose a reasonable way for the person to get out of the situation and save face in the bargain, the person may take it. This process may, however, take considerable time.

When asking questions, the clinician should try not to challenge the ability of the person in crisis to perform a task; for example, he or she should avoid asking: "Could you do that?" or "Can you give me the gun?" The questioner wants to know whether or not the person *will* do something, not whether he *can* or *cannot*. To question another person's ability is insulting and puts the person questioned into a child's position. Questions like that often make an adult (particularly an adult who has low self-esteem) feel angry or insulted without his or her being aware of why it is happening. Another important point to be aware of when communicating with someone in a crisis situation is not to say things that guarantee or promise, unless one is sure that one can do what has been promised. If the guarantee fails or the promise is not performed, credibility will have vanished. A humble stand is preferable, i.e., "I'm going to try to do what I can."

Whenever limits must be set with a person in crisis, they should be framed in the way suggested by this example: A therapist who is trying to convince an agitated, psychotic patient to surrender a weapon and agree to go to the hospital might say, "I want to help you, but you need to go to the hospital for me to do so. I don't think the police out here are going to let you shoot anyone, and I don't think they are going to let you go. So what are you going to do?" In this way, the interaction does not remain one-up/one-down or superior/subordinate anymore, and this approach can be used in many situations. This manner of speaking conveys to a person in crisis that the clinician is concerned and will try to help; but, at the same time, the person should not think the clinician so "involved" that he or she can be manipulated.

Suicidal people can be manipulative in this way, if they think that a person is very concerned about them. They will threaten self-destructive things to make the other person feel guilty or sorry, so that he or she will do what they want. The clinician can respond to a suicidal person with this basic message: "I am concerned; I don't want you to hurt yourself, but it is really your business if you want to do that." It is an honest and a credible statement, and it is also one that the person cannot use for manipulative purposes. The same idea applies to other potentially violent situations because, if the therapist overreacts and shows too much concern when someone acts out and threatens to harm another person, that overreaction can reinforce the prior threat. If someone is hurt and a clinician hears a scream and overreacts, the person who is acting out may have decided that the best way to put pressure upon the clinician is to harm the person again. In this sort of situation, the therapist should try to take the focus off the injured person and, instead, place the focus upon what the acting-out person wants and needs. The reason is that keeping the focus upon the person who has been hurt, and reacting primarily when something has happened or when a threat is made, can make the acting-out person *even more reluctant* to release or stop hurting the other. A therapist can inquire concerning the health of the injured person, but it is better to do that at a time when the acting-out person is not interacting with the victim if possible, or at a moment when the stress level is relatively low.

Effective communication in emergency situations often demands time in abundance, and with it considerable patience and careful thought. These requirements may be difficult to meet, especially because many people who do emergency work are oriented toward action. But the slower the pace of communication in such a situation, the longer it will last and the more likely it is to be successful. Waiting and listening carefully to what is said will give a therapist more time to frame responses precisely. A response can either stimulate more acting-out behavior or encourage calm behavior and thus lower the stress level of the situation. When deliberate and thoughtful, a therapist's own behavior gives this subtle but important message: "I want to listen to you; what you say is important."

When communicating, the therapist should try to avoid predicting future events and making promises, but rather talk only about what is known. If it is necessary to talk of the future, it is preferable not to sound optimistic because the acting-out person knows that his or her future prospects are probably not bright, and thus the clinician will not be believed. Do not give guarantees. When speaking of something the therapist is planning to try in the future, he or she should always acknowledge that there will probably be a measure of difficulty in getting it done. In case a significant positive change in the situation occurs, it is better to try to plan it so that the person in crisis can be given credit for the change. In that way, he or she can feel responsible for the eventual successful outcome of the negotiation, and the therapist can avoid being seen as someone who has the power to make things happen. The correct position of the clinician is neutral, not that of a person who possesses power. The reason is that if the clinician is seen as having power, the acting-out person is going to try to manipulate the clinician into doing what he or she wants done, for example, making concessions or granting favors. This neutral position is sometimes difficult for an action-oriented person to take, but it is of vital importance in potentially violent situations.

The power of praise is too often misused in high-stress interactions. Praise should be formulated thoughtfully and expressed with care. Self-reflection will confirm that it is very, very hard to accept praise from someone whom one does not know and does not trust, particularly when frightened or angry. In fact, there are times when praise can make a person angrier than either a neutral statement or criticism—if the person does not trust or believe the praise. Since most of us have at least potentially successful careers and positive life scripts, it is easy for us to forget how threatening praise can be to some people in certain contexts. A therapist is probably not someone who has been in and out of clinics or hospitals or jails all his life, nor someone whose life has meant continual humiliation, failure, and loss. When communicating with a person whose own sense of self-esteem is obviously low, the therapist may wish to insert a compliment between two neutral or two negative statements—for example, "You've had a rough life and you are in a very bad spot, but it's amazing that you have managed as long as you have. You're probably a strong person, but I don't know if you are ready to hear that right now." Embedded in those statements is a compliment. By framing or embedding compliments in this way, the clinician can compliment a person in crisis in a way that is compatible with the negative view that the person has of himself or herself. By contrast, lavishing a person who is really insecure with praise will cause the other to become uncomfortable in short order.

A related point is to avoid the common error of trying to cheer up a depressed person. It is well known that many people in crisis are suffering from acute depression at the time of the incident. By trying to cheer that person up and get him or her to "see the bright side," the therapist is disqualifying his or her view of reality, and acting as if his or her problems are small or are nothing to worry about. On the contrary, those problems are so important that the person is going to hurt someone or himself or herself because of them. So the first thing for the therapist to do is to let the person know that he or she hears what the problem is, acknowledge it as a problem, and then let the person talk about some of the things that he or she is hurt or angry about. A therapist can even give the person some credit for "standing it" for so long, by saying something like this: "I don't know if I could have taken it as long as you have." Thus, the clinician shows recognition that there is a problem and that the person has worth in his or her eyes. At this point, the person in crisis may be more willing to start communicating in an active, positive way.

It is vitally important that the person in crisis feel that he or she is understood, or at least that the clinician is willing to try to understand his or her view of reality. In short, a therapist wants someone to trust enough to take a great risk, the risk of stopping his or her pathological behavior and trying a new approach to problem resolution.

REFERENCES

Erickson, M. H., Rossi, E. L. and Rossi, S. I. *Hypnotic Realities*. New York: Irvington, 1976.
Watzlawick, P. *An Anthology of Human Communication; Text and Tape.* Palo Alto: Science and Behavior Books, 1964.
Watzlawick, P. *How Real Is Real? Confusion, Disformation, Communication.* New York: Random House, 1976.
Watzlawick, P. *The Language of Change.* New York: Basic Books, 1978.
Weakland, J. H. and Jackson, D. D. Patient and therapist observations on the circumstances of a schizophrenic episode. *Archives of Neurology and Psychiatry,* 79:554-74, 1958.

3

Clinical intervention in emergency situations

THE FIRST TELEPHONE CONTACT WITH A PERSON IN CRISIS

When someone calls for help in an emergency (no matter who that person is—a police officer, a mental health professional, a runaway teenager in a phone booth, a suicidal adult, or a woman who has been beaten by her husband), the person has already defined that situation as beyond his or her resources to control. Too often emergencies have been dismissed or mishandled because the person who received the call for help was not sensitive to the needs or feelings of the caller. A professional person may be concerned or fearful that a situation may be in process of escalating beyond the possibility of establishing control, but because these encounters with persons in emergency situations are extremely critical, they must be met with considerable sensitivity. As a general rule, it is wise to look upon the caller as a person who is experiencing a true emergency—simply by virtue of the fact that the person has spoken of the situation as such.

The beginning of this chapter reviews some basic telephone procedures for this first contact. It describes the kinds of information that it is advisable to gather when first talking by telephone with a person

31

who is involved in an emergency situation. How to ask for and make use of police assistance in a potentially dangerous situation is also discussed.

Upon receiving an emergency call, the first priority is to try to get the name and telephone number from the caller. This may seem trivial, but on several occasions obtaining a phone number has saved a person's life. Many people who are extremely upset may panic and hang up suddenly: e.g., suicidal persons often change their minds about talking and hang up, and the therapist may find himself or herself knowing full details of the sad story but not knowing who the person is or how to recontact the person. Usually people will provide their name and telephone number fairly easily in an automatic way, if it is requested early enough in the conversation and in a matter-of-fact manner. The best method to accomplish this is to refer to a "bad connection," i.e., pretending to be worried about being cut off will help to induce an agitated person to give the telephone number without thinking about what he or she is doing. Then, even if the person does hang up suddenly, the address of the person can be traced through a "reverse directory," which lists addresses by telephone numbers and is generally available through a local police department at night and on weekends, or from the telephone company. There is a commonly held misconception that telephone calls can be easily traced if the caller can only be kept on the line. However, calls are extremely difficult —and often impossible—to trace. In the best of circumstances such a procedure requires at least an hour and it often requires two or three hours.

After obtaining this important information, the therapist should try to get a clear description of the problem from the caller and try to find out how many people are involved in the emergency situation. How many people are there in the family and how many people are present at the moment of this call? Next, the therapist should ascertain whether or not there are weapons present and whether drugs or alcohol have been involved in the problem. It is not necessary to be blunt or obvious in asking these questions—mentioning weapons directly, for example, may frighten or make the caller suspicious. The therapist can ask, "Has anyone been hurt?" and "Are you hurt?" and, if the answer is yes, "Did they hit you with their hand or did they hurt you with something?" A therapist can usually obtain this information while talking in a general way or asking questions about the problem in a conversational tone of voice, thus avoiding the implication that the person is being interrogated in some way.

As a general rule, the therapist should try to speak briefly with each person present before going to the home. This approach does not require a lengthy conversation; it is only necessary to gain each person's general consent to be visited. This step also lets everyone know that the therapist is interested in him or her and respects the family members' individual rights. Meanwhile, it is also wise to determine whether or not someone has already left the scene in anger, i.e., a person who may be likely to return later and be surprised by the presence of a third party in the home. Of course, this is a situation which it is best to avoid, if necessary by planning to meet the caller outside of the home or away from the scene of the emergency. The only situation in which ETC therapists do not gain the consent of everyone present before making a visit is when there is a life-or-death issue: when someone has attempted suicide or is going to hurt himself or herself; or when someone is behaving in an acutely psychotic manner and may be capable of hurting another person; or, in the case of a family emergency, when someone announces that a person may be severely battered at any moment if an intervention does not occur immediately. But in most cases when making an emergency response to the home, it is vital to respect people's civil liberties—above all their right to privacy—and to gain consent for such a visit. In short, the therapist should have the consent of each person who is present in the home when possible, unless someone's life is at stake.

In many cases, such as that of a battered spouse or a severely acting-out adolescent, one or more family members may not be pleased about having a therapist visit the home. For example, an abusive husband may be most unwilling to talk with anyone about his conduct, and yet there are good reasons for trying to get his consent. By doing so, a clinician can indicate that he or she is prepared to treat the husband as a person, and thus the therapist may be seen as less of a threat. In addition, this unexpected or paradoxical approach may help to change the husband's set way of thinking about therapists, so that some of his resistance can be bypassed.

If consent is given and it appears to be reasonably safe, the clinician can go directly to the home. If the husband does not consent in a spouse-beating case, it may be wiser and safer to offer meeting the wife at some place outside the home, e.g., at a friend's house, a coffee shop, or any place that is neutral territory. In those instances in which there is an extremely enraged person in the home, who has been actively violent or has used a weapon recently, it may be wise to call for police assistance.

Before a therapist does emergency work, or if the therapist often treats high-risk or potentially violent persons who may become involved in emergencies, it is wise to establish a good working relationship with the local police, the ambulance service, and the fire department. (Unfortunately, many mental health professionals have an antagonistic— or at the very least indifferent—attitude toward their local police.) If a therapist is dealing with an emergency situation that involves a young child or adolescent, and emergency police assistance is needed during the day, the local Juvenile Officer can usually be asked for assistance. In most police departments, there is a Juvenile Officer who has had special training in working with young people. When a therapist is working with an adult in, for example, a battering situation, he or she can ask for someone in the Detective Bureau; and, the department may have an officer or officers who work on sex crimes. These officers wear plain clothes and have some special training in helping people who are extremely upset and in crisis situations. If none of these specialist officers is available and it is necessary to go through the regular complaint desk, it is advisable to try to explain to the officer on duty that this is a family emergency situation and that it would be helpful if the officer who responds to the call is one who is experienced in dealing with families and doesn't mind doing family crisis work. If possible, it should be an officer in plain clothes and in an unmarked car. It is useful to recall, in such situations, that the people who called for help asked for the help of a therapist or a counselor and were *not* calling the police; also, they may have had a good reason for not asking the police to intervene. Even so, the therapist must take reasonable precautions for his or her safety, as well as that of the client.

How a therapist coordinates the emergency response with the police is often critical, and how the police are brought into the emergency situation is of extreme importance. Of course, if the therapist is dealing with a situation in which someone is actively violent and has injured someone or is holding a person hostage, the police must be summoned immediately. But if, for example, a call has been received about a psychotic person or a violent family fight and the description of the situation is such that the therapist does not feel comfortable responding alone, in such a case it is equally appropriate to call the police for assistance with the visit. Should it not be advisable or wise to inform the family or person that the police are on their way, it will be a good idea to meet the police at a corner near the house or apartment, i.e., one that is completely out of sight of the house. It is not wise to simply call the police and tell them about the incident and ask them to respond to the scene, because information about the problem may be conveyed incorrectly to police officers in the field by a dispatcher, and these officers may be the ones to arrive first, with an incorrect view of the situation. If this happens, the person or family member who called is likely to feel angry and betrayed, and any attempt to establish a therapeutic relationship will be difficult or impossible.

Whenever one person must tell another something in a hurry, confusions and distortions readily occur. One unfortunate miscommunication of this sort happened when an ETC therapist called for help with a large, and potentially explosive, psychotic adolescent in a parking lot. The message that the police in the field received was, "Sniper with a gun at a parking lot." Much to the clinician's surprise and consternation, the SWAT team arrived. So, when calling the police, it is important to be aware that a request for assistance often may be passed along by two or three people and can become distorted in the process. Consequently, if a situation is particularly sensitive, the dispatcher may have the officer in the field call back. In this way the therapist can speak to the officer directly before he or she responds to the call, in order to be sure that the problem is understood. The therapist should plan to meet the officer at some distance from the scene and proceed there with the officer on foot. Upon arrival at the scene, an explanation can be given to the person who called concerning why the police were brought in. If the situation appears to be calm, the therapist may choose to ask the officer to leave; or, the officer may be asked to remain for a while, until the problem has deescalated to the point at which the therapist feels safe without an officer present.

It is usually advisable to establish a secure communication link between the therapist(s) who are responding to the emergency scene and the office, so that they can call in for help or assistance should an unexpected problem occur. The communication system should be sufficiently discreet to enable a therapist to notify the office that he or she needs help, while at the same time the people at the scene do not know that help has been called for. The Emergency Treatment Center has experienced frightening moments when therapists were threatened, but fortunately the ETC staff member was able to talk his or her way out of each situation. In one instance, a therapist responded to a call from a battered spouse; later, her husband returned, drunk and armed with a knife (despite the fact that the police had removed him from the home to a friend's apartment on the previous day). The clinician was able to make a telephone call back to the office on false pretenses and was able to convey, subtly, to the office staff that he was in serious danger and needed police assistance. The police were asked to respond to the call immediately.

After another, similar instance which involved a battered child, we decided to institute the following telephone call-in system at ETC. When staff members respond to an emergency in the field (any emergency occurring in which there is some indication that there may have been violence or there is the potential for violence), as soon as they arrive they tell the people whom they are visiting that they will have to telephone the office. If a situation is dangerous, the counselor will first say (upon reaching the office), "This is Jane Doe calling in. Were there any calls for me?" When that happens, the office staff (at night, the answering service) will know that a therapist in the field is in trouble and will send police assistance immediately. If, by contrast, the situation is relatively calm, the clinician will merely (for example) identify herself by first name, and that informal method of identification will let the office staff know that the staff member is all right. In puzzling or ambiguous situations, the counselor will identify herself by first name but will add "Thank you. I'll call back in fifteen minutes" (or whatever time span is appropriate). The office staff is thus alerted that, if no call has been received fifteen minutes later, police assistance should be dispatched.

RESPONDING TO AN EMERGENCY

Before proceeding to offer some recommended procedures for the emergency response, it will be useful to reflect upon considerations which cause this sort of clinical work to be somewhat unique. When a clinician responds to the scene of an emergency, there are many aspects of that kind of scene which differ from emergencies that take place in a hospital, clinic, or private office. Some of these differences are quite subtle and, if overlooked, can affect the course and outcome of treatment in a negative way. This section will review these differences, in addition to discussing nontraditional ways in which it is possible to work with families who would be resistant to the more traditional methods of psychotherapy.

In a majority of emergency incidents, clinicians are often surprised to find that a family may be receptive to change if the therapist is cautious and sensitive about how he or she approaches the family system. In fact, the family that has been struggling with a problem for a long time may be more receptive to change, merely because that family has been in pain longer than some others. And no matter how angry or polarized a family may appear to be on the surface, at least one family member usually recognizes that outside help can be useful in resolving problems. What is critical here is that a clinician who enters the family system should be extremely sensitive to the pride and self-esteem of the family members; it is vital not to jump to conclusions or to humiliate or "corner" a family member, however inadvertently.

Paradoxical as it may seem, the sooner a therapist can see the family in an emergency the better, even if one or more of the family members is still acting out or is agitated. (The only exception would be if a family member was too drunk to communicate coherently or was under the influence of drugs. In such a situation, it would obviously be wise to wait until each person is clearly sober and coherent.) If the clinician has this opportunity to see a family while the actual emergency is taking place or very shortly thereafter, so much the better because the family's resistance to intervention will be lessened. The people in-

volved are in emotional pain and, because of that, are much more motivated to change or to work on their problems. After time passes and
the family members are not experiencing as much discomfort, they
may then be more reluctant to do something about a problem. Another reason for seeing a family as soon as possible is that it gives
the family members a message that someone genuinely cares about
them and is concerned about what will happen to them. This point
cannot be emphasized too much. Many families that ETC has successfully treated would never have gone to a traditional clinic. We
were able to help those families primarily because we reached out to
them when they were experiencing great pain.

It is important to consider what steps must be taken by someone
who is seeking help for a personal or interactional problem. First, the
person must be aware (at least to some extent) that the problem is psychological in nature. Second, the person must be able to figure out
what kind of agency or profession can be of help—not an easy task
when one considers the proliferation of social agencies and programs
both public and private. After deciding which agency is appropriate to
his or her needs, the person must find and visit the agency (assuming
that it is during regular working hours), a prospect that may be frightening for various reasons, such as language or cultural barriers or socioeconomic class distinctions. He or she must then explain, to a total
stranger (in what may be an intimidating setting), intimate details of
his or her personal life. Under these circumstances, it is a matter of
some amazement that people find help for their troubles at all.

When undertaking a home visit, it is well to remember that, in essence, a therapist is entering the other person's *space*. This applies
even when meeting the person in a public place, because many of the
key aspects of a professional's role and authority are not present in a
public or neutral place. Many assertive and/or confrontive interventions that can be accomplished by a therapist in the office with great
ease may be misperceived as a threat or as an insult when the therapist
is visiting someone's home or has met the person in a public place.

A therapist who does emergency work needs to be aware that even
though his or her self-perception is that of someone who is nonthreatening and who wishes to help others, some people in crisis may
view the therapist as a very real threat. For example, accidentally sit-

ting in someone's favorite chair may make that person uncomfortable or angry without the person knowing why. Assuming a strong authority role too quickly in a family situation may possibly offend a mother or father, who may feel that his or her role is being challenged because of not being able to solve the family's problems himself or herself. A therapist can take more liberties in his or her own office, mainly because the clients have come there (more or less) because they wanted to and have entered the therapist's domain.

However, when a clinician goes out on an emergency call, he or she is often responding to the request of someone else, e.g., another family member, a neighbor, a probation officer, or the police. Since the people involved in the emergency probably did not originally intend to see a therapist, they have probably not yet defined their problems as psychological in nature. Even though they have given their consent to see a counselor or therapist, it may have been a tentative or reluctant consent; their first reaction to the arrival of a clinician may be fear or anger or both. They may be full of misunderstandings about what a therapist is and does, and they may find such a person threatening in addition to the upset and humiliation occasioned by the emergency itself.

Consequently, it is usually advisable for the therapist to move at a much slower pace than usual when working in the home, and to set therapeutic goals much differently. Sometimes new ETC staff members become discouraged after an emergency visit or after the second visit of a case that began as an emergency, thinking that they have not really accomplished much. But in fact, if a therapist can get a family to permit him or her to come back or can persuade the family to come into the office the next day or a week later for a follow-up session, the therapist has achieved a very large and very important goal during the first visit.

The following description of a family, which is typical of those seen by the ETC, will serve to illustrate some points made above in this section. Harry and Mabel have been married 18 years and have two adolescent children—a boy, Wayne (16) and a girl, Debby (14). Both Harry and Mabel have drinking problems and once or twice a month they have violent fights. Harry lost control one day about a week ago and "slapped around" his daughter when she "talked back" to him.

Debby is an unhappy girl who smokes marijuana and sometimes has been known to overuse pills. She has had an abortion that neither of the parents knows about. Debby's brother, Wayne, is not home very much these days, but his parents don't seem to notice. He has also used drugs and was arrested once for shoplifting, which his father dismissed as boyish fun; lately, he has been selling grass and pills. Mabel sometimes mixes tranquilizers with alcohol, and twice she had to go to an emergency room for what was called an "accidental" overdose.

The police are fairly frequent visitors to Harry and Mabel's home, because when Harry drinks too much he often loses control and beats Mabel up. Harry was laid off last year for six months and things got pretty bad at home, but Mabel was too ashamed and afraid to tell anyone about it at the time. She called a social agency once but didn't keep the appointment. The school counselors and the Probation Department are concerned about the family, but what can they do? Friends and relatives have suggested that the family needs help, but Harry and Mabel have ignored them. If someone dared to advise these people that theirs is a "mental health" problem and that they need psychotherapy, either Harry or Mabel would more than likely tell the person to "go to hell" because they are not crazy!

One day, this man and wife will have another fight. They will both be drunk and Mabel will be threatened with a beating again. When she realizes that she is in physical danger—during the most explosive phase of the struggle—Mabel may well call the police. The thought of asking a mental health professional for help would not occur to her. The police, in their turn, would act to quell the marital crisis, but once that had been accomplished would have little to offer the embattled couple. If Harry and Mabel were lucky, the police would call for assistance from an agency such as ETC. Obviously, for people like Harry and Mabel to permit a therapist to visit their home and later agree to a second visit, considerable rapport will have to be established within a short time. In order to be able to reach out to the many people who are similar to Harry and Mabel, clinicians need to develop highly flexible and readily adaptable techniques. Many approaches taken by traditional schools of psychotherapy would tend to confuse and alienate people like Mabel and Harry. That is a good reason for the therapist to adopt therapeutic interventions that fit within Harry and Mabel's perceptions of reality and their system of values.

When talking with people like Harry and Mabel, it generally makes more sense for a therapist to speak in terms of difficulties and problems, rather than to use traditional psychological terms. It will be understandable to talk about managing difficulties in a better way so that they do not escalate into serious problems. A clinician may reassure the person that it's normal to have difficulties in life and that no one is without them. The therapist may add that people generally mismanage difficulties in three ways: 1) They may make too little of a major problem, such as when a mother dismisses her son's drug abuse and petty thievery as just an adolescent "stage"; 2) they can make too much of a minor difficulty, thus causing it to grow out of proportion, e.g., a parent's overreacting to some minor acting-out on the part of a teenager, leading the teenager to think that the magnitude of his crime should be increased to fit the magnitude of his punishment; and 3) they often mismanage a problem by applying a "commonsense" remedy that may make it worse, e.g., trying to "cheer up" someone who is depressed, which is exactly the wrong thing to do because it conveys the message that he has no reason to be depressed when in fact he thinks he does. In effect, it tells the depressed person that, for one reason or another, he or she has not been listened to.

In order to reach people like Harry and Mabel, a clinician needs to learn to talk with them in terms that they can understand. Emphasis needs to be placed upon real issues of the here and now, rather than on intrapsychic processes grounded in the past, which they would not see as being relevant. Further, a therapist needs to gain insight into the person's perceptions of reality, keeping in mind that what someone considers to be "reality" is, for the most part, his or her highly personalized concept of what reality should be. In fact, a clinician's perceptions of reality may differ greatly from those of someone who is experiencing an emergency; and if a therapist and a person in crisis are going to communicate, the therapist needs to be aware of what differences exist in their two separate realities and must be able to speak according to the client's point of view. It is also necessary to be cognizant of the fact that people who are traumatized or are experiencing the stress of an emergency tend to think in a rigid and concrete manner. That is, when they are agitated or frightened, people tend to cling more rigidly to their private reality or world view. So, in an emergency it is even more important to decode the perceptions of reality of the person in crisis and to frame the therapeutic intervention in terms appropriate for that person's reality.

While most of us go through life with the awareness that life has its tragedies as well as its joys, most of us do not have to contemplate the possibility of being attacked by another person in the course of our work. For some reason many people think that this sort of thing happens only to others, and that is particularly true of people in the helping professions, i.e., those who are basically humanitarian in character and optimistic about the human spirit. We at the Center have often found that psychotherapists are reluctant to take some of the precautions necessary in responding to emergency calls. Nevertheless, this fact should not imply that all people in crisis are potentially dangerous, for many are frightened people who feel trapped and desperate because they have been hurt beyond endurance; some are people who, in other circumstances, would never dream of hurting another person. Even so, people in the heat of an emergency can more easily become inflamed and act out in a blind, aggressive, or violent manner. Because of that, it is wise to observe certain precautions.

First, it is not advisable to go to an emergency alone, particularly at night. Even the police do not respond to violent family fights or to obviously dangerous situations alone. Police officers invariably ask for "cover" (that is, another officer or a police team) when they respond to emergencies. Now, if the police don't respond alone (with their radio, gun, mace, and other accoutrements) to family emergencies, it stands to reason that mental health professionals who lack this kind of equipment should not respond alone.

We have found that a team of a man and a woman is best for working with family emergencies. Our rationale is that it is often necessary, at first, to separate the various members of the family and to talk with each person alone, for the purpose of permitting each to ventilate feelings and calm down before any kind of therapeutic intervention, with the whole family present, begins. It is usually easier for a female therapist to talk with the woman who is involved in the conflict, without causing any feelings of anger or jealousy on the part of her husband or lover, and for a male therapist to talk with the man in question, also without arousing jealousy and suspicion.

When arriving at the scene of an emergency situation, it is wise to proceed in a cautious and well-planned manner. Even though what a clinician has heard on the telephone from the person calling for help may have sounded very fearful or desperate, it is important that his or her response is well thought through; in other words, as the song says, he or she is best advised not to "rush in where angels fear to tread." The following plan of action is recommended. Park a short distance away from the house, and walk to the house slowly and quietly. Listen for sounds of a disturbance or active violence. Continue listening carefully while walking up to the door and do not enter the home without being invited. Even when responding to someone who has expressed profound distress, do not rush pell-mell into that person's home; remember that it is the other person's territory and that suddenly entering someone's home may be interpreted as aggression rather than concern. In addition, the person who called for help may not have been telling the truth or may have distorted the situation to suit his own needs. A hurt family member who has called in anger may have painted a picture of the situation that is completely inaccurate. An example would be that of a battered spouse or adolescent who wishes to put the person who hurt him or her "in their place." The injured person may be unaware that he or she has distorted the facts and has misled the clinician about the behavior of the other family members.

People who call for help in family emergencies are usually grateful that someone has come to the home, and often are pleasantly surprised that someone cared enough to respond to them in a moment of need. But occasionally something very unexpected and possibly dangerous may be waiting for the therapist, and so it is best to approach these situations with utmost care. When going to someone's home, as noted earlier, the therapist should concentrate on the awareness that it is *their* home. When waiting to be let in, it is wise to stand back a little way from the door. By doing so two things will be accomplished: 1) The person who answers the door is given "space," so that he doesn't feel crowded or threatened; and 2) if he or she does become angry, the person waiting will not be as much of a target and will have room to move out of the way. It is wise to bear in mind that a clinician does not have the same rights and privileges (under the law) as a police officer. If, for example, a therapist walks into someone's house without permission, the therapist is technically trespassing. Hence legally, as well as ethically, it is wise to wait and use caution.

If a house is extremely dark it may be necessary to enter even more slowly in order to adjust to the darkness. When first entering the home, the therapist should introduce himself and give the person(s) present some form of identification. Meanwhile, it is important to look around for any signs of violence, e.g., broken things on the floor or overturned furniture. Also, the clinician should be very cautious of the "space" of the person(s) with whom he is talking. Generally, in American and European cultures under nonthreatening circumstances about one-and-a-half to two feet of personal space is considered to be safe and comfortable. In an emergency situation it is not advisable to get much closer than three or four feet, unless the person gives a clear message that he or she would be agreeable for someone to come closer.

If the emergency has calmed down enough so that it appears that the family members are ready to talk with a therapist, it will be best for the clinician to choose an appropriate room for the meeting. It is usually a good idea to avoid the kitchen because there are knives and a variety of small, dangerous objects that could be used as weapons, should things become heated. Around the dining-room table or in the living room are generally good places to discuss things. If the living room is chosen, the therapist may wish to select a straight-backed chair or to bring one into the room. In that way the therapist can avoid choosing someone's favorite place and thus inadvertently annoying that person. Also, it is a good idea for the therapist to be stationed at a fair distance from the person in crisis, without being obviously distant, until the situation can be fully evaluated. The therapist might say, "I want to move this chair so that I can see everyone," and few people will find this to be unusual or take offense. During this period it will be possible to determine whether or not the people can discuss their problems as a family group. If it is impossible for them to talk as a family without someone becoming angry, the therapist might suggest that the group discussion stop (temporarily) and talk with each person individually to help him to ventilate enough anger so that he can eventually return to the group.

In determining whether or not a family or couple can talk calmly together, the therapist may wish to use the "only one person speaks at a time" rule: i.e., each family member can describe his or her perception of the problem, in turn, without having another member interrupt or become agitated. When a family is capable of following this rule, the members can usually work together as a group. Moreover, this rule can serve to convey to each person the message that the therapist wants to hear each side of the story. It is a good idea to ask the most potentially explosive family member to speak first. By doing this, the clinician will convey recognition and respect and, in addition, will find out fairly rapidly if this person can be worked with in the family context or will require individual attention.

BASIC STEPS AND GOALS

The first important step in making an emergency response is to gain the rapport and trust of the person in crisis. This point cannot be emphasized too strongly. It means that someone who is going to be working in the field of emergency psychology needs to be able to establish rapport with many types of persons from many differing backgrounds. An emergency therapist should be able to talk with anyone from the young "street person" to the alcoholic to the fundamentalist Christian to someone who lives in a very elegant, upper-class home. In emergency work, particularly when responding to police emergency calls, a therapist must be flexible enough to respond to *anyone* who may be present at the scene. There is no selectivity in the clients accepted in a crisis situation, as often occurs in private clinics or private practice. So the initial step is to gain rapport with the person in crisis; and if this is the only accomplishment of the first visit, it can be considered a success.

The next step, after establishing rapport, is attempting to formulate a clear definition of the problem: What actually is the problem and how can it be described in behavioral terms? It is surprising to realize that many people have not really thought through what their true problem is, nor what has brought it to the current status of an emergency. Now there may be two definitions of the problem: A clinician may define the problem one way and the person experiencing the emergency may define the problem another way. In fact, the therapist may not always wish to share with the family his or her own definition of the problem at first. It may be wiser to propose a definition of the problem that the family can understand in clear, behavioral terms—in simple language, what is being done wrong and who is doing it?

Next, it is important for a clinician to know what this person or this family has done in the past, or is currently doing, to cope with or to resolve the problem. Obviously, it is a waste of time and energy to recreate a strategy for change that was unsuccessfully tried in the past.

The therapist will then want to establish some goals for treatment. One way to obtain a behavioral description of the problem that will help in the formulation of goals is to ask the question, "What will be different when the problem stops?"—i.e., how will the family know that things are different, that the problem has gotten better or has gone away? Goals, like the definition of a problem, need to be stated in precise behavioral terms. Goals such as "I really want to get my head together" or "I want to be less depressed" are patently not acceptable. Less depressed, less miserable—these are vague strivings, not objectives or goals. But therapeutic change requires clear definitions and specific goals that can be understood and measured by all parties to the current state of affairs. The therapist needs to know what the people in crisis will be enabled to do if things change, as well as what kinds of events will no longer take place if change occurs. In particular with people who are depressed, it is essential to direct them toward thinking about concrete, behavioral changes that can be observed (in light of the goals they want to accomplish), because depressed people tend to negate what progress they make unless progress is demonstrated to them unequivocally.

Finally, it will be important to focus upon the person's (or the family's) perceptions of reality. When people are in a crisis state, their perceptions of reality become quite limited and rigid as a result of the intense stress that they are experiencing. This phenomenon might be described as emotional "tunnel vision." Because of this, people in crisis are more susceptible to techniques such as those of Milton Erickson (Erickson et al., 1976) and the indirect or paradoxical techniques of the Brief Therapy Center (Watzlawick et al., 1974). Some of the more traditional therapeutic approaches which require insight, reasoning, and interpretation may cause agitated or angry persons in acute crisis to become even more defensive and resistant. In other words, it is patently unreasonable to expect people in crisis to be reasonable. Consequently, we suggest that a therapist attempt to convert the person's perceptual rigidity into a clinical advantage, by means of methods recommended below.

STRATEGIES FOR DEFUSING EMERGENCIES

The therapist should try to incorporate the person's world view and self-perception into the design of an interaction. Immensely valuable clinical information can be gained from the person's use of language, such as what his or her values are, what the person is afraid of, and what the person's perceptions of self and people in general are. Since people are tenaciously wedded to these perceptions when they are in a state of crisis, a therapist who is facile can have enormous freedom of movement in the crisis situation by redefining desired or undesired behavior according to the person's rigidly defined reality. For example, if being strong and manly is a vital part of the person's perception of himself, then restraint and self-control can be reframed (redefined) as manly, and aggressive behavior can be reframed as childish or unmanly. (A concise definition of reframing is the one given by Watzlawick, 1978, p. 119.)

Another example of reframing a person's reality is that of someone who wishes to punish a loved one for abandoning him or her by committing suicide. A therapist may redefine the suicidal person's reality in these terms: If the suicidal person really wants to punish the former lover, he or she should try to find a new lover and establish a happy relationship with this new person. Thus the former lover would be shown as less important and in fact readily replaceable. And the formerly suicidal person can have the exquisite pleasure of being present to witness this revenge.

Since reality is a subjective phenomenon, a clinician can work toward altering the person's view of reality by reframing certain components of this perception, as described by Watzlawick:

> In this changeability of subjective "realities" lies the power of those therapeutic interventions that have come to be known under the rubric of reframing. Let us remember: we never deal with reality *per se*, but rather with *images* of reality—that is, with interpretations. While the number of potentially possible interpretations is very large, our world image usually permits us to see only one—and this *one* therefore appears to be the only possible, reasonable, and permitted view (1978, p. 119).

The description aptly pertains to people in crisis, who are especially resistant to clinical interventions and to change. Because they are frightened and confused, they cling to their habitual but neurotic behavior patterns which usually only serve to perpetuate a problem.

Traditionally direct or "rational" attempts to persuade the person in crisis to give up old and unsuccessful problem-solving techniques will often prove to be useless, because what is familiar—even if unsuccessful—usually feels safer. Thus it will be wiser to accept the patient's defensiveness and to incorporate this resistance into the clinical intervention. An example of making use of resistance is the following.

An Emergency Treatment Center therapist was called to the home of a young couple for the purpose of deciding whether or not the husband would require hospitalization. Upon arriving, the clinician was told that the husband had been rolling around on the floor and yelling that he wanted to die because he found out that his wife had had an affair. Being a woman of fairly small stature, the therapist realized that any direct approach would be unwise and ineffectual, since the husband was quite large. Also, he was gaining considerable emotional "payoff" from his actions, which served to stimulate humiliation and grief on the part of his wife. The therapist therefore decided to accept the husband's resistance and try to "pre-empt" (Watzlawick, 1978, p. 151) any further acting-out on his part by several means.

First, she said to the wife, in a serious tone of voice (and loud enough to be heard by the husband), that she felt that the wife had "wounded" her husband very deeply. In addition, the husband needed to roll around on the floor in order to express his deep feelings of anguish concerning what she had done to him. In fact, he would probably need to roll on the floor for another hour before he would be able to express himself fully and thus experience some relief. Then the therapist began encouraging the husband to shout louder and to roll around more furiously. After a few moments of this intervention the man stopped rolling and said (to the therapist), "What's the matter with you? Are you crazy?" The therapist replied that she was not crazy but knew that he was deeply hurt and needed to express to his wife the intensity of the emotional pain he was feeling. The husband agreed to the latter comment.

In this situation, if the clinician had insisted upon taking a more direct approach to gaining control over the husband, the emergency would have probably had a very different outcome. In all likelihood the police would have been called and the husband would have been sent to a psychiatric facility for observation. While the intervention itself may sound simplistic and scarcely adequate for defusing such an emotionally charged situation, it may have been this very quality of simplicity that led to its success. In any event, the therapist was able to avoid a confrontation by accepting the husband's behavior first and then giving him a reason to change it himself.

Another concept (previously noted in Chapter 2) that is useful for defusing acute emergency situations is that of the "illusion of alternatives" as identified by Weakland and Jackson (1958), Erickson and Rossi (1975), and by Watzlawick (1978), who defined the concept as follows:

> . . . establishing a frame within which a seemingly free choice is offered between two alternatives, both of which amount to the same outcome—that is, therapeutic change. An illusion is thus created, suggesting that there are only these two possiblities, or—in other words—a state of blindness is produced for the fact that there indeed exist other possibilities *outside* the frame (p. 120).

This kind of intervention can be used to therapeutic advantage in emergencies precisely because the person in crisis lacks perceptual flexibility. For example, this technique could be used in a situation in which the clinician has decided that someone should be hospitalized and the person is hesitant. In the course of negotiating this important event in the person's life, the clinician can offer to arrange transportation to the hospital either by ambulance or in a police car, and give the person in crisis free choice between the alternatives.

There will be times when a therapist will feel stymied during the initial stages of treatment and will seek to make more efficient the process of obtaining information on the nature of the problem. One way is to ask the people not to change right away—providing it is safe to do so. (This is clearly not a wise intervention technique for situations in which violence has occurred.) The therapist can ask people to take notes or keep a journal of certain kinds of behavior, between one session and the next. The subject of these records will be actions or incidents that the therapist needs to know more about, and thus during this period people's attention will be focused upon observing their own behavior and their interactions more closely. In the process a certain kind of change will in fact have occurred, because their concentration will be diverted from escalating the conflict to documenting it. Admittedly this may be only a slight change, but perhaps it will prove significant if it yields information that the clinician can use to formulate new interventions.

Should an emergency situation begin to escalate once more, the following tactics of distraction can be quite useful in bringing a crisis back under the therapist's control. He can ask a series of trivial but professional-sounding questions about the life of each person in the family—in effect, taking a quasi-psychological history by asking, for example: "How many children were there in your mother's family?", "What was your father's profession?" and "What high school did you go to?" Most of us are accustomed to visiting a physician and having him or her ask us odd but innocuous questions. They elicit automatic kinds of responses and clearly establish that the professional person is supposed to ask the questions and the client is supposed to reply. Generally, within a few minutes the clinician will have structured the situation so that he or she is in control once more and can proceed to work out an intervention.

Another technique that may be of help in calming people is for the therapist to feign being slightly "thick" or confused, or to act as though he or she is not quite clear about what the people are trying to convey. The rationale is that most people, despite being upset or angry, want others to understand their side of an issue. If the clinician acts in a concerned but uncomprehending manner, the angry person will usually put more effort into attempting to clarify his or her point of view. Of course, caution is in order so that the person who is speaking doesn't become annoyed. The therapist could say, "I want to make sure that I understand you correctly," and then repeat to the person what he or she has just said but slightly incorrectly. As a consequence, the angry person will have to expend some effort and energy in explaining what he or she has been trying to say. This process can divert some of the person's energy away from anger into clarifying his side of the issue for the therapist.

An additional device that may be used to calm someone or to get a person to listen in a tolerant way is to frame behavior in a more positive light. This doesn't mean "painting things rosy" or acting in a Pollyannaish manner; what it means is looking for the positive aspects of a person's behavior and calling attention to that part in order to gain his or her trust. For example, with an aggressive and possibly assaultive husband, the therapist might refer to his behavior as that of a man who is "strong" and comment on the importance of being strong. The therapist may tell him that he gives the impression of being someone who wants to control his environment, and who wishes to have some authority over what is going on around him. This tactic can point out positive aspects of the husband's behavior that he may be able to "hear," and may give the clinician some leverage toward inducing him to pay attention.

Yet another method that may be used for getting people to settle down and listen is that of paradox. Sometimes a paradoxical intervention can change the situation or a person's "set" just enough to break the escalating cycle of anger and violence. For example, the therapist may, when visiting a person's home, ask politely for a cup of coffee or a glass of water. This somewhat unusual request can immediately change the role of antagonist in a crisis to the person's more usual role of host or hostess. Such a disarmingly simple or unexpected request may often be successful because it serves to divert the person's attention long enough to de-escalate the anger. An ETC staff member once stopped a couple in the middle of a very heated fight by saying, "Do you smell gas? I think I smell something strange." All at once their attention was focused upon something other than their conflict. It gave the clinician a chance to break the escalation of anger and to move the communication in a different direction.

Finally, humor can be a marvelous way to divert, calm, or slow down angry behavior. But humor has to be used with great caution and sensitivity to the pride and dignity of others. Care must be taken so that the humor itself, as well as the manner in which it is used, will not be misunderstood or taken as making fun of the other person. Some therapists and counselors can use humor in a natural way and some cannot. If the use of humor is something that a therapist does well and easily, it can often be most valuable in an emergency situation. If it does not come naturally, a therapist will be well advised not to use it.

REFERENCES

Erickson, M. H., Rossi, E. L., and Rossi, S. I. *Hypnotic Realities*. New York: Irvington, 1976.
Erickson, M. and Rossi, E. L. Varieties of double bind. *American Journal of Clinicial Hypnosis*, 17:143-57, 1975.
Watzlawick, P., Weakland, J., and Fisch, R. *Change*. New York: Norton, 1974.
Watzlawick, P. *The Language of Change*. New York: Basic Books, 1978.
Weakland, J. and Jackson, D. Patient and therapist observations on the circumstances of a schizophrenic episode. *Archives of Neurology and Psychiatry*, 79:554-74, 1958.

4

Hospitalizing persons in crisis

One of the more critical clinical decisions that a therapist will make is the choice of hospitalizing or not hospitalizing a person in crisis. This decision, of course, is most serious when it involves involuntary hospitalization. Frequently clinicians who are comfortable in a hospital setting forget how terrifying hospitalization can be to a "patient," and what hospitalization will mean to that person's life in a real or a symbolic way. Hospitalization means that for a period of time a person's life is being placed under the control of other people who, in most cases, are unknown to the person. Also, putting someone in a mental hospital exposes that person to the threat of a stigma which could be lasting—considering the proliferation of data banks and automated record-keeping systems, compounded by inadequate protection of the privacy of client records. Hence one hospitalization could affect someone for the rest of his or her life.

In critical situations such as those described in this chapter, considerable pressure is often placed upon a therapist by the friends or family of the client to hospitalize, or not to hospitalize, the person. The therapist must weigh each consideration independently and base a decision upon what he or she believes to be the best interests of the client. This chapter is intended to be useful to a therapist in making this difficult decision on clinical grounds. Legal aspects of the hospitalization decision-making process will be addressed in Chapter 13. The current chapter reviews general procedures for preparing to hospitalize someone, either voluntarily or involuntarily, and presents some guidelines for assessing the extent of a client's potential for violence toward other people. (See Chapter 12 for information that may be helpful in assessing suicide risk.) Two case studies are presented to illustrate the hospitalization process. In addition, suggestions are offered on how to handle the situation when a therapist decides, contrary to the desires of the client or the family or friends, that hospitalization would *not* serve the best interests of that person.

DECIDING WHETHER OR NOT TO HOSPITALIZE

Even if the therapist has had a long-term relationship with a client, the hospitalization process will not always be an easy one. Essentially the decision should be based upon considerations such as these: whether or not the therapist believes that a client's condition is at serious risk of deteriorating unless he/she is placed in a protected environment; whether or not the client is so mentally ill that he/she poses a threat to self or others; whether or not the person is so gravely disabled by mental illness as to be no longer able to care for himself or herself.

This critical decision should not be made merely because the client wishes to enter a hospital. Some people use hospitalization to punish or manipulate those around them, and some chronically ill persons use the hospital as a refuge from the responsibilities of living. Moreover, the decision to hospitalize should not be made because a person is merely bizarre in manner or difficult to live with. It can be hard for a therapist to resist the pressure that friends, neighbors, or relatives apply in favor of putting an annoying or odd person into the hospital. In such cases a therapist needs to return responsibility for the care of this kind of person to the family or friends where it belongs. The therapist should help these "significant others" to realize that a period of hospitalization may temporarily relieve them of some pressures, but will not necessarily change the person nor make it easier to live with him or her. Instead, changes in their own behavior toward the client will have a better chance of altering the unacceptable behavior eventually.

ASSESSMENT AND PLAN

If the person in crisis is unknown to the therapist who is assessing his or her condition to determine whether or not hospitalization will be necessary, the situation will often require considerable skill. First it will be wise to observe the person carefully, while approaching him/her slowly. While observing his/her nonverbal behavior, it is important to be careful to allow enough personal space so that the person does not feel trapped or confronted. Disturbed or agitated people can easily feel threatened and may act out suddenly if someone gets too close to them. In such situations, the usual range of one to two feet of comfortable personal space should be increased to a range of four to six feet of space. As with other emergency situations, the therapist should focus first on gaining rapport, while also trying to understand what has caused the person to become agitated. The therapist should bear in mind that this person has not chosen him/her as a therapist, and quite possibly this person may not have defined the present situation as an emergency. Often the person who is being assessed was not the one who called for help, and he or she may also have been treated in an insensitive or provocative manner before the therapist arrived. Thus a clinician may face not only the problem of gaining rapport with a disturbed person, but also the added task of trying to undo the cruel or insensitive treatment of others. There is an additional possibility that the person in question may have been hospitalized previously, which may have been a personally bad experience.

To begin the actual assessment process, it is useful to remember Salamon's advice to "deal with the healthy" (1976, p. 110), because even acutely disturbed people have some ego strength. It is wise to try to approach the situation in a manner that inspires confidence, and to convey to the person that his/her safety and well-being are the primary concerns. Next, the therapist should try to discover what the person's reasons are for his/her behavior. Even acutely disturbed people who are behaving in a bizarre manner have some reasons for their actions, and often behavior which appears to be bizarre is quite reasonable when one grasps the logic behind it. It cannot be emphasized too strongly that acutely disturbed people—even those who may be acting in a violent or abusive way—are usually very frightened people. They are not only frightened of their own impulses, but of the imagined or real impulses of others as well. How well this process unfolds will depend largely upon a therapist's ability to inspire trust in, and develop good rapport with, the disturbed person.

Disturbed people are acutely sensitive to (and perceptive of) the behavior of others, even though they may not be able or willing to behave appropriately themselves. Hence, they are often very aware of mixed messages or deception on the part of the clinician: for example, when a therapist claims falsely that he/she is not afraid of the disturbed person, or when a therapist claims falsely to like the person. A wiser course, in such a situation, is for the therapist to admit some of his/her feelings in a neutral manner. For example, the therapist can say that a person is making him/her uncomfortable instead of saying that he/she is unafraid—which could be misunderstood as a challenge to act out more. This kind of neutral admission of discomfort is advisable because, if a disturbed person is angry and is trying to express that anger or keep the therapist at a distance, it lets the person know that the therapist got the message. By contrast, a denial of discomfort may inadvertently provoke more anger because the disturbed person will be resentful that the intended message was not heard. Above all, it is a more honest answer which, in the long run, the person will appreciate.

A clinician needs to adopt a firm but reassuring manner and to control the direction and flow of this kind of conversation. Initial questions need to be uncomplicated, direct, and capable of being answered by simple answers. The therapist can then slowly move on to more open-ended questions as the conversation progresses, and as the disturbed person becomes less anxious. If the person refuses to talk, a therapist can relieve some of the tension and avoid a confrontation by suggesting that the person may wish merely to nod or shake his or her head "yes" or "no." If the person still refuses to speak, the therapist may pursue a paradoxical approach by pretending to "order" the person not to talk. A therapist can say, for example, "It appears to me that you are upset and that talking may be too stressful, so I think that it would be best if you did not talk." This paradoxical approach may accomplish one of two things: If the person subsequently talks, the clinician has avoided a possible confrontation; or, if the person remains silent, he or she may have been relieved of considerable pressure.

It is most important that a clinician both maintain control and behave appropriately, no matter what the disturbed person does. Acutely disturbed people may be very skillful at provoking the anger or disgust of others, and frequently they use this means to control a situation or to make others leave them alone. Such persons are often very perceptive and are able to choose just the right word or action to frustrate or anger someone. Consequently, a therapist needs to be well aware of himself or herself in the situation, and other members of a staff need to be sensitive to and supportive of their fellow clinician in these emotionally demanding moments.

In the course of an assessment interview, a therapist should convey to the person being assessed that he or she will do what is necessary to help, but even if the person does not agree about what is the wisest course of action, the clinician will take whatever steps he or she believes to be necessary. In short, a therapist *will* use an external control such as hospitalization if the person cannot control himself or herself. Even though initially protesting, a disturbed person will often be relieved to learn that the clinician is willing to take full responsibility for seeing that control is restored.

Once the decision has been made to hospitalize someone, it should be undertaken in a thoroughly planned manner (when possible), and the plan should be presented to the client firmly but positively. Ideally, the arrangements themselves should have been made before the client is informed. The reason is that when someone loses control or decompensates to such an extent as to require hospitalization, the experience of entering a hospital itself can be terrifying. Even very belligerent or violent people may be frightened by their own impulses and their own expanding loss of control. It can be quite reassuring in such a situation (even if the person protests vehemently at the moment), when the hospitalization process is conducted in a humane but well-organized manner. In fact, disorganization and lack of direction on the part of a clinician may inadvertently provoke more acting-out on the part of a disturbed person. Consequently it is advisable, when possible, to call the hospital in advance to check available bed space and, if the therapist is not a physician, to discuss the situation with the on-call psychiatrist. Should the therapist later decide not to hospitalize, it will be a simple matter to telephone the hospital and say that the person will not be arriving.

INVOLUNTARY HOSPITALIZATION

The actual statutes may vary from state to state, but almost all states permit involuntary hospitalization because of danger to the self (being suicidal), danger to others (being homicidal), or being gravely disabled (see Chapter 13). State regulations also vary in respect to which licensed mental health professionals may sign an order for involuntary hospitalization, but in most states police officers may also sign these orders. Thus, if a clinician is not empowered to hospitalize the person involuntarily, the police may be of assistance. If the therapist is not a physician and the client is to be evaluated by an on-duty psychiatrist, it will help the psychiatrist to have the following kinds of information—because even very disturbed people may behave quite differently once they have arrived at the hospital:

1) Identifying information: i.e., name, sex, date of birth, address, phone number, marital status, referral source.

2) General appearance.

3) A brief history.

4) Current problem.

5) Client's attitude toward the current problem, toward the clinician, and toward going to the hospital (submissive, resistant, etc.).

6) Motor behavior: e.g., posture, gait, possible tremors, or posturing.

7) Manner of speech.

8) Affective state(s): e.g., anger, fear, elation, and whether or not appropriate.

9) Thought processes: i.e., whether or not the person's thoughts are logical.

10) Thought content, including delusion(s).

11) Perception or distortion(s) of perception.

12) Intellectual functioning.

13) Orientation in terms of identity, place, and time.

14) Judgment (ability to make and carry out plans).

15) A clear description of the person's behavior during the emergency situation.

THE HOMICIDAL OR DANGEROUS PERSON

As referred to above, many people who lose control, even those who become aggressive or homicidal, are fearful of their own impulses. In many instances this may seem an unwarranted assumption, especially if the disturbed people are rather large, powerful, and/or agitated. Nonetheless, no matter how formidable the people are, they may be astonished and confused by their own actions. So it will be a good idea to protect this kind of person from as many aggravating or provocative stimuli as possible. Thus the therapist should talk with the person in a quiet but not closed-in place, since an enclosed area may cause a person to panic if he or she feels trapped. It is also wise, as Salamon (1976) noted, for a therapist to give an aggressive person free access to the door, so that if a person tries to run out he or she will be less likely to attack the therapist en route to leaving the room. In most cases a person can be brought back by the police or a security guard if he or she runs away.

If a person does become agitated and must be restrained, the clinician should attempt to avoid a one-to-one confrontation, trying instead to muster enough assistance to make resistance futile. Salamon (1976, p. 111) also warned that a therapist should be careful to restrain an aggressive male in such a manner that he does not feel this restraint to be a challenge to his masculinity: i.e., when three or four people are involved in the restraining process, the odds are good that he will not see it as a challenge. Of course, a therapist should try to arrange for this necessary support in advance. A disturbed person may be encouraged to act out more violently if the clinician recommends hospitalization and then is not able to back up this statement because no one else is there to provide support.

The following are some guidelines for making an assessment of the potential dangerousness of a person. It should be noted that the person in question may simply not appear to be violent when being seen by a therapist. Some paranoid people are quite capable of controlling their violent tendencies for a period of time when necessary. In such a case it may be helpful to include one or more significant others during the interview, because the disturbed person may not be able to mask his/her thoughts or actions as easily around people with whom he/she is emotionally involved. Yet no amount of clinical skill will be able to penetrate the calm demeanor of some paranoid persons.

Because not all violent people are homicidal, the following critical questions, as suggested by Salamon (1976, pp. 113, 114), may help a clinician to differentiate between the merely violent and the homicidal person. First, what is the *meaning* of the current violent behavior? Is it the venting of nonspecific rage, or is it clearly directed toward someone in particular? Obviously, violence that is directed toward a specific victim represents the more serious situation. Did the violent behavior invite discovery because it was so blatant, or did the client attempt to conceal his/her true intentions? Is the intended victim an innocent party, or did he or she do something to provoke this aggression? How delusional is the disturbed person: i.e., does he or she have any remaining capacity to test reality, or does the person have such a bizarre and well-formed delusional system that it could justify homicidal violence? Does the person have a well-defined plan and access to some means (e.g., a weapon) to carry out this plan?

A disturbed person's personal history can help the clinician to assess potential dangerousness. Does the person come from a violent family background? Was he or she the victim of abuse or brutality? Had the person ever been placed out of the home (removed from the parents' care), or have the parents died or abandoned him or her? Has the person exhibited the "triad" of fire-setting, bed-wetting, and cruelty to animals, as described by Salamon (1976, p. 115)? Since a person's past behavior is the best indicator of future behavior, is there a history of some form of domestic violence? In addition, because driving a car can function as a symbolic outlet for aggression, a history of frequent auto accidents or incidents of drunken or reckless driving may suggest poorly controlled aggressive impulses.

If a clinician discovers that the disturbed person is carrying a weapon, the first thing to bear in mind is that the person is carrying it to protect himself or herself *from* other people. Thus the therapist should be extremely careful not to do anything that this person would view as aggressive or frightening. It may seem paradoxical, but a person who carries a weapon is more afraid of the clinician than vice versa, because the person must carry a weapon in order to feel safe. With this concept in mind, it will be easier for a therapist to negotiate with an agitated client who is carrying a weapon, because the fear and desperation that lie behind it can be understood clearly.

It is wiser to ask why the person is carrying a weapon than to request that he or she surrender it. After learning why a person is carrying a weapon, the therapist can attempt to convince the person that it is not necessary, because he or she will not be harmed. A clinician may then say that he or she would be more comfortable if the person handed over the weapon or placed it on the table. Under no circumstances should the therapist try to disarm a person. If the person refuses to relinquish a weapon, the therapist should see to it that this problem is turned over to the police or to a hospital security service.

Finally, a vital component in assessing a person's dangerousness is how well he or she responds to the offer of therapeutic assistance. A person who is receptive to help and has the support of family and friends is a better risk than someone who is resistant to help and does not have a well-functioning support network.

A CASE STUDY ILLUSTRATING THE HOSPITALIZATION PROCESS

The Emergency Treatment Center was called by a police Watch Commander at about 8 p.m. and asked to send someone to the police station. The Watch Commander explained that a young man had wandered into the station and was behaving very strangely. He did not know what to do with the man, although he obviously had a problem. When the ETC therapist arrived, he was shown into an office where Richard McMillan was waiting. The Watch Commander introduced the clinician and asked Richard if he would tell his story. At first

Richard was suspicious, complaining that he had already told his story three times. The therapist reassured Richard that he had come to the station for the purpose of helping him, and that this would be the last time he would have to tell his story. After some hesitation, accompanied by exaggerated gestures, he agreed to tell the story once more.

Richard said that a man who was impersonating his father was living in his father's mobile home. When the therapist asked him what he thought had happened, his answer was that he didn't know, but he knew that the man was not his real father. Richard said that, although his father had blue eyes, the impersonator's eyes were brown. The therapist asked him if the man looked like his father. Richard replied, while gesturing and grimacing, that this impersonator was extremely clever and knew a lot, but that his car was the wrong color. When the therapist asked if there were friends or relatives living in the area who could identify his father, Richard explained that all of his relatives were impostors. He said they were clever too and, while they thought they knew all about him, they were really lying. Although they were friendly to him and often invited him to visit and have dinner, he knew they were being nice so that he would not expose them. Richard added that these relatives would try to bring up his "past," but that it didn't matter. The therapist asked what those people would try to bring up. At that, Richard became very agitated and exclaimed, "We just won't talk about that because it has nothing to do with this."

The clinician explained that they would have to figure out a way to obtain proof of whether or not his father or those other people were impostors. At first Richard objected because he felt it was not necessary since he already had proof that they were impostors. Even so, the therapist explained, it would be better for legal reasons to decide upon some positive means of identification. The therapist asked Richard if he would draw up a list of names of the relatives whom he thought were being impersonated, and if he would supply the address, telephone number, and a description of each of those people. Richard hesitated, initially, to give addresses and telephone numbers because he was afraid that someone would call or visit the relatives. He said they would be very angry if anyone called them late at night. When the therapist offered to telephone only during the daytime, Richard gave him the numbers. When the therapist asked Richard if he lived nearby and if he had a job, he replied that he had been living in this area for four months and had just moved into a hotel nearby; he did not have a job, but instead received an income from Social Security. Richard added that he was completely alone and desperately wanted to find his "real" father.

The clinician told Richard that there probably wasn't much more they could do that night, especially since he was reluctant to permit anyone to telephone the people who were impersonating his family. The therapist decided to invite one of the (alleged) relatives to visit the ETC office next morning, so that Richard could identify him or her. While he was still somewhat suspicious, Richard reluctantly agreed to the meeting. The clinician's purpose in arranging this meeting was to gain additional information because, despite the fact that his behavior was quite bizarre and clearly delusional, Richard was not at that time so disturbed that he required hospitalization.

When the therapist asked if he had thought about finding another place in which to live than his hotel room, Richard answered that he was looking for a place and "for a lady to live with." He said he had thought about finding a halfway house temporarily, so that he would not be alone. The clinician told Richard that the Emergency Treatment Center could possibly help him find a halfway house where he could stay until he found a job and an apartment. He took the name and telephone number of Richard's hotel and said he would call him before noon the next day. When the therapist offered to walk with him to his hotel, Richard appeared to be greatly relieved that someone was trying to help him. The therapist thought that Richard, although schizophrenic, was still functioning on a level at which he could be treated as an outpatient. He wanted to find a placement for Richard in a halfway house, and enroll him in a day treatment program to prevent the young man's schizophrenic episode from escalating.

As the therapist and Richard walked along toward the hotel, Richard became increasingly fearful. He stopped outside the hotel door and said, "Please, could we talk some more? I don't want to go back because I won't sleep." Richard asked if they could go to a bar around the corner, have a beer, and talk a while longer; he seemed much relieved when the therapist agreed. The therapist spent another half hour with Richard, reassuring him that he would not be deserted. When he asked Richard if he had taken some kind of medication before, Richard replied that he had but couldn't remember the names of the drugs; besides, it didn't matter because he was never going to take drugs again. He talked at length about the fact that his mother had died and how much he missed her. Although Richard was 26 years old, his speech and manner were those of a confused, 12-year-old boy. After about an hour's conversation, he said that he thought he could go back to the hotel and sleep.

The next day the clinician began trying to locate members of Richard's family and to find a halfway house for him. Eventually he located an older brother named Ralph, a married man who lived nearby, and also found a halfway house which had a vacancy. The only requirement for admission was that the client appear voluntarily for a psychological interview and a financial interview. The staff felt it important that potential clients initiate contact with the house, as a demonstration of their motivation.

The therapist then telephoned Richard and told him he had spoken with his alleged brother Ralph and that Ralph would be willing to come to ETC's office in the afternoon of the next Saturday. He added that in this meeting they would be able to identify Ralph as either an impostor or as Richard's real brother. When Richard agreed to come to the meeting, the clinician told him about the halfway house placement. Richard was not particularly excited about the latter idea, reiterating that he would rather find a woman to live with, but he said that he would think about the suggestion.

By the end of that week Richard had still resisted telephoning the halfway house, despite several attempts by the clinician to get him to do so. When Richard arrived at the ETC office for Saturday's meeting, the therapist placed a long-distance telephone call to Richard's (alleged) father. Richard spent some time talking with the father and, when he finally asked him to meet with him and the therapist at some later time, the father agreed. Richard's only comment after the lengthy telephone conversation was, "He's a pretty good impostor." The meeting between Richard and his brother Ralph was not a successful one—the brother suddenly became extremely angry and left, saying that he was "through" with Richard and his "crazy nonsense." The therapist guessed that a show of warm acceptance and concern, suddenly being transformed into angry rejection, was a typical dynamic in the family system.

A meeting was arranged between Richard and his father, and this meeting repeated the same acceptance-rejection theme that had characterized the earlier one between him and his brother. The therapist learned that Richard's father had, some years ago, spent 10 months in a state mental hospital; he apparently felt insecure and ashamed of that illness and hospitalization. In the meeting, the father would coldly reject Richard (because he reminded him of his own schizophrenic break), and then feel guilty for rejecting him and make vaguely fatherly gestures. But when Richard responded to his father's overtures of friendship and tried to feel closer to him, the father would reject him again. Throughout the meeting, the father's manner was brusque and businesslike, while Richard obviously expected that his father would indicate some concern. The father did not say it but made it perfectly clear that he wanted nothing to do with Richard. He stayed for about half of the scheduled one-hour appointment and then left, claiming that he had to go to a business meeting.

Following these rejections by both his brother and his father, Richard's condition began to worsen. The therapist was reluctant to permit him to remain in an unsupervised living situation, but Richard had neither family nor friends to help or lend their support at that time. For that reason, the clinician repeatedly urged him to enter the halfway house. Richard stubbornly refused, insisting that he had to find his real father. The therapist finally decided to hospitalize Richard involuntarily because he was deteriorating rapidly, to the extent that he could no longer care for himself properly. When this decision was made, the therapist made the necessary preparations before informing Richard about them, because he was aware of Richard's intense feelings against hospitalization. The hospital had been called and the case discussed with an on-duty psychiatrist who assured the therapist that there would be an available bed in a locked ward. The therapist asked that the hospital have two strong ward attendants at the ready, should assistance be needed, because Richard was above average in size and quite athletic.

When the clinician presented this plan for hospitalization to Richard, he became quite agitated and began pacing around the office. At this point the therapist rang for assistance; when two other ETC staff members arrived for help, Richard jumped up, grabbed a cup from the therapist's desk, and smashed it in defiance. But when he saw that the staff members were determined, he agreed to go to the hospital. The therapist accompanied Richard through the entire hospitalization process. He visited regularly and had several consultations with the staff of the psychiatric ward. At first Richard was extremely resistant to treatment, but after about a week he began to make progress. When Richard was to be transferred out of the locked facility, the ETC therapist was consulted in the decision about where he sould be sent. Richard agreed voluntarily to enter an unlocked residential facility that provides aftercare treatment for patients who had once been acutely disturbed.

Richard responded well to treatment. Even his brother Ralph commented that he could not remember when he had seen Richard "in such good shape." The brother has also made some progress in establishing a better relationship with Richard. Even so, the attitude of Richard's father toward his son did not change. Richard subsequently made several telephone calls to the ETC in order to express his thanks and to tell the therapist about his progress.

A CASE ILLUSTRATING THAT THINGS ARE

NOT ALWAYS WHAT THEY APPEAR TO BE

Dan Wilson was a 51-year-old chronic alcoholic, who was first brought to the attention of the Emergency Treatment Center by a police officer who had become his friend about two years before. Unknown to any of Wilson's family or friends, he had noticed that a growth on his upper lip had become inflamed and enlarged. He went to his physician, who referred him to a surgeon. The surgeon looked at him briefly and said he thought that Wilson had a carcinoma on his lip; he would have to go into a hospital the following week for surgery. After the surgeon said that, he excused himself to see another patient. Wilson was told to talk with the secretary, who would make the necessary arrangements for his hospitalization. Since Wilson had heard of carcinoma, he thought that he had an incurable cancer, that the operation would disfigure him greatly, and that he would soon die an agonizing death.

Wilson purchased a gun after he left the surgeon's office, and later that evening he began drinking heavily. He attempted suicide by driving his car into a cement wall at high speed. The car was wrecked, but miraculously Wilson was not hurt. The next day his family (i.e., his son and daughter-in-law) tried to get him to enter the alcoholism ward of a local Veterans Hospital, but when they took him to the hospital he became frightened and refused to commit himself. Thereupon the family members became so angry with him that they left him at the hospital.

Wilson walked several miles to the house of a friend, who drove him home. As soon as he was home, he called his son and told him that he had a gun, and if anyone tried to hospitalize him, he would shoot anyone who came near him and then commit suicide. The son, in turn, called Wilson's police officer friend because he thought that his father had simply gone crazy and needed to be locked up. When the officer telephoned Wilson, he repeated his threat that he planned to barricade himself in his home and commit suicide. The officer then called upon ETC for assistance, and two therapists who were on duty met him at Wilson's house. The three of them began talking with Wilson through the front door. With time, the story about the feared carcinoma came out; it became clear that Wilson was not a violent person who wanted to harm others. Instead, he was terrified about the growth on his lip causing him to be horribly disfigured and, eventually, suffering a painful, prolonged, and terminal illness. The clinicians eventually convinced Wilson that he had other options and that he should at least obtain a second medical opinion. Grudgingly, he agreed to go voluntarily to the psychiatric ward of a general hospital (since by then he was completely sober).

When the ETC therapists visited Wilson at the hospital that evening, they found him to be an extremely pleasant man. He said that he was very sorry that he had caused everyone so much trouble, but he was obviously fighting very hard to control his terror about the cancer on his face. He recalled that the surgeon had told him that he had a carcinoma and that half of his entire upper lip would have to be removed. One of the therapists then suggested that the general hospital staff could help him find another surgeon. Wilson agreed that it would be sensible to consult another surgeon and added that at one time he had worked as a surgical technician. He had seen too many cancer operations that were not successful. He appeared to be somewhat relieved to be able to talk about his fears concerning the operation.

After this interview with Wilson, the therapists believed that he was still suicidal. They asked the head nurse not to release Wilson until after a second surgeon had evaluated the growth on his face. She agreed, saying that she would find someone to accompany him to visit a surgeon's office. The next day Wilson was examined by a highly regarded cancer specialist.

Two days later Wilson called one of the ETC therapists to report that he had seen the specialist, who had taken enough time to explain the problem to him. The surgeon had said that while he could not be sure whether or not the growth was a carcinoma until he did a biopsy, he would remove the growth in his office and then conduct a biopsy. The surgeon added that Wilson would have the biopsy results by the following week; if the growth were a carcinoma, he would take a little more tissue out to be sure that all was removed.

Dan Wilson called ETC again on two occasions. The first time, he told us that the operation had gone well. With the second call, he reported that the biopsy had shown that he did not have a carcinoma. In this case, a suicide or barricaded situation had been prevented, an involuntary hospitalization had been avoided, and a contributing factor to an alcoholic binge had been identified and alleviated.

REFERENCE

Salamon, I. Violent and aggressive behavior. In R. Glick, A. Meyerson, and J. Talbott (Eds.), *Psychiatric Emergencies*. New York: Grune & Stratton, 1976.

5

Domestic violence

Family violence has been considered to be a "private affair" or an event that "doesn't happen" in nice families. Often participants (both victim and perpetrator) will go to great lengths to conceal the violence within their family from outsiders. Gelles (1972) noted that persons may publicly disapprove of violent behavior which they may privately permit or condone. Similarly, Marsden and Owens (1975) described the "Jekyl and Hyde" type of husband who is at one moment friendly and affable, particularly in public, but later in private can suddenly become violent to his family. Most victims think that they are the only people who have experienced this. In fact, family violence is an international affair, and in many societies it is overtly or covertly condoned.

Only recently have many people been willing to acknowledge the extent to which domestic violence exists. For centuries the family realm has been considered to be a sanctum that no one, least of all a person from outside the family, had a right to invade. When wife-beating and other forms of intra-family violence were first brought into the open, they were often dismissed as rare occurrences, except in poor or foreign families. Or, they were blamed upon "provocative" women

The authors wish to thank Dr. Arthur M. Bodin for his significant contribution to this chapter. His ideas formed the basis of the section on couples who fight violently.

who really wanted to be "put in their place" once in awhile. But in the past few years, as a result of the efforts of researchers such as Gayford (1978), Steinmetz and Strauss (1974), and Strauss (1973, 1974), and notably the moving work of Pizzey (1974), family violence has finally been recognized as a reality of far more complex dimensions than were ever thought to exist in the past.

A major factor that has contributed to family violence internationally is the nuclearization of families. Modern industrial society has inexorably caused the large extended family group to break down into smaller (nuclear) families. We at ETC, as well as Glick (1975), have noticed that there tends to be less violence in the large extended family. When there is fragmentation, the support system that often serves to prevent intra-family conflict soon disappears. Without grandparents, uncles and aunts, cousins, et al., the family is an even more "private place" where feelings of hurt, anger, and frustrations can become acutely focused upon one or two people. Because the nuclear family can become progressively more isolated from relatives, fewer and fewer people will be aware of whether or not violence is taking place within the family.

Most of us would prefer to think that violent acts such as wife-beating and child abuse take place only in "sick" or deviant families. This commonly held misconception further serves to isolate the victims of family violence, so that they continue to think that violent acts are only being done to them. And because violence can only be happening to them, something must be wrong with them. A possible source of this commonly held myth may have been found by Steinmetz and Strauss (1974), who reviewed the mass media (especially television and movies) to see how domestic violence was portrayed; they discovered that violence was never portrayed by a "normal" or average family. By contrast, when family violence did occur, the acting-out person was portrayed as a deviant, a criminal, or a foreigner.

Many would prefer to believe that violent families are ethnically different or, at the very least, from a different social class than theirs, but our clinical experience and that of Freitas (1979) and Gelles (1978) (the latter wrote that 50 percent of all married women will be assaulted by their husbands during their marriage and that, at any given time, nearly one million American children are being abused or neglected) suggest that this myth is a far cry from reality. Other relevant evidence was provided by Wolfgang's (1958) classic study of homicide: He found that, while only 12 percent of homicide victims had been slain by strangers, a majority had been slain by friends and relatives; also, 94 percent of murderers and their victims were of the same race. Gelles (1978) put the matter succinctly: ". . . the most common relationship between murderer and victim is a family relationship" (p. 172).

Apparently, violence tends to be closer to home than most of us would prefer to believe. We are more vulnerable to violence in the midst of our friends and relatives than with the (mythical) stranger of another race. Possible causes of the misconception being described here are complex. One such cause may be that many behavioral scientists have difficulty in accepting and understanding the fact that "normal" people, like themselves, in certain circumstances could be violent towards their spouses or children or close friends. It may have been this same reluctance that in the past caused some clinicians to relegate true accusations of incest to the realm of fantasy, because the subject of incest was too unpleasant for them to face as reality.

A further indication of our reluctance to view family violence candidly is the fact that this species of behavior was not a common topic of public concern, academic research, or even discussion by therapists until at least 1962, when Kempe et al. published their landmark paper on battered children in the United States, or until 1974 when Pizzey published her dramatic *Scream Quietly or the Neighbors Will Hear*. Since then, several events have brought the unpleasant subject of family violence forcefully before the public eye, e.g.: 1) the National Commission on the Causes and Prevention of Violence was formed after the Kennedy and King assassinations, and it produced startling information on the nature and extent of violence in American life (see especially Mulvihill et al., 1969); 2) the women's movement served to raise the public's consciousness that many women were victims of violent assault in their own homes. Those developments drew support from the revelations of Gelles and Wolfgang (noted above), namely that the most common relationship between murderer and victim is that of family member or friend. Further, it has become known in recent years that family violence is the reason behind a majority of calls to police departments. This kind of call is considered by police to be the most dangerous, because more officers are hurt or killed when intervening in family disturbances than in any other single type of case that is dealt with by police (Parnas, 1967).

One factor that we have found to be strongly associated with family violence is substance abuse. In fact, in about 40 percent of ETC cases of intra-family violence, alcoholism or another form of substance abuse is a contributing factor. Our findings at ETC are consistent with Gayford's (1978) study of violent families, in which he found that alcohol abuse was involved in about half of the cases of wife-beating in his sample. That is not to say that substance abuse is by itself a direct cause of family violence, but alcohol or other kinds of drugs do tend to interfere with people's ability to control themselves under stressful conditions; in effect, they permit fear, anger, or jealousy, which had been controlled and hidden below the surface, to erupt into violent acting-out.

Although it should be reiterated here that it is not our opinion that family violence is a product of social class or culture, it has been noted by others who are involved in the study of violence (e.g., Gelles) that relatively more people from working-class and lower-income families are found to experience violence in the home. The reason for this is not that these people are inherently more violent, but instead, as Gelles (1972, 1978) aptly pointed out, working-class and lower-income families are more vulnerable to social pressures such as those caused by unemployment and financial insecurity, overcrowded housing, unplanned pregnancy, and a host of other problems. As a result of these pressures, they sometimes turn on each other and victimize each other. In addition, working-class families cannot afford the private services that middle- and upper-class families can, and thus they are more likely to take their problems to a public agency, thereby becoming a part of the record-keeping system and public statistics.

A most significant factor in the etiology of family violence, as reported in a large body of research (e.g., Bakan, 1971; Gayford, 1978; Gil, 1971; Gelles, 1976; Kempe et al., 1962; Levine, 1975; Sears, Maccoby, and Levin, 1957; Steele and Pollock, 1968) in the United States and abroad, is that the more violence a child experiences while growing up, the greater the likelihood that the child will become a violent adult. What a sad fact it is that these, the children of violent families, will probably become the violent adults, spouses, and parents of tomorrow unless something is done in a humane and realistic way to stop the tragic cycle.

Unfortunately few social, medical, or mental health programs currently provide appropriate, effective services for violent families. Professionals in the criminal justice system, including police officers, usually indulge in the excuse that, because these are private or "civil" (i.e., not "criminal") matters, they themselves should not get involved. In some parts of the country, attitudes are slowly changing, but in many communities some archaic notions (such as, "Women need and even like to be struck once in awhile, to be shown who's boss" and "Parents have a right to punish their child, however they see fit") still persist. Eventually, in the authors' opinion, there will be a much-needed reversal of this reluctance of society to become involved in "private" family affairs. Even though "a man's home is his castle," he does not have a right to beat his wife or his children.

COUPLES WHO FIGHT VIOLENTLY

Many disagreements between the partners of a couple result in violent fights in which one strikes or hurls an object in the direction of the other. This kind of chronic violent fighting is a quite different phenomenon from the battered wife syndrome which will be described in Chapter 6. The present section is confined to a discussion of chronic fighting between spouses.

Violent behavior is likely to occur when some factor (or interaction of factors) that normally prevents acting-out decreases in strength. Or, the person who becomes violent may have had poor impulse control in the first place. Some factors which may cause a breakdown of control are chemical (i.e., drugs or alcohol) and some are neurophysiological (e.g., brain damage), while others are psychological and sociological. The following discussion will focus on the psychological (e.g., communicational) and sociological factors that lead to violence.

In describing family violence, the word "escalation" is commonly used. Unfortunately, this term has come to have more than one meaning, and it will be useful to distinguish between the two meanings and define the term precisely as it is to be used in this discussion. Watzlawick et al. (1967) used "escalation" to describe a type of pathology that occurs in "symmetrical relationships," in which either partner in a relationship can become extremely uncomfortable if the relationship is perceived as the slightest bit "unequal." This form of competitiveness is often referred to as the "I can do anything better than you can" aspect of a symmetrical relationship. A second sense in which the term "escalation" is used refers to the exacerbation of an ordinary life *difficulty* into what begins to be experienced as a *problem;* this can occur when the way in which people choose to deal with a difficulty merely serves to intensify it. As Weakland et al. wrote, "The action meant to *alleviate* the behavior of the other party *aggravates* it; the 'cure' becomes worse than the 'disease'" (1974, p. 149). This second usage of the term "escalation" is actually closer in meaning to the terms "intensification" or "exacerbation." Yet there is a connection between how the term "escalation" was originally used (to describe the excessive competition in a symmetrical relationship) and the second usage of the term, i.e., when a "commonsense" remedy turns an everyday difficulty into a major problem. The connection is that an initial, unconscious exacerbation of some minor difficulty or disagreement can bring to the awareness of the family (or couple) a major problem. This awareness having occurred, there often ensues a highly motivated struggle for control. It is in that sense—of a chain of events, sometimes intentionally and sometimes unintentionally begun, which leads to a very conscious struggle for control of the situation—that the term "escalation" will be used in the discussion to follow.

One way in which escalation can occur is by means of the violation of "family rules" or patterns (cf. Jackson, 1965). Such rules may be unspoken and idiosyncratic to each family, by contrast with the more commonly held family rules such as fidelity, privacy, and parental authority. Certain family rules are consciously acknowledged and others are not. Examples of some of the more subtle rules are the total avoidance of certain topics (or their avoidance in the presence of certain people), and the family myth or "shared untruth" that family members secretly agree to accept and protect. Family rules may also involve the status or power of certain family members. Violation of any one of these rules, whether of the consciously acknowledged or the unconscious variety, may instigate the process of escalation. That is especially likely when one member of the family attempts to repair the damage or restore the family status quo by a commonsense (i.e., misguided) remedy.

Usually an escalation will proceed in differing ways depending upon whether the broken rule was of the conscious or unconscious variety. Violation of a consciously acknowledged rule is more likely to initiate an immediate outburst of anger, while violation of an unconscious rule is more likely to result in delayed outbursts of anger. The fact that a slower escalation should result from the violation of rules which are followed *without* conscious awareness is understandable because a person who is on the "receiving end" of the rule-breaking (called here the recipient) only becomes aware of the broken rule later on (after it has been broken); not until then do the resulting feelings of hurt or anger surface. In effect, the one who vaguely suspects that a rule has been broken may feel uneasy, wronged, or in some sense "violated," without being able to articulate to others precisely why. This recipient may retaliate with anger toward the rule-breaker and feel quite justified in doing so. Further, the recipient may not be able to articulate clearly any acceptable "reason" when he or she is directly challenged on this point by the rule-breaker, since the recipient probably feels "right" in having retaliated. And since the retaliation appeared to have no justification discernible to the rule-breaker, the rule-breaker may then retaliate in kind, because of being "attacked for no reason."

Thus do spouses or two family members often become indignant combatants, each one claiming to be the innocent victim of the other's provocation. What both fail to realize is that each is right in a sense, and that each is wrong to a degree. Each person is responding to a stimulus that was provided by the other, and naturally each will prefer to interpret an escalation sequence in a way that can support his or her view of the reality of the situation. This kind of situation is even more complex and difficult to decode when one person holds one set of unconscious rules and the other holds a conflicting set of rules. Then the two will continue their battle, as each excuses his or her own "responsive" behavior as justified by the "provocative" or "unjust" behavior of the other. Each person feels that he or she has been wronged by the other, but neither can clearly specify why or how it began. In this way, an interaction sequence that begins by the breaking of an unconscious (or extremely subtle) rule can suddenly evolve into a very conscious and competitive struggle for power and control.

A salient psychological factor that we at ETC have observed to be capable of provoking violent acting-out among couples is the conscious or unconscious manipulation of fear of loneliness or abandonment. People who already suspect that they are unloved or unlovable —partly due to the behavior of the loved one and partly because their early training caused them to doubt their lovability—are particularly vulnerable to real or imagined threats of abandonment. Because they are unable to face the prospect of this worst possible event (being abandoned), it is not surprising that a situation involving that kind of threat possesses a high potential for violent behavior. This is particularly true when other psychosocial factors (e.g., violent childhood role models, economic pressures, or fear of social humiliation) combine to tear down what controls the person may normally have been able to muster.

A stressful situation may be exacerbated further by the person's attempts to solve a problem by one or more of the well-intentioned, but potentially dangerous, commonsense remedies, for example: "If I hit her a couple of times, she will realize how much I love her"; "If I throw something at him he will know how much he has hurt me and stop"; or 'If I threaten to leave, it will scare him and he will change." Other commonsense myths that are sometimes believed in by people who doubt their ability to be loved concern sexual matters, such as the notion that "sex is better after a fight." Notions of this kind are usually based upon the feelings of one or both partners that one of them is not sexually adequate under more normal circumstances. So the couple develops a pattern or set of rules based upon the tacit agreement that intimacy will be preceded by a fight. But if during one of these battles, staged as a prelude to intimacy, one person "strikes a nerve" by saying something truly wounding to the other, this "mock" fight can easily become quite violent and ugly.

Since anger is notoriously contagious, these pathetic common-sense measures, which are naively designed to elicit demonstrations of love and affection, can produce a paradoxical outcome. Actually, each partner, in order to respond in the desired manner, would have to know the feelings of fear and desperation that lay behind the other person's mask of angry behavior, requiring a degree of perceptiveness that is rare in these couples. In general, this sort of commonsense attempt to manipulate the other person to provide needed reassurance is doomed to fail because it requires that one angry person "read the mind" of another. The needs of the would-be manipulator are not going to be met for still another reason: Many of these needs for nurturance on the part of an adult result from dependency needs that were not met as a child. Few of these needs can be adequately met by a marriage partner.

The following is an example of how a fight between two people can escalate when there are differing or conflicting perceptions of the reality of the situation. A couple in their late twenties were frequently involved in vicious fights. They had been married for five-and-a-half years, and since the first six months of marriage they had occasion to quarrel almost daily. About once every two months their word fights erupted into physical confrontations which reached the threshold of actual violence. The problem, according to the wife, was that the husband ignored her and would not give her the affection she needed, so that she was forced to take extreme measures to make him pay attention to her. Periodically she was reassured of his need for her by the outbursts of jealousy which she would consciously provoke in him when she became fearful. He, in turn, claimed that he was unable to be affectionate toward her because she constantly kept him at a distance. He said that, when he was feeling most insecure and most fearful that she might be interested in another man, she would leave the house and refuse to tell him where she was going or when she would return. When he demanded to know where she was going, she would say, "Where I go and what I do are my business!" At this point, the husband would tear her away from the door and usually a heated struggle would follow.

Many family fights, which on the surface appear to involve an easily identifiable "victim" and an equally obvious "villain" (depending upon which family member is asked), have their true origin in a shared, interactional context. Since family members and marital partners share considerable history, they have had plenty of opportunities to learn the patterns that constitute family rules. In effect, the husband in the case described above had good reason to know that if he ignored or was not affectionate to his wife, she would become enraged (thus reassuring him that she needed his love). But because he was not capable of providing her with the reassurance *she* needed, her fear and anger would continue to grow until she would make her provocative "parting speech"; to that, he would respond by trying to restrain her physically. By the time that happened, the wife would be far too enraged to see that her husband's attempts to restrain her were no more than a misguided attempt at affection. In the struggle, she would respond with still more rage and resist his restraint. The husband would retaliate by striking her to "make her realize" how much he loved her, so that she would not actually go.

The wife also had had plenty of opportunities to notice the pattern of her husband's jealous and violent responses to her parting speech. But, as mentioned above, two entirely different descriptions of the situation would be given, depending upon which person was being questioned. To review, the wife's image of the situation was that of being a loving person who was ignored and emotionally starved by her cold, self-centered husband. His perception of reality was that he had tried to be affectionate to her in his way, but she had kept him at a distance by being vague and secretive.

The fact that these patterns of interaction had been going on for more than five years suggests that either partner could have interrupted the cycle if either had perceived it as being too painful. The fact that neither did anything to stop the cycle of their increasingly more violent fights (at first they were quite resistant to outside intervention, despite complaints from neighbors and several visits by the police) further suggests that some need was being satisfied by this repetitive pattern. For example, the husband may have acted so as to induce his wife to "jar" him out of his usually unexpressive, withdrawn shell of self-protection. Also, the husband's jealous rages provided the intensely dramatic, emotional display that the wife required to feel that she was loved by someone.

In order to treat such a couple successfully, a therapist should first decode the two disparate "realities." The clinician can then interpret how these two realities interact in a healthy way, as well as how they interact in a neurotic or destructive manner. Next, the therapist may explore what each person is capable of perceiving in respect to the other—considering the status of their current self-images. Because people tend to think in a more rigid manner when frightened or angry, each person's behavior will, in turn, need to be clarified, interpreted, and reframed (that is, put in terms that will fit within each person's cognitive set and will not threaten the current self-image of either). Finally, the therapist needs to encourage alternative behavior that will create new and healthier interactional patterns.

In the example of the couple described above, the ETC therapist first focused upon the transparent fact that the two partners actually cared for each other, but did not express their affection appropriately and did not request affection in terms that the other person could understand. The husband had been raised in a blue-collar family in which men were tough and not talkative; they expressed their affection by working hard and by being "good providers." Because of his background he thought that he was being what a good husband should be, and he perceived himself as a loving husband. In addition, he thought that his wife's constant demands for attention or affection meant that she did not appreciate him.

The wife, by contrast, came from a family in which the father and mother were alcoholics. She was forced to grow up quickly, in order to care for her younger siblings because her parents were seldom at home. She was attracted to her husband because she thought him a strong, stable, and loving man who would never abandon her as her parents had done. The clinician helped clarify that she had created an idyllic fantasy, the theme of which was that everyone outside her terrible family of origin was loving; once she left her parents' home, she thought, everything would be different. The therapist helped the husband to realize, as time went by, that it was all right—possibly even manly—to show affection. Eventually, the therapist helped this couple to communicate with each other in terms that each could understand and that would not require loss of face on the part of either person.

This case shows one typical way in which conflicting self-images may contribute to an interactional situation in which family rules can fuel the escalation of domestic violence. If the couple is especially unfortunate, these periodic eruptions of violence will satisfy enough of each person's needs so that each will allow it to continue. Occasionally, they will actively restart the cycle and resist any attempt to stop it from rolling relentlessly on.

There follow two case studies of therapy with people who had violent family fights, describing some intervention techniques that were useful in working with these families.

A VIOLENT HUSBAND

The Emergency Treatment Center was called by a police officer who had responded to a violent family disturbance. ETC was asked to respond immediately, because the couple (Mr. and Mrs. Campbell) were still actively combative. The officer met the therapists in front of the Campbell home with the news that the situation inside the house was still very "hot": The husband had tried to stab his wife earlier, but a friend had stopped him. The officer added that the husband was sitting in a corner, swearing and mumbling about flowers.

When the ETC staff members entered the Campbell's dimly lit, lower-middle-class home, furniture had been thrown about and there were empty bottles and beer cans on the floor. Mr. Campbell was sitting in a far corner of the living room; Mrs. Campbell was in the next room with a second police officer. The police had concluded that this couple would not stay apart without supervision. At this point, it was decided that just one officer would remain on the scene with the two ETC therapists.

The staff members decided to interview the husband first because he was by far the angrier of the two and the one more likely to explode violently. After Mr. Campbell had settled down a bit, one clinician asked him what he thought the principal problem was. He answered that he could not stand the sight of his wife. When asked how long he had not been able to stand the sight of his wife, Campbell replied that for the past three years she would not let him "live down" his drinking. He said that he was currently unemployed, but that he was looking for work. The clinicians talked for a while with Mr. Campbell, but it was obvious that he was too intoxicated to be interviewed effectively that night. A therapist then decided that Campbell should, if possible, go to an alcoholism facility for detoxification immediately, since he had been drinking heavily for a long period of time. When the idea was proposed to him, Campbell reluctantly agreed to go to the inpatient facility.

Next, a therapist talked with Mrs. Campbell in order to learn her view of the problem. She said that when Mr. Campbell got drunk he became irrational and violent. She said that he was too proud and too "blind" to see the impact of his drinking upon his family and his work. She said that he had been laid off from a foreman's job, which he had held for 11 years, because of his drinking. She added that she was fed up with him and had threatened him with a divorce. When the clinician presented the idea of hospitalizing Mr. Campbell, Mrs. Campbell agreed that it would be a good idea, considering the extent of her husband's recent drinking.

We called a local detoxification facility to reserve a bed and asked the workers at the facility to send a car to fetch Mr. Campbell. He was quite cooperative at first, but when the car arrived he refused to leave and became belligerent again. Finally, the police officer had to intervene, informing Mr. Campbell that if he did not go he would be hospitalized involuntarily, because of his earlier attempted assault upon his wife with a knife. After Mr. Campbell had been taken to the facility, an ETC therapist stayed to talk with Mrs. Campbell, the teenage children, and the friend of Campbell's who had taken the knife away from him. The friend said that he, himself, was an ex-alcoholic who had been "dry" for six years. He said that Campbell suffered from the "nice-guy" syndrome because he was nice to his enemies and strangers but was nasty to his friends and family. The friend said that Mr. Campbell had bullied his wife and children mercilessly. He added that Campbell picked on the children incessantly, but bragged about their accomplishments when they weren't around.

After some summary discussion, the clinician made a follow-up office appointment with Mrs. Campbell for two days later. He also suggested that Mrs. Campbell call her lawyer the next day about a restraining order and her wish to begin divorce proceedings. The therapist also offered to talk with the lawyer about writing a special type of restraining order, i.e., one that would contain a specific message from the judge to the police, directing them to enforce the order at her request (instead of their usual practice of informing the woman that the problem is a civil matter and that she should go to court). He also reminded Mrs. Campbell that the police believed she should change the locks on her doors, in case her husband decided to come back for revenge.

At the first follow-up visit, Mrs. Campbell said that during his first day in the detoxification facility, her husband had called her and had been talking in a suicidal manner. He asked her how much life insurance he had and whether or not the policy would be paid if he committed suicide. The ETC therapist advised her not to respond to the suicidal threat, because it could provoke more acting-out. Mrs. Campbell also said that her husband was being transferred that same afternoon to a private residential clinic for alcoholics. She added that the clinic operated an intensive, three-month program.

The therapist asked Mrs. Campbell how long Mr. Campbell had had a drinking problem and if she knew of anything in particular that could be associated with the onset of his alcoholism. She answered that her husband had been drinking for 12 years and that four things had happened at about the same time he started drinking heavily: 1) their son was born; 2) Mr. Campbell's mother died; 3) they bought a house; and 4) she (the wife) had started a new job. She said that Campbell was deeply remorseful at not having shown more affection to his mother before her death. Mrs. Campbell added that her husband was fearful of growing old and that he dyed his hair; but he wouldn't allow himself to "let go" or be playful. After some hesitation, Mrs. Campbell told the clinician that she had had an abortion two years before and that her husband strongly resented her for that. She also said that Campbell frequently referred to her as a "bastard" because he had formed the belief that she had been an illegitimate child.

As the therapist continued to talk with Mrs. Campbell, it became clear that her husband was a man who felt he had lost control of several aspects of his life—in particular, his wife, his family, and his job. Because of her anger at her husband, Mrs. Campbell was unconsciously doing things that intensified his feelings of helplessness. During the next session, although she was still quite angry about her marriage, she began to deal with some of the problems which had led up to the current crisis. She was able to see that both she and Campbell had contributed to these problems. The therapist explained to her that she had repeatedly rescued and forgiven her husband and by doing so had hindered him, in some respects, from stopping his drinking habit. When Campbell was drinking, she had more control in the family and played a sacrificing role in the eyes of outsiders.

At the next visit, Mrs. Campbell told the therapist that she wanted to try to save her marriage. She said her husband was making amazing progress and that his progress was forcing her to look at herself. Now she had to learn how to relate to a man who was not completely dependent upon her, as well as a man who was not always making empty promises. She said that Campbell finally realized how childish he had been and that he had become more understanding of their children.

An ETC staff member who had made the original emergency home visit continued to see Mrs. Campbell (and, on two occasions, the children) occasionally for about four months. A few times Mr. Campbell came in for individual sessions while he was still a resident of the alcoholism program. When Campbell was released from the program, he returned to his family and later joined family therapy sessions with an ETC therapist. Subsequently the Campbells have had few difficulties. On one occasion Mr. Campbell became angry at his eldest son for disobeying him, became fearful of his impulses, and called the police. When they arrived Campbell explained what had happened and the police officer told the boy that his father had a right to discipline his children, so long as he was not cruel or abusive which, on that occasion, he had not been. Except for this minor incident, the Campbells have become a successfully integrated family, and there have been no subsequent calls to the police.

A CASE OF MURDER RECONSIDERED

Madilyn Leggett called the police one rainy evening in November, because she was fearful of being alone. A week earlier this woman in her fifties had been the victim of attempted rape by a man who had broken into her home, and what she was afraid of was that the rapist would come back and attack her again. Her daughter and son-in-law had been staying with her since the attack, but on that evening they were preparing to leave and return to their own home. Since the responding policeman was unable to calm her fears and had to return to his patrol duty, he called the Emergency Treatment Center for assistance.

When the ETC therapists arrived and were briefed on the details of the case, the officer left and Madilyn Leggett gave her account of the attempted rape and her present insecurities. As she talked, she seemed to become gradually more calm and poised, and for some reason decided to give us a tour of her small house. She took special pleasure in showing the library which contained an enormous collection of books on the occult, esoteric religions, etc.

While Madilyn showed the therapists around, the figures of a man and a woman were observed passing by from time to time. The man and woman did not seem to be getting along well with each other. They were avoiding each other, and when Madilyn invited them into the living room, there was obvious tension between them. We learned that these were Madilyn's son-in-law and daughter and that they had been experiencing a problem in their marriage. When we asked them if they were interested in marriage counseling, they said they were, and we made an appointment for them to see an ETC therapist in the office on the following day. When we felt that Madilyn Leggett was sufficiently reassured by persuading the daughter and her husband to stay on for at least another night, we took our leave.

The next day the therapist met with Mrs. Leggett's daughter and son-in-law. Anthony Rivera, 31 and a machinist by trade, and his wife Gabrielle, 32, had been married for 10 years. Gabrielle had a daughter by a previous marriage who was 13, and she and Tony had a nine-year-old daughter, Maria-Teresa. Over a period of three weeks they were seen several times by the ETC therapist, both together and separately, in the course of which the following personality dynamics emerged. Gabrielle Leggett Rivera was convinced that she possessed two identities: 1) that of an angel or equivalent of the Virgin Mary; and 2) that of a whore or agent of the devil. In her angelic state she was a dutiful wife and mother, and in her devilish state she indulged herself with a lover. The lover, Buddy Baker, was a 25-year-old whose sole ambition in life was to be accepted into the Hell's Angels. For a while the therapy with Gabrielle focused upon her relationship with her mother, Madilyn, who was said to have read thousands of books on the occult. In this context, the therapist asked whether or not the Leggetts had a "family secret" or "myth," and Gabrielle responded by saying that, in fact, she was the victim of a family curse which she explained as follows. She had discovered in a family album a newspaper article from 20 years before which was about her grandmother. The grandmother (whose middle name was Gabrielle) had murdered her husband in collaboration with a lover. The lover had been executed and the grandmother had been sentenced to 20 years in jail. This was a curse that to Gabrielle represented her own certain destiny. She added that Tony had once taken a wild rifle shot at Buddy Baker when Buddy had been discovered at their home.

For his part, Tony Rivera admitted that he was a murderously jealous person concerning his wife. He said that Buddy Baker had once been a friend of his, and he acknowledged having fired a shot at him in a fit of rage. Once, in fact, he and Buddy had engaged in a furious chase around town in their cars, bumping into each other in a mad version of the game of tag. When asked what weapons he kept in the house, Tony replied that he had six guns in all. When asked whether or not he was planning to take a shot at Buddy Baker again, he replied that the answer would depend upon what Buddy did in the future. The therapist asked Tony if he would promise to telephone first if, at some time in the future, he had an urge to shoot someone. To the clinician's surprise Tony agreed.

Two weeks later, precisely at midnight, Tony (whose voice the therapist recognized at once) called to announce: "Tonight's the night." The therapist asked, "How soon can you meet me at my office?", and Tony's answer was, "In 15 minutes and I'll have my gun with me." The therapist took a deep breath and said, "I can meet you in 15 minutes but please leave the gun in your car." When Tony agreed to this condition, the therapist asked if it would be all right if he invited his two ETC colleagues to join them at the meeting, and Tony acquiesced.

At the appointed time, Tony appeared at the bottom of a stairway leading to the therapist's office. When asked, "Have you left your gun in the car?", his reply was "Yes, but I brought the barrel inside with me because some kid might break into the car and get hurt." During the long session that followed, Tony kept the gun barrel tucked under his jacket. From time to time it was visible, and the three therapists soon realized that it was part of a sawed-off shotgun.

In their work with Tony that night, the clinicians began with the premise that Tony was a neurotic young man whose jealous rage had reached the breaking point. He was not psychotic nor likely to become so, but his potential for violent acting-out was acute. Even so, because he had clearly designated the target of his rage, the therapists felt assured that he would not harm one of them.

As the hours dragged on, Tony was tearful and angry by turns. He alternated between berating himself for his murderous thoughts and summoning up courage for what he knew he must do: "I got to do it. I know I'm crazy, because I got to do it." The therapists let him know that they did not think he was crazy and that what he was feeling was understandable because of what his wife had put him through. But with the passage of time, the clinicians felt that they were not weakening Tony's resolve to kill Buddy Baker, and since they knew that he had been a frequent drug user, they surmised that he had taken some kind of "upper" that night, because his energy level and stamina were formidable.

At one point Tony related, with some pride, the story of an incident that had taken place the previous day and which demonstrated the desperate lengths to which he was willing to go to "settle things." He wanted the therapists to know that he had given Buddy Baker fair warning that he was going to kill him: Only yesterday he had taken Buddy with him to the local police station and had insisted that the officer put him (Tony) in jail, saying, "Arrest me because I'm going to kill this guy." The policeman had remained unconvinced and had asked both men to leave the station.

At about two o'clock in the morning, when the intervention was becoming totally unproductive, one of the clinicians asked Tony if there was one person in the world whom he truly loved. When he replied, "My daughter," the therapist said, "Lean back and close your eyes and imagine this scene: You are in prison because you have killed Buddy; you are pleased with yourself and you are basking in the glow of your accomplishment; now Maria-Teresa comes to visit you in jail and you ask her, 'How are you, honey?' and she says, 'OK, Daddy,' and you say, 'Tell me what's wrong, honey,' and she says, 'The kids at school sing a song like this [here the therapist began to sing softly and in a few seconds his colleagues joined in]: "Your daddy is a murderer. Your daddy is a murderer. Your daddy is a murderer." ' " They sang in unison for about 30 seconds, while Tony slumped in his chair, obviously shaken. He sighed and after a silence took a deep breath. After another long silence came the nearly whispered words "All right, I won't do it." Later on, at about four in the morning, the therapists let Tony leave, convinced that he would keep his promise—especially because by then he was extremely tired and emotionally spent.

The next day when the ETC staff members conferred about the events of that night, they had some second thoughts about the propriety of what they had done. On the one hand they wished to preserve the confidentiality of their meeting with Tony, but they were also mindful of the requirements of the *Tarasoff* decision (see Chapter 13), which mandates the duty of a therapist to warn the intended victim of a dangerous client. In addition, they agreed that something should be done about Tony's sawed-off shotgun, the mere possession of which is a felony in every state.

After seeking the advice of an attorney, an ETC therapist telephoned the chief of police in the town where Tony lived. The therapist explained the situation without giving Tony's name, and the chief decided that the best thing would be for ETC to try to get this man to give up his guns. If we could deliver the guns, the police would store them for an indefinite period and, more importantly, would take the sawed-off shotgun into custody without charging its owner with illegal possession.

For the purpose of providing a timely warning to the possible victims, the therapist who had been seeing the Riveras most recently asked Gabrielle to come in that same day and bring Buddy Baker along. When they arrived it soon became obvious that the *Tarasoff* warning would not likely be heeded. Buddy, in fact, greeted the news with belligerent disdain: He said that he was willing to confront Tony at any time and that he had no intention of breaking off his affair with Gabrielle. For her part, Tony's wife did not seem alarmed and showed no inclination to change her behavior.

The therapist then telephoned Tony, asking him to visit the office at about nine that same night for the purpose of persuading him to give up his guns. The issue was as follows: Since Tony had agreed the previous night not to kill Buddy, what was the purpose of keeping the guns, especially since they were a source of temptation to do what he had promised not to do? It took a while before Tony gave his permission for the guns to be turned over to the police temporarily, and it took even longer to convince him to let the therapist follow him home in order to confiscate the guns that very night.

It was quite late when the two men arrived at Tony's house. The six guns, fully loaded, were lying on a table and on the top of a cabinet. Slowly and with care Tony unloaded each while the therapist compiled a list of the type of gun, its caliber and serial number, and listed the 450 rounds of ammunition by type and quantity of each type. Naturally the list did not contain the owner's name, but the therapist gave Tony a signed receipt for his guns and ammunition. Then a solemn Tony helped the therapist to carry his arsenal to the car. After driving at an extremely slow rate of speed to the police station, the therapist asked to see the Watch Commander and said, "Please come out to my car. I have something to give you."

The delivery of guns and ammunition to a police station marks the beginning of the last chapter in this story of murder reconsidered. Next day, Tony appeared at the station and asked to have his guns back, but the police refused to give them to him. The therapist continued seeing Tony on a regular basis for a while. Once, Gabrielle came to the office for a visit, and the therapist reminded her that her life script called for a murder to take place and warned her to break off the relationship either with Buddy or with Tony; again, Gabrielle was adamant that she would not leave either man.

In therapy with Tony, the clinician was able to reframe the situation so that Tony could see that the stronger (or more "masculine") resolution of his problems would be to get a divorce from Gabrielle. Subsequently, after a period of indecision Tony filed for divorce and continued to visit the ETC therapist during the six-month waiting period. He again asked to retrieve his guns, but the therapist refused on the grounds that Tony was too agitated at that time. Later on when he was more calm, Tony asked again and the therapist got the guns (except for the sawed-off shotgun) from the police and returned them to Tony.

About five years later, Tony asked to see the ETC therapist once more. He was then divorced and had obtained custody of both his daughter and stepdaughter. The stepdaughter, now 18, had been experiencing "growing pains," and Tony was seeking advice about how to be a better father.

Thus ended ETC's involvement with Tony, Gabrielle, Buddy Baker, and Madilyn Leggett. A case which had begun with a grandmother's experience of attempted rape had ended with her granddaughter's adolescent crisis. This case is relevant to the emergency therapist because it demonstrates that:

1) Help for one kind of problem may not only serve to solve that problem but permit another quite different and much more serious problem to emerge and be given attention.

2) Successful therapy can be reached by many routes, often by taking the opposite direction from that usually taken; for example, thinking processes can be influenced *by means of* changing behavior instead of the other way around—the more customary direction of therapy.

3) In respect to providing protection for the community, it may be that mental health professionals, instead of the police, will be called upon to play a major role more often in the future. When clinicians are prepared and willing to take on the task, they can be successful in this role of deterring violence.

4) A gun is a gun is a gun; this and any other potentially dangerous weapon cannot be ignored, even by the clinician. Indeed, if a therapist's client does possess a potentially dangerous weapon, this fact should not be ignored in therapy; when in doubt, a therapist should make the assumption that the client is capable of using it against someone (or as a means to suicide).

5) The alleged or identified client may not always be the person in the family constellation who most needs help.

In sum, there will be times (often very inopportune times) when a therapist cannot *not* act, when a clinician must commit his or her total energy to a life-or-death intervention. Finally, remember that people *are* capable of changing, and some of them can become as opposite to their former selves as day to night.

REFERENCES

Bakan, D. *Slaughter of the Innocents: A Study of the Battered Child Phenomenon.* Boston: Beacon Press, 1971.

Freitas, J. Family fights: A social cancer must be cured. *San Francisco Sunday Examiner & Chronicle*, May 13, 1979, Sec. B, 3.

Gayford, J. J. Battered wives. In J. P. Martin (Ed.), *Violence and the Family.* New York: John Wiley and Sons, 1978.

Gelles, R. J. *The Violent Home: A Study of Physical Aggression Between Husbands and Wives.* Beverly Hills, California: Sage Publications, 1972.

Gelles, R. J. Abused wives; Why do they stay? *Journal of Marriage and the Family*, 38:659-668, November, 1976.

Gelles, R. J. Violence in the American family. In J. P. Martin (Ed.), *Violence and the Family*, New York: John Wiley and Sons, 1978.

Gil, D. G. Violence against children. *Journal of Marriage and the Family*, 33:637-648, November, 1971.

Glick, P. C. A demographer looks at American families. *Journal of Marriage and the Family*, 37:15-27, February, 1975.

Jackson, D. D. Family rules: The marital *quid pro quo. Archives of General Psychiatry*, 12:589-594, 1965.

Kempe, C. H., Silverman, F. N., Steele, B. F., Droegemuller, W., and Silver, H. K. The battered child syndrome. *Journal of the American Medical Association*, 181:17-24, 1962.

Levine, M. B. Interparental violence and its effect on the children: A study of fifty families in general practice. *Medicine, Science and the Law*, 15:172-176, 1975.

Marsden, D. V., and Owens, D. The Jekyll and Hyde marriages. *New Society*, 32:333-335, 1975.

Mulvihill, D. J., Tumin, M. M., and Curtis, L. A. *Crimes of Violence*, Vol. II. National Commission on the Causes and Prevention of Violence. Washington, D.C.: U.S. Government Printing Office, 1969.

Parnas, R. I. The police response to domestic disturbance. *Wisconsin Law Review*, 914-960, 1967.

Pizzey, E. *Scream Quietly or the Neighbors Will Hear.* Baltimore: Penguin Books, 1974.

Sears, R. R., Maccoby, E. E., and Levin, H. *Patterns of Child Rearing.* Evanston, IL: Row, Peterson, 1957.

Steele, B. F., and Pollock, C. B. A psychiatric study of parents who abuse infants and small children. In R. E. Helfer and C. H. Kempe (Eds.), *The Battered Child.* Chicago: University of Chicago Press, 1968.

Strauss, M. A. A general systems theory approach to the development of a theory of violence between family members. *Social Science Information*, 12:105-125, June, 1973.

Strauss, M. A. Leveling, civility, and violence in the family. *Journal of Marriage and the Family,* 36:13-30, February, 1974.

Steinmetz, S. K., and Strauss, M. A. (Eds.) *Violence in the Family.* New York: Harper and Row (originally published by Dodd, Mead & Co.), 1974.

Watzlawick, P., Beavin, J. H. and Jackson, D. D. *Pragmatics of Human Communication: A Study of Interactional Patterns, Pathologies, and Paradoxes.* New York: W. W. Norton, 1967.

Weakland, J., Fisch, R., Watzlawick, P. and Bodin, A. M. Brief therapy: Focused problem resolution. *Family Process,* 13:141-168, 1974.

Wolfgang, M. E. *Patterns in Criminal Homicide.* Philadelphia: University of Pennsylvania Press, 1958.

6

Battered spouses

This chapter separates spousal battering from the situation of couples whose fights periodically erupt into incidents of violence such as pushing, shoving, throwing small objects, or slapping. The authors believe it is useful to distinguish between these two major types of violence for the sake of clarity. It is necessary to show how markedly different kinds of family systems function, and how the couple that fights violently may later evolve into a couple in which battering occurs. This distinction does not mean that the authors do not consider any situation in which one human being strikes another as being an extremely serious matter—we do.

For the purpose of this chapter, Gayford's definition of a battered spouse is very much to the point: ". . . a woman who has received deliberate, severe, and repeated demonstrable physical injury from her marital partner [or cohabitant]" (1975, p. 237). Gayford went on to explain that "battered" husbands do exist in the full sense of the word, but that such cases are extremely rare for two reasons: 1) Men are usually stronger than women; and 2) men can usually leave the home more conveniently. Even though Strauss (1980) has pointed out that more violence is directed at men by women than was formerly suspected, it has been the authors' experience that what violence does occur fits better into the category of fighting than of battering as defined above: i.e., deliberate, severe, and repeated demonstrable physical injury.

To clarify the phenomenon of the battered spouse, Gayford's

(1978) moving study of 100 battered women will be summarized and discussed in detail. Each woman suffered bruises and 44 of them suffered lacerations; in 17 cases the lacerations were inflicted by a sharp instrument such as a knife or broken bottle. Twenty-five of the women suffered fractures, e.g., of the nose, teeth, or ribs; and eight women suffered fractures of other bones such as those of an arm, a finger, the jaw, or the skull. Two women had dislocated jaws and two others had dislocated shoulders. Internal organ damage was evident in two cases, and one woman became epileptic because of the injuries inflicted by her husband. Eleven women were burned or scalded, and seven were bitten. Even though each of the women was attacked by at least a clenched fist, kicking was a part of the assault in 59 cases. The abdomen was a frequent target of the attacker, and abortions were caused in several cases. In 42 of the cases a weapon was used, and in many instances it was presumably the first available object. But in 15 of these cases it was found that the same weapon (such as a belt) was repeatedly used on the woman. Many of the attacks were sudden, uncontrolled outbursts of rage, but some were viciously premeditated, with injuries inflicted in such a manner that they left no visible marks: e.g., blows above the hairline, upon the ears, or upon the lumbar-sacral area of the back.

The children of these 100 battered women also presented a sad picture. Many were described by workers at the shelters to which they had been taken as being "disturbed"; they exhibited a variety of problems such as temper tantrums and bed-wetting. Vandalism and stealing were common occurrences, as well as "fighting in a vicious way" with each other, a fact which points to the legacy of future domestic violence that parents such as these may bequeath to their children.

It is compelling to note that each of the 100 women in Gayford's study thought that her situation was unique and that 20 of them had tolerated the battering for 10 or more years. This finding raises the question of why some battered women behave in this paradoxical way, namely returning time and again to the husband who has beaten them. Upon review of the horrific list of injuries suffered by these women, it is apparent that in no way could they have enjoyed any part of the beatings. It appears that an interaction of several factors causes the women to stay or return. One relevant phenomenon is that many battering husbands love their mates; on occasion they feel tremendous remorse, and some even make great demonstrations of affection after an attack. Certain of these men rationalize their behavior by explaining that the woman caused the beating to occur. Others argue that they did it because she "needed" it. In some subcultures a beating is actually interpreted as a demonstration of love. After a time, a battered woman's thinking becomes distorted in a way similar to that of the victims of brainwashing (Gayford, 1975), in that she begins to accept whatever the abusive spouse tells her. Also, considering that many adults who remain in abusive relationships had parents who were themselves abusive, it is not surprising that some people associate loving interaction with abuse. Their thinking becomes so distorted that they make statements such as, "He beat me because he loves me."

In order to understand more about how two people become enmeshed in this type of relationship, it will be useful to consider Bateson's (1972) view of the "complementary" system, in which one person is dominant and one is subordinate. In its most pathological state, such a system deteriorates as follows:

> . . . submissiveness will promote further assertiveness which in turn will promote further submissiveness. This schismogenesis, unless it is restrained, leads to a progressive unilateral distortion of the personalities . . . which results in mutual hostility between them and must end in the breakdown of the system (Bateson, 1972, p. 68).

When this kind of breakdown occurs, some spouses are battered because they are too dominant or competent and pose a threat to the submissive or "inferior" partner; thus, they provoke the battering by their very being. Others are battered because they, themselves, are too submissive or "inferior"; this frustrates the dominant member of the system, who in turn does the battering. A woman may be battered, in essence, for the role that she plays in a complementary system which has gone out of control.

In one all-too-familiar scenario, the husband will originally have been attracted to the spouse because she was so sweet and naive; but, this same naivete and passivity has led to frustration with her because she cannot cope with domestic responsibilities. This, in turn, leads to the battering. For her part, she attempts to placate and please him by being even more submissive, which leads to his greater frustration, and further beatings ensue. What the wife has done in an attempt to make the situation better has in fact made it worse. Because each spouse is unaware of what the other is thinking and feeling, each becomes more and more bound to this escalating, cyclical pattern. As the pattern progresses, both partners appear to develop an almost fanatical fear of breaking free from the system, while at the same time the system oscillates farther and farther beyond control.

A differing form of complementary system may exist when the abusive husband has chosen his spouse because of his own dependency needs and because she was so strong and capable. It is that spouse's competence which eventually will threaten him and provide a stimulus to the assaults. On one level he wants her to be competent and to take care of him, but at the same time he hates her for her competence. His threshold of frustration is, at the best of times, very low; alcohol may disinhibit him, and when his anger and resentment rise beyond the level of tolerance, a beating is the result. The woman, in turn, tries to placate and please him by doing what she thinks he wants, and this ultimately activates the cycle of battering again. Once more, what each spouse thinks can make things better will in reality make the situation worse and has unwittingly provoked violence. At the core of this situation is a (pathological) complementary relationship to which both partners are obsessively attached. Each goes to extraordinary lengths to preserve this unhealthy pattern of interaction, and with time each develops the overwhelming delusion that neither could survive without the other. This irrational fear that one could not survive without the other is a critical component of the system, as evidenced by the lengths to which each will go to preserve the system as long as possible.

A BATTERED WIFE

This case is not a typical one from a socioeconomic standpoint, because the majority of battered wives are working-class or poor; but it is a typical case from a psychological standpoint. It is presented to clarify several misconceptions that are commonly held about battered women and to demonstrate that the dynamics of *battered spouse syndrome* cross all socioeconomic boundaries. It is not unknown for women to return home from their professional jobs and face battering by their husbands.

Joyce was 35 years old when she consulted an ETC therapist because of chronic headaches and depression; her physician had suggested that hypnosis or relaxation training might be of help. She had been married for 10 years and had two children, a boy of eight and a girl of six. Joyce was quite anxious and rather vague when describing the frequency and symptoms of her headaches. She was also evasive about her current family situation. The clinician had a sense that there was a more serious, hidden problem in Joyce's life, but if pushed into disclosing more than she was prepared to tell, she would not return.

Joyce did give consent for the therapist to consult the physician who had referred her, in order to obtain information about medical aspects of the chronic headaches. Joyce also revealed that she was an attorney with a local law firm and that she specialized in civil litigation. Her husband, Steve, was an architect. She subtly indicated that even though both their professional lives were quite successful, their married life was at times turbulent and unstable. She made an appointment to return the following week.

When the therapist called Joyce's physician to obtain more information about her headaches, the doctor was most cordial and said he was glad that Joyce had followed through with the recommendation to see a psychotherapist. He explained that while he was concerned about Joyce's headaches he was also very much concerned about her situation at home. She had required medical treatment for several unexplained falls and other odd accidents during the past few years. While the physician was genuinely worried about Joyce, he didn't know what he could do to help. He described Joyce's husband, Steve, as a self-assured, obviously successful man who was difficult to approach on a personal level, and added that Joyce had been extremely secretive about her marriage. This conversation with her physician served to confirm the therapist's suspicion that Joyce was hiding a family secret.

During the next few weeks of treatment, Joyce's story slowly came out. Her headaches were caused by beatings which had begun about a year after her marriage to Steve—a history of nine years of abuse. In telling this, Joyce tried to be protective of her husband and went to great lengths to give reasons why he periodically beat her. She described Steve's childhood as having been traumatic and tragic. His parents were alcoholics and he had been on his own at an early age, refusing any help from the parents. Joyce had met him when they were in college, and she had admired his determination. She described Steve as someone who was energetic and hardworking, but was really very shy and awkward in showing his feelings. Joyce went on to say that she had "mothered" Steve and tried to make up for the lack of love in his childhood. Because of this mothering, he had come to need her very much.

Joyce described her own family as having been completely opposite from that of her husband. Her family was solidly middle class and entirely stable. Even though she had two siblings, she had clearly been her father's favorite. Joyce said that she felt almost guilty for the happiness and stability of her own childhood, by contrast with Steve's. They had been married shortly after she was graduated from law school, and as long as they had to struggle to make ends meet they had been happy together.

A few months after she passed the bar exam and had taken her first job, Joyce came home about an hour late from work and found her husband in a rage. He accused her of having an affair with one of the men at the law firm where she worked. The more she tried to explain why she was late and to insist that she had no interest in any of the men where she worked because she loved and needed him, the more violent Steve became. He struck her several times, knocking her to the floor. The next morning he said he was deeply sorry for what he had done, adding that the only reason it happened was that he loved her so much; if she would forgive him, it would never happen again. It didn't happen again for about a year, and by this time Steve was rapidly becoming successful in his own business and Joyce had given birth to their first child. The next beating took place shortly after the birth of the baby, and resulted from Steve's feeling that Joyce was paying too much attention to a business acquaintance of his during a dinner party at their home. Steve, who had too much to drink, had burst into a jealous rage. This beating resulted in a black eye and cracked rib that caused Joyce to stay home from work for a period of time, during which Steve was extremely solicitous and remorseful. As before, he swore it would never happen again and she forgave him because she felt so deeply sorry for him.

More than one year passed before another beating occurred, shortly after the birth of their second child. It was presumably provoked by the threat of another child taking more of Joyce's attention and love away from Steve. This time Steve, in a drunken rage, threw her down the stairs and broke her arm. As Joyce explained to the therapist, it was as if the more successful he was in his work, the more fearful and easily provoked he became. Joyce said that she had a deep sense of tragedy in her thoughts of this man who had worked so hard for his success in life, only to find himself unable to enjoy it when it came. She did not seem aware that the births of their children had been threatening to Steve because of his feeling that the children would take some of her nurturance away from him.

Joyce described her life as "living with a time bomb" which might "explode" at any moment. She said that every minute of her time had to be accounted for to Steve, and thus she could only meet with the therapist during the noon hour (she frequently missed appointments). Joyce added that her husband completely controlled the family finances and that she did not know in which banks the family had accounts. She gave Steve her paychecks and he would give her an allowance, plus additional cash if she needed anything more. Joyce had accepted this situation and tried to rationalize Steve's need to control the finances as a result of his childhood poverty. She saw it in terms of Steve always wanting to make sure that the family had enough money, rather than as his need to control her.

In its initial stages, therapy was somewhat ineffectual due to Joyce's fearfulness and resistance, as well as to her failure to keep regular appointments. She was terrified that Steve would discover that she was seeing a therapist and flatly refused to discuss the possibility of his entering treatment with her. Despite Joyce's resistance, the therapist believed that if she were given time to develop trust, she would eventually be able to face the need to make some changes in her situation. The therapist was well aware that many battered spouses are reluctant clients and that it is difficult to persuade them to enter a therapeutic relationship which can truly facilitate change. These women require a combination of patience, deep understanding of their situation, and firmness. The woman must be led to face the fact that eventually she will have to take steps to end the violence, either by leaving her home or insisting that the husband receive treatment as a condition of her remaining in the home. But this takes time in many cases, since rarely is the battered spouse capable enough or ready to accept or carry through these necessary prerequisites for change in a system. A clinician needs to be aware that many battered women are not emotionally prepared for separation from their spouses, nor from the violence-producing, complementary system in which they are trapped. They usually need to make several attempts before eventually breaking the cycle. Too often therapists become discouraged with these women and prematurely dismiss them as being unmotivated, at the instant when they are making their first tentative attempts toward separation.

It is possible to interrupt a cycle of battering on the first try, but the ETC experience suggests that this would be an exceptional outcome. A battered woman usually makes, on the average, between three and five attempts to leave home before she is capable of staying completely away or is able to insist upon the spouse's receiving treatment as a prerequisite to her return. It will be helpful for the clinician to view these early attempts to end the batterings as a learning process which, in the long run, will have a cumulative effect to assist the woman in making her final break. Battered women need to learn gradually to counter the psychological effects of their battering; these effects are similar to those of brainwashing in that they distort the victims' views of reality and debilitate them emotionally. Changing a woman's previously distorted view of reality requires that she experience a different reality. For example, she needs to know that there is a place of refuge for her, such as a woman's shelter where professionals and volunteers will try to assist her.

Even though Joyce was herself an attorney and knew her rights on an intellectual level, getting her to stand up for them proved difficult. Over the years (even though she was in a sense the strong, nurturing woman whom Steve depended upon) she had become, psychologically, totally dependent upon her husband. It was as though Joyce were two people: the working woman who was competent, successful and had developed a reputation as a person who tolerated no nonsense; and the woman at home who, in her wifely role, was a fearful spouse who nourished and protected the husband's every whim and desire. To a certain extent, Joyce thought of Steve as a child who, in his fashion, had become hopelessly dependent upon her.

Joyce made several attempts to leave her husband. The first came one night when Steve arrived home in a drunken state. After he went to sleep, she ran away with the children to a friend's house. At about four in the morning, the clinician received a telephone call from an hysterical Joyce. Steve was on his way to the friend's house to get her and the children, and she didn't know what to do. The therapist agreed to come to the friend's house and try to talk with both Steve and her. At the very moment when the therapist arrived, Steve was forcefully escorting a sobbing Joyce and her two children to his car, and in a controlled but angry voice he warned that the clinician should "stay away from [his] wife."

Joyce did not call the clinician for about six weeks after that incident, and when she did she was apologetic and afraid that the therapist would be angry with her and refuse to see her again. The therapist reassured her that this was not so and made an appointment for them to meet again. During this renewed course of treatment, the therapist made several attempts to bring Steve into treatment, but each attempt was unsuccessful. Subsequently, Joyce made two other unsuccessful attempts to leave her husband. The final separation came after a beating in which Joyce's jaw and cheekbone were broken and she had to be hospitalized. A major reason for her making the decision to leave was that her six-year-old daughter had been injured by Steve in the course of the latest incident of battering. In an attempt to reach Joyce, he had grabbed the girl and dislocated her arm as he pulled her away from her mother.

This injury to one of her children was more than Joyce could tolerate. When the clinician met her at the hospital next morning, Joyce was barely able to talk. The therapist helped her plan where she would go after her release from the hospital. The therapist also convinced Joyce that she should contact a new attorney and have a restraining order issued against Steve, to prevent him from harassing or harming her or the children. At first she was reluctant to do so, but she finally agreed to have the restraining order prepared. The therapist then made arrangements to visit Joyce's children, who were staying with a friend.

This time Joyce stayed away from her husband. Even though she eventually resolved to end the relationship entirely because Steve still adamantly refused any form of treatment, the entire process of separation, divorce, and rebuilding a life was not easy for her. Joyce remained in treatment for about a year, during which time much therapy was devoted to working through how she could have permitted the battering to happen to her for so long, and how she could have been one kind of person at work and another kind at home. One reason was that Joyce had come from a traditional but loving family in which the father was unquestionably the dominant figure. In addition, because she was her father's "pet," she came to believe that male authority figures were mostly benevolent; thus, if they became angry, it must be because someone had done something wrong. When Joyce saw that she did not make similarly naive assumptions in her professional life, she felt quite free to assert herself for a change.

It is worth reiterating that the present one is not typical of the majority of battered spouse cases, but shows that the dynamics of battering transcend socioeconomic boundaries. The reality of a typical battered spouse is that she does not have a career nor does she have any prospects for one. Most have major responsibility for the care of one or more children. Without resources, either financial or emotional, the woman feels as if she is isolated in every sense from the help and concern of others, and thinks herself totally trapped in a battering situation which, to her, is unique and seems without possible remedy.

REFERENCES

Bateson, G. *Steps to an Ecology of Mind.* New York: Ballantine, 1972.
Gayford, J. J. Battered wives. *Medicine, Science and the Law,* 15:237-245, 1975.
Gayford, J. J. Battered wives. In J. P. Martin (Ed.), *Violence and the Family.* New York: John Wiley & Sons, 1978.
Strauss, M. A. Wife-beating: How common and why? In M. A. Strauss and G. T. Hotaling (Eds.), *The Social Causes of Husband-Wife Violence.* Minneapolis: University of Minnesota Press, 1980.

7

The battered child

Before recommending treatment strategies for use with families in which child abuse or neglect may be occurring, it will be useful to introduce the topic by means of a clear and concise definition of what "abuse" is in this context. When that is done, it will be possible to present a description of the kinds of people who abuse their children, as well as the psychological dynamics within a family system that can set these pathologic events in motion. In general terms, parental abuse of children is not a sex-linked phenomenon. It has been said that more mothers abuse their children than do fathers, but it is also said that abuse by fathers is far more brutal and devastating to the child. The dynamics referred to here, as well as recommended strategies of therapy, are assumed to apply equally to abuse by fathers. And even when the actual abuse is carried out by only one of two parents, the other bears a considerable measure of responsibility for acquiescence in the assault.

WHAT IS CHILD ABUSE?

Child abuse is neither strict punishment, nor spanking, nor rough handling. Although corporal punishment is permitted in our culture, corporal punishment, in and of itself, is not child abuse (no matter what someone's personal views on the subject of corporal punish-

102

ment may be). Child abuse can be said to have occurred *when corporal punishment has caused bruises or other injury to the child,* or *when the child has been injured in such a severe manner that medical attention is required.* To amplify this definition, these "guidelines for the diagnosis of physical abuse" from the *Child Protection Team Handbook* (Schmitt and Loy, 1978) will provide useful details:

> . . . physical injuries inflicted by a caretaker, sibling, or baby sitter. Also called non-accidental trauma. These could be rated as *mild* (a few bruises, welts, scratches, cuts, or scars), *moderate* (numerous bruises, minor burns, or a single fracture), or *severe* (large burn, central nervous system injury, abdominal injury, multiple fractures or any life-threatening abuse). In its extreme, the result is death. Often the injury stems from an angry attempt of the parent to punish the child for misbehavior. Sometimes it is an uncontrollable lashing out at the child who happens to be in the way of an adult when some unrelated crisis is occurring (pp. 188, 189).

It is evident that injuries such as those described above clearly go far beyond what would be considered the result of normal punishment for a child's misbehavior. Just about *every* adult has had the urge or impulse to strike a difficult or unruly child at one time or another. Child abuse, by contrast, transcends this acute but temporary arousal of angry feelings that most adults are capable of keeping under control.

What kind of adult is not able to control himself or herself? What species of adult anger, hurt, or confusion can spill over onto children, and can eventually lead to their abuse and/or neglect? In many cases this abusive behavior has had its genesis in the parent's own childhood. There is considerable evidence that a majority of abusive parents were once abused or rejected children themselves (Feinstein et al., 1963; Johnson and Morse, 1968; Nurse, 1966; Silver, Dublin, and Lourie, 1969; Steele and Pollock, 1968). Many of these abusive parents possess an exceptionally low sense of self-esteem, having the tendency to feel that they are failures as people; also, they are persons who tend to be frequently depressed (Court and Okell, 1970).

The following vignette indicates how a mother's low self-esteem

and deep-seated feelings of inadequacy can contribute to abusive behavior. The sad scenario begins in this way: A young girl feels a terrible sense of inadequacy while going through the process of growing
up. She feels rejected by one or both parents, may have been abused
by one or both of them. This girl probably marries early, in effect because she is trying to fulfill her acutely felt needs for affection and love.
As a woman she develops a deep-seated conviction that she is not
capable of doing anything right. But having reached physical maturity, she experiences the feeling of being able to "do something right"
by conceiving a child who will love her. She feels even greater worthi-
ness by carrying the child to full term and by giving birth. Upon this
baby are projected the sources of love and affection that she missed in
her own childhood. She gives birth to this child expecting that there
will be at least one human being in her life who will love her without restraint or qualification.

When she has taken the baby home, this woman may begin her
career as a mother by holding the baby awkwardly or fearfully (because of an inward awkwardness or fear), and the child may respond
by feeling uncomfortable and squirming or crying. But instead of perceiving this squirming or crying as a natural result of the child's feeling
uncomfortable, this mother may believe that the child is screaming at
her or is trying to escape from her. On a symbolic level, she may experience the fantasy that the child is blaming her, leading to obsessional thinking such as, "I have failed; while I may have thought for a
moment that I succeeded, instead I have failed."

Parents of this kind have such great needs within themselves and
such hope that their children will make up for all they have lacked as
children themselves, that they are unable to see or understand the
needs of their own children (Green, Gaines and Sandgrund, 1974;
Morris and Gould, 1963; Steele and Pollock, 1968). As parents who
have frustrated dependency needs themselves, they displace their
anger at their own parents for lack of nurturance and love onto their
children, as a further episode in this unhappy chronicle of abuse.

Many abusive parent have a marked lack of understanding of (or
empathy for) their child's moods and behavior. They often project
adult motives onto a child's actions, when in fact the child may be upset because he or she feels sad or wet or hungry (Allen, 1978). This

naivete may account for the fact that there is a considerably higher risk of child abuse in young couples than in older couples (Lynch, 1975; Oliver et al., 1974; Skinner and Castle, 1969; Smith, 1975). Further, abusive parents seem to have a lack of knowledge of a child's capabilities. That is, they are largely unaware of what is appropriate behavior for a child at the various age levels (de Lissovey, 1973). Because they are so lacking in understanding of children, they have acute deficits in the most basic parenting skills. They often make very unrealistic demands of their children in terms of obedience or skill or intellectual ability (Court, 1974; Ounsted et al., 1975).

Often abusive parents are isolated people, having little or no support system to back them up or assist them when they are experiencing stress or are caught up in a crisis. Many such parents have serious marital problems that may not be obvious upon first meeting. Some of them put forth the pseudo-appearance of having a very tightly knit, loving, "us against the world" kind of family. This, upon closer inspection, is revealed as a family in which there is great fear of intimacy and closeness. Some mothers who abuse their children are themselves being battered by their husbands (cf. Smith, 1975). Other abusive parents will "scapegoat" a child as the cause of problems in the marriage relationship (Gibbens, 1972). For example, the abused child may be seen as a competitor, by a dependent and jealous parent, for the spouse's attention (Court, 1970; Wasserman, 1967).

There appear to be fewer instances of child abuse in large or extended families, and several good reasons can be found for this. First, in a large or extended family there is a ready-made social network to assist in child care when a mother is experiencing stress or having some difficulty: e.g., when there are sisters or aunts or nieces who can assist in child care or relieve the mother for a period of time from the duties of parenting.

Second, in a large or extended family children have more experience in caring for other children so that, by the time they are themselves adults and married, they have had considerable practice in caring for a child. Also, these children can form a good understanding of what is normal and appropriate behavior for a child at the differing developmental stages. We have noticed in many child abuse cases that an abusive parent's first experience of caring for a child has occurred when the first child arrives. In other cases the abusive parent has had few opportunities, because of the social isolation of his or her own childhood, even to be in the company of small children. These circumstances can lead to vastly unrealistic expectations of a child's capabilities and needs.

Another factor that research has found to play a role in child abuse is that many abusive mothers had given birth prematurely or had had much difficulty in giving birth (Elmer and Gregg, 1967; Lynch, 1975; Oliver et al., 1974; Skinner and Castle, 1969). Because of the complications of a premature or difficult birth, children are often isolated from the mother shortly after birth, and thus the child and the mother are not together for a critical period during which "bonding" between mother and child normally takes place. Perhaps as a result of this lack of infant-mother bonding, the research suggests, child abuse may occur later on (Klein and Stern, 1971).

The image of a pathetic, isolated, lonely, and fearful parent emerges as a portrait of those who abuse their children. Most are people who themselves were once victims of neglect or abuse. Many lack friends or family members who live nearby and can provide support during stressful times. Owing to their isolation, loneliness, and low self-esteem, when they are under stress they have considerable difficulty in asking for the help that they so desperately need. This inability to ask for help is often carried over into their daily lives, in that they have great difficulty in asking for assistance with everyday problems. For example, going to a neighbor and asking to borrow something that they need for the house (a cup of sugar or some coffee) is a relatively simple matter for most people, but for the abusive parent—because of lack of self-esteem and fearfulness—this relatively simple request becomes an overwhelming task. These are people who fear closeness and intimacy, probably because they have not experienced it themselves as children. Or, when they did experience intimacy, it was often interrupted by episodes of violence.

Many abusive parents are idealistic and upwardly motivated people. They desperately want to succeed but, at the same time, perceive themselves to be failures in life and see their task as parents to be virtually impossible. They tend to be impulsive people who have great difficulty in controlling themselves when they are hurt, frightened, or frustrated. And while the reader may find it a difficult leap of faith, it is helpful to be aware that these people who lash out at or injure children are not sadists; that is, they are not people who take pleasure in hurting their own children. Quite the opposite is true of abusive parents. Most are people who love their children very much but who are so troubled and are experiencing so much psychological pain that they cannot control themselves in even mildly stressful situations. They often use the defense mechanism of denial to protect themselves from facing what they have done (or are doing) to their children. They will claim not to remember when or how the actual injuries to the child were sustained.

GENERAL DIAGNOSTIC INDICATIONS

This section reviews some of the indicators which may assist a therapist or counselor in determining whether or not child abuse is taking place. Here are condensed some of the diagnostic signs that were presented by Barton D. Schmitt in the chapter, "The Physician's Evaluation," from *The Child Protection Team Handbook* (1978, pp. 39-57), as well as guidelines that are used by the Emergency Treatment Center. If, when involved with an emergency situation, a therapist encounters a family in which there is evidence of two or three of these indicators, there is probably a case of child abuse which should be investigated more thoroughly.

1) An unexplained or unexplainable injury: if a parent is reluctant to explain the cause of the injury and makes statements such as "We just found him like that"; or if the family is unwilling to discuss details of how the child was injured. Most parents are very concerned when their child is injured and go to considerable lengths to find out how and why the injury occurred.

2) A discrepancy between the descriptions, on the part of each parent, of how the child was injured, when the parents have been questioned separately; or a difference between the explanation given by one or both parents and an explanation given by the child when questioned separately.

3) A discrepancy between the type of injury or wound of the child and the reported "accident": e.g., when the parents say

that the child tripped over a chair and fell down, but the child is covered with severe bruises over several areas of his or her body, or with long narrow welts which indicate that he or she has been beaten with a belt or ruler.

4) Suspicious injuries that are said to have been self-inflicted. Children who are not emotionally disturbed rarely injure themselves intentionally, and the child may have injuries that could not have been self-inflicted, e.g., if the parents claim the baby rolled over and broke his or her arm while asleep, or imply that the child is masochistic or has hurt himself or herself in a temper tantrum.

5) Injuries inflicted by a third party, as when parents blame someone such as a baby-sitter, friend, or neighbor. These accusations should be investigated thoroughly. Other suspicious third-party injuries are those said to have been inflicted by rough siblings or playmates; if, after making such an accusation, the parents are unwilling or unable to produce the name of the third party who injured their child, the accusation should be regarded with suspicion. Few parents will permit their children to continue to play with or be cared for by persons who injure them.

6) A delay in obtaining medical care for the child's injury. Most parents seek medical treatment immediately when they discover that their child has been injured; if a parent waits 12 to 24 hours before obtaining treatment for a child's injury, this fact by itself may strongly suggest that the injury was inflicted by one of the parents.

7) A history of repeated suspicious injuries: if the child has suffered unexplained injuries on more than one occasion or if a sibling exhibits similar injuries. Many children such as these are referred to by the parents as "accident-prone," "clumsy," or "rough."

PHYSICAL INDICATIONS

Wounds that are considered diagnostic of child abuse include bruises, welts, lacerations, and scars. (Bruises and other injuries that are predominantly located on the buttocks and lower back are usually the result of punishment, that is, of spanking.) Numerous bruises on the cheek and pinpoint bruises on an earlobe are usually the result of being slapped or cuffed. Similarly, most wounds on the inner thigh and genital area have been inflicted by another person. (While *accidental* falls rarely cause bruises in the soft tissue, they usually result in bruises or scrapes that involve bony prominences such as the forehead, the cheekbone, or the hip.) In addition, if fresh bruises are accompanied by fading or yellowish other bruises, abuse should be strongly suspected. Handmarks and pressure bruises resembling fingertips or an entire hand, often found along the arm or the legs of a child, or pinch marks which appear as two small crescent-shaped bruises facing each other are also injuries that are diagnostic of child abuse. Human bite marks also take the form of paired, crescent-shaped bruises; this type of injury should be carefully examined since parents usually claim it was inflicted by a sibling or playmate. Strap marks are often rectangular-shaped bruises of varying lengths. Bruises that appear on several different bodily planes are usually inflicted wounds, unless there is clear evidence of a tumbling accident. Tumbling accidents often do cause minor bruises and abrasions, but they will appear predominantly on elbows, knees, or shoulders.

Approximately 10 percent of physical abuse cases involve burns. The most common burn is that inflicted by a cigarette; these generally consist of more than one circular, pinched-out burn. When a child accidentally bumps into a cigarette, it will normally make only one circular burn mark unless a cinder catches the clothing on fire. Smaller but similar burns can have been inflicted by a hot match tip. Another form of burn which is very suspicious is one that has been caused by immersion in hot water. Such a burn will leave marks above the ankle or wrist but no splash marks. Children do not put their limbs into hot water and keep them there voluntarily.

Eye damage, in respect to this syndrome, can include acute hyphema, dislocated lenses, or detached retinae. Retinal hemorrhage is a clue to subdural hematoma in children who may have unusual central nervous system symptoms. Retinal hemorrhaging in children (absent clinically important intercranial hemorrhage) can also result from sudden compression of the chest.

The worst possible injury, in terms of potential lethality, is subdural hematoma: victims often have convulsions and may enter a coma.

The typical subdural hematoma is associated with a skull fracture re-sulting from a direct blow by hand, or from being hit against a wall or door. External bruises related to the same blow are usually present. Intra-abdominal injuries are the second most common cause of death in battered children. Children who have been beaten in this way tend to have recurrent vomiting and/or abdominal distension, among other symptoms. A most common finding is a ruptured liver or spleen.

"Failure to thrive" manifests itself in an underweight, malnourished child. These children usually have prominent ribs, wasted buttocks, and spindly limbs. Failure to thrive usually occurs in the first two years of life because this is normally a time of rapid growth and dependence upon adults for feeding. This syndrome has been detected in babies even before they have reached the age of eight months. The causes of failure to thrive are estimated as being organic in 30 percent of the cases, underfeeding due to understandable error in 20 percent of the cases,and deprivation resulting from maternal neglect in as many as half of the cases.

If a child is extremely passive or seems catatonic, this may also be an indicator of neglect or abuse. In fact, abused children may exhibit a wide range of abnormal psychological symptoms. Some appear "flat" emotionally, with depressed mood; they seem to lack the color and energy of normal children. By contrast, some abused children can be-have in an impulsive or aggressive manner. But one fairly consistent element in the behavior of abused children is that they do not easily trust people and are acutely distrustful of strangers.

ASSESSING THE SAFETY OF A HOME

In some cases it will be necessary for a clinician to determine wheth-er or not it is safe for a child to remain in his or her home. In other cases, if for example a child has been temporarily removed from the home, it may be necessary for the clinician to decide whether or not the child should return. Some risk factors that may affect this often dif-ficult decision are addressed below.

The first factor to take into consideration is whether one or both of the parents fits the description of the abusive parent referred to above.

Were they themselves abused or neglected as children? Are they isolated and lonely people or are they fairly well-adjusted socially? Are the demands which they, as parents, place upon their child appropriate or inappropriate? Do these people have reasonable parenting skills? Are they able to discipline their child effectively? Are they able to differentiate their own needs and feelings from those of their child?

Another key factor to consider is the age of the child. Most research on the subject of child abuse suggests that children are extremely vulnerable between the ages of three months and three years. This is the period in a child's life when he or she is most demanding, most helpless, and places relatively more demands upon the parents. Also, during this period of life a child is virtually unable to get away from an abusing parent to ask for help, while an older child would be more capable of seeking help or assistance should a crisis occur. These considerations suggest that it is wise to take a more conservative stance in deciding whether or not to allow a child to remain in the home when the child is under the age of three, because the risk is so much greater for a child of that age.

It is necessary to consider if this child is "difficult" or sickly. Does the child, because of some limitations or handicap, put unusual demands on his or her parent(s)? Or does a parent perceive this child as being "strange" in some way, or capable of making extreme demands? Have there been prior incidents of abuse in the family? Has this or another child of the family ever been removed from the home in the past? If that has happened, considerable caution is in order unless there is evidence that the parent or family has made significant changes.

Eventually it will be necessary to assess the adjustment level of the parents. If one parent is a chronic or borderline schizophrenic, that fact plus evidence of abuse may definitely indicate that the child should be removed from the home. Even so, being schizophrenic should not by itself disqualify a person from parenthood. A more important factor is the severity and duration of proven abuse. If a parent loses control and strikes his or her child once and then not again, the situation is different from one in which the parent injures the child repeatedly for a long time. The essential difference is between a moment's loss of control, under extreme pressure, and serious psychopathology.

Finally, a vital factor in assessing the resources of a family to decide whether or not an abused child should remain there is: Does this family have a support network of relatives, friends, or professional advisors to whom it can turn in time of stress; or are the parents isolated and reluctant to seek help? When a majority of the factors discussed above is present in a family in which an incident of child abuse has occurred, the indication is strong that at least a temporary separation of abusive parent and child will be appropriate until a further, more thorough assessment of the family can be conducted.

TREATMENT OF CHILD ABUSE

Discovery of child abuse in the course of an emergency intervention can be a brutal, shocking relevation. It is extremely important for a therapist, in such a situation, to be able to monitor his or her own feelings of anger and disgust and keep these emotions under control. If they are not contained, a clinician's feelings may only serve to isolate (further) and wound the abusive parents who may have been abused children themselves. It is also necessary to accept the difficult awareness that these people are not horrible monsters. Instead, they are persons in need of compassion and understanding, who in their own pathetic way are crying out for help.

Initially most will deny the abuse, and the clinician should avoid being drawn into their anger and rage but remain, instead, detached from the pathological system. A therapist should be prepared to find that the family members will not like him or her. An abusive family will fear and resent any outsider—including the therapist—for invading and disrupting the family system, and this resentment is likely to persist for quite a while. Though it may be tempting for a therapist to agree not to report abuse in an effort to gain the trust of a parent or as the result of angry threats, failing to do so is a serious error of judgment that will not help the child victim in any way (see Chapter 13 on legal requirements for the reporting of abuse).

Usually the clinician will be called into a suspected abusive situation by a third party. Sometimes a member of the immediate family calls for help, but we have found this to be quite the *unusual* occurrence in child abuse syndrome families. One way in which a therapist or other professional often discovers an abusive family is by means of treating a family member for another problem, in the course of which child abuse is revealed. The main thing to realize at the beginning of an intervention is that many abusive families do not seek or want help, will be defensive or secretive, and will try to conceal the abuse. The clinician should try not to appear outwardly suspicious in such a way that a parent will become even more guarded about admitting possibly abusive behavior.

During the initial encounter with a parent who is suspected of child abuse, it is important for a therapist to avoid acting impulsively or emotionally, no matter how worried he or she may be about the child in question. One reason is that a need may arise to prepare the foundation of a legal case. But if the parents are warned of the therapist's suspicions in advance, they may attempt to cover the evidence or try to prevent the therapist from seeing their child a second time. In many cases it will be necessary to visit with the child more than once in order to confirm suspected abuse. Another vital issue is that of gaining the trust of the child—i.e., children who have been abused not only are fearful of strangers but may distrust adults in general. Moreover, most abused children "love" their parents very much, and thus any outsider who threatens the family will be perceived as an enemy.

Above all, before taking action it is important to consider what may happen to the child if this attempt to help fails. What if the professional person rushes into a situation too quickly, and the family is able to conceal the abuse or escape detection by moving to a different address? What if a child finally learns to trust an adult—the clinician—but the help so desperately needed is not forthcoming?

The first encounter with a family in which there is suspected abuse should be as nonconfronting and nonthreatening as possible. If necessary, this position can be changed to a more assertive one later. The clinician should try to learn as much as possible about each of the family members and their backgrounds. Using the profile of the abusive parent presented above, it is wise to examine how closely these parents fit the profile. Next, the clinician should weigh the seriousness of any apparent injury and reflect on the age of the child. When a child needs to be removed from his or her family, it may be best to arrange this during a natural separation time, such as when the child is at a day-care center or school. If possible, the therapist should try to avoid the dramatic scene of separating a child forcibly from his or her parents. In many cases, children who are suspected of being abused can be more easily taken out of a school setting (and brought to a pediatrician for an examination) than by confronting the parents directly.

The following is an example of a first intervention with two abused little sisters who will be called Annie (seven years old) and Carolyn (eight-and-half years old). This case study also serves to illustrate types of behavior which are characteristic of abused children. ETC was called by a teacher who was concerned about these two little girls: According to the teacher, their clothes were always dirty, they had not been sent to school with lunches for at least six months, and there were bruises and scratches on their arms and legs. An ETC therapist went to the school to meet the girls, both of whom were very reluctant to speak to her. From their teacher, the therapist learned that each girl had had serious behavioral problems at school. Annie was very withdrawn and would intentionally hurt herself, commenting, "See, it didn't hurt." One day she even stabbed herself with a pair of scissors. Carolyn, by contrast, was an extremely aggressive and destructive child; she would be quiet at one moment and then act out explosively. Carolyn had attacked other children on several occasions, and had once destroyed a classroom display in an outburst of rage.

The clinician met with each girl separately, and during the second meeting with Annie, asked her how her parents punished her if she did something wrong. She replied, in a very matter-of-fact manner, that they would strap her, and if she was "real bad," she would have to sleep outside of the house (on the ground) all night. When the therapist met with both girls toward the end of this session and repeated what Annie had disclosed earlier, Carolyn suddenly jumped up and attacked her sister, screaming "I hate you, you liar."

By the end of this second meeting with the little girls, the therapist had decided that there was sufficient reason to send both of them to a pediatrician and to report the suspicion of child abuse. The pediatric examination revealed that each child had, in fact, been beaten. Annie's nose had been broken previously, but she had received no medical treatment for the injury. Both children were suffering from malnutrition and each had bruises, welts, and scratches that could not have been self-inflicted.

After learning of this finding, two ETC staff members had a meeting with the parents, who were quite young: The mother was 24 and the father 25. As a couple, they were both struggling to "make ends meet"; he worked at a garage and she worked as a waitress at a fast-food restaurant. At the beginning of the meeting with them, they became furious and threatened to sue the Center. One of the clinicians explained that, because of the results of the pediatric examination, they had no choice but to report the abuse and to arrange for both children to be placed in a children's shelter until a thorough family evaluation could be done. That visit with the parents lasted approximately three hours, most of which consisted of reassuring them that we wished to help the family members live together in a healthy, supportive way. Even though the parents continued to be angry with us for some time, we were able to persuade them to continue in therapy. Later, the children were returned to the home and presumably there has been no recurrence of abuse in the family.

Early in therapy with abusive families, it is fair to state clear ground rules for treatment. Because many of these families are receiving treatment involuntarily, the parents may have exaggerated or distorted fantasies about what therapy is and is not. Hence it is advisable to clarify what the role of the therapist will be, and what the family can and cannot expect from a therapist. The following is a combination of some of the basic therapeutic ground rules that ETC has found helpful, with those suggested by the work of Saruk (1979).

An incident of child abuse which occurs *in the course of treatment* does not necessarily mean that therapy must terminate, that the parents must be jailed, or that the child must be removed from the home. But while such an incident should be confronted clinically, the highest priority must be given to child protection. The clearest message that needs to be given to the parents from the start is that a clinician will not help them cover up their abusive behavior. From now on they will have to learn nonviolent ways of coping with life stress and raising their children. These parents must learn to admit their problems and difficulties and to accept help. Lending force to these requirements, we have found it necessary to have the support of the local criminal justice system and/or the child protective service of the local welfare department, in order to ensure that these families remain in therapy during the critical early stages of treatment.

Because abusive parents have a chronic inability to control their aggressive impulses, it is vital to establish the rule that not only this but also any subsequent incident of abuse will be reported. The rule will apply to each person who is involved in the therapeutic situation, and there can be no reprisals between or among members of the family. Further, if the parents quit therapy before a therapist feels that they are ready to do so, that fact will be reported—which may result in the child's being removed from the home. Our policy is to recommend to the court that a therapy requirement include these provisions: Not only should a minimum duration of time be established for therapy, but a minimum number of sessions should be specified; if the family members fail to attend this number of sessions, they must make them up. By building therapy on a firm foundation in this way, we seek to overcome the parents' lack of motivation for change.

Every attempt should be made to coordinate the therapist's efforts with schools and other agencies that will be working with an abused child, for several reasons. For example, many abusive parents cannot deal with any type of stress, and possibly a teacher or agency worker could inadvertently provoke a new child abuse incident by sending home a note complaining of the child's poor performance or poor behavior. When feasible, a clinician should ask that messages such as this be channeled through him or her and thus be dealt with as a part of therapy.

We have found the following arrangement of therapy appointments to be the most advantageous for abusive families: weekly individual sessions for each of the parents and one session per week for the parents as a couple. If the abused child is old enough to participate in therapy, either family therapy or a multifamily group (with other abusive families) is recommended in addition. We have also found that it is best if at least two clinicians are involved with each family or multifamily group, because treating an abusive family can be very stressful for a therapist. Two or three therapists who coordinate their work can support and relieve each other during some of the more demanding phases of treatment. In many cases, individual play therapy sessions for the abused child will be useful, and for this to be feasible a team of several therapists may be required. Multifamily groups have proven to be a promising modality for treating abusive families because they serve more than one therapeutic function: The arrangement helps to break each family's isolation and prevent the family members from feeling that theirs is the only one to whom this tragedy has happened; it also helps to dispel the belief that the parents' abusive behavior is a result of some peculiarity that is unique to them.

When we treat abusive parents, we let them know that we shall be available to them at any time of the day or night, should an emergency occur or an overwhelming problem arise. This can often be of considerable importance because, by beginning in this fashion, a clinician can establish the combined role of "good parent," helper, and teacher. These parents need to have someone whom they can call upon when they find themselves to be overstressed and are fearful that they may act out once more against their child. The therapist should be aware that events which most people would consider to represent minor difficulties may be catastrophic to abusive parents.

In general, treatment of abusive families proceeds as follows. At first, there is a stage during which the parents are frightened and angry and will deny the abuse as best they can. It is best not to fight this but allow it to run its course. A clinician should try to avoid asking why the parents did what they did, how or when or where it was done, or any question that may imply an accusation of blame during this initial phase. The primary aim is to "ride out" the anger and be as supportive as possible, in an attempt to gain some trust. While the parents' anger will appear to be capable of going on forever, usually within four to six weeks this anger will turn (in many cases quite suddenly) into dependency. During this stage of dependency, it is important for the therapist or co-therapists to be readily available to these parents. It is a period when the family can be thought of as most vulnerable to stress. For the first time the parents have allowed someone to enter their hermetic family system, and thus it is important for a therapist to "be there" at those significant moments when they permit themselves to ask for help.

Some initial requests for assistance may appear on the surface to be trivial. For example, a parent may want to find out the name of a good medicine for colds, or perhaps one of the children has asked a question and the parent wants advice about how to respond. The point is that many events which most people can take in stride are exaggerated in the case of those who are as deeply psychologically impoverished as abusive parents are. Finding them overwhelmed by these momentary crises, perplexed and unable to cope, the therapist soon realizes that they, themselves, are needy children who require re-parenting to become healthy adults. This stage of dependency in therapy will be a time when the abusive parents, having passed through phases of anger and denial, will feel much relieved, and the clinician will very likely be able to make substantial therapeutic gains. But the therapist must be aware that this course of treatment will proceed slowly and will very likely be time-consuming to complete.

Our work with abusive families consists of three essential roles: the first is that of therapist, the second that of re-parenter, and the third that of teacher. As teacher, a clinician endeavors to explain appropriate and realistic expectations of children, since abusive parents know so little about normal child development. In order to help abusive parents improve their parenting skills, we focus much attention upon the concepts of punishment and praise. Abuse often begins with a parent's simple attempt to stop undesired behavior by punishing the child for something he or she has done. What the parent lacks is knowledge of a means of punishment that does not require violence. For example, the parent should know about alternatives such as "time out," i.e., putting the child in his or her room for a period of time as a form of punishment. Another alternative is to establish a point system by which the child may win or lose points for good or bad behavior. These approaches to behavioral control can serve to make violent punishment unnecessary.

For many of these parents, it is useful to provide "empathy training," a method intended to teach people to recognize and understand the feelings of others. We have observed that abusive parents are so consumed by their feelings of personal inadequacy that they are unable to recognize feelings of sadness or pain in others. In order to learn empathy, the person is asked to recall incidents in which he or she was hurt by someone, as well as incidents in which he or she was made to feel joy or happiness. The object is to focus attention upon the interaction (positive or negative), thus showing how one person's behavior affects and influences the behavior of another.

Finally, working with abusive parents requires teaching them new ways to respond when they feel anger. The goal is to persuade them to restrain their impulsive and volatile reactions to challenge or stress. One way to do this is to use "guided fantasy," and another is to ask the person to keep a diary or journal. In guided fantasy a person is encouraged to recall moments in life that were the most gratifying. It is not suprising to find that many abusive parents have considerable difficulty in recalling periods of time in their lives that were happy, considering their own histories of deprivation and abuse. Later, the parents are asked to remember incidents in their lives when they knew they weren't supposed to do something and, in fact, did not do it because it was "wrong." Then we suggest that they recall how good it felt to be able to control themselves in this manner. A final step is to persuade the parents to connect these positive feelings from the past to events and situations that are occurring in the present. This approach can be extended even further by asking the clients, in the course of treatment, to report moments in their present lives when they have delayed in acting out their frustrations or anger.

Moreover, asking parents to keep a diary or journal can be useful as a device to get them to record anger-producing incidents. Part of the problem is that many such parents are largely unaware of the kinds of events which cause them to act out in an aggressive manner; some respond so rapidly that they lose track of the chain of events that led to their violent behavior.

In this stage of treatment, our aim is to teach the parents to follow a more problem-solving approach to coping with angry feelings, instead of permitting a provocative stimulus to "trigger" anger time after time. We encourage them to believe that, when experiencing pressure or stress, they are capable of discovering the cause of the problem and of making a more rational decision about what will be accomplished by their behavior. Lastly, they can choose what is the most appropriate action to take.

REFERENCES

Allen, J. J. Child abuse: A critical review of the research and the theory. In J. P. Martin (Ed.), *Violence and the Family.* New York: John Wiley & Sons, 1978.
Court, J. Psycho-social factors in child battering. *Journal of the Medical Women's Foundation,* 52:99-106, 1970.

Court, J. Characteristics of parents and children. In J. Carter (Ed.) *The Maltreated Child*. London: Priory Press, 1974.

Court, J. and Okell, C. An emergent programme to protect the battered child and his family. *Intervention*, 52:99-104, 1970.

Elmer, E. and Gregg, G. Developmental characteristics of abused children. *Pediatrics*, 40: 596-602, Part 1, 1967.

Feinstein, H. M., Paul, N. and Esmiol, P. Group therapy for mothers with infanticidal impulses. *American Journal of Psychiatry*, 120:882-886, 1963.

Gibbens, T. C. N. Violence to children. *Howard Journal*, 13:212-20, 1972.

Green, A. H., Gaines, R. W. and Sandgrund, A. Child abuse: Pathological syndrome of family interaction. *American Journal of Psychiatry*, 131:882-86, 1974.

Johnson, B. and Morse, H. A. Injured children and their parents. *Children*, 15:147-52, 1968.

Klein, M. and Stern, L. Low birth weight and the battered child syndrome. *American Journal of the Disabled Child*, 122:15-18, 1971.

Lissovey, V. de High school marriages: A longitudinal study. *Journal of Marriage and the Family*, 35:245-55, 1973.

Lynch, M. Ill health and child abuse. *Lancet*, 317: 16, August, 1975.

Morris, M. G. and Gould, R. W. Role-reversal: A necessary concept in dealing with the battered child syndrome. *American Journal of Orthopsychiatry*, 33:298-99, 1963.

Nurse, S. M. Familial patterns of parents who abuse their children. *Smith College Studies in Social Work*, 35:11-25, 1966.

Oliver, J. E., Cox, J., Taylor, A. and Baldwin, J. A. Severely ill-treated children in North East Wiltshire. Research Report No. 4, Oxford Record Linkage Study, Oxford Regional Health Authority, England, 1974.

Ounsted, C., Oppenheimer, R. and Lindsay, J. The psychopathology and psychotherapy of the families: Aspects of bonding failure. In A. W. Franklin (Ed.), *Concerning Child Abuse*. New York: Churchill Livingstone, 1975.

Saruk, S. Group therapy with child abusing parents. Paper presented at the Western Psychological Association Convention, Los Angeles, 1979.

Schmitt, B. D. The physician's evaluation. In B. D. Schmitt (Ed.), *The Child Protection Team Handbook*. New York: Garland STPM Press, 1978.

Schmitt, B. D. and Loy, L. L. Team decisions on case management. In B. D. Schmitt (Ed.), *The Child Protection Team Handbook*. New York: Garland STPM Press, 1978.

Silver, L. B., Dublin, C. C. and Lourie, R. S. Does violence breed violence? *American Journal of Psychiatry*, 126:404-407, 1969.

Skinner, A. E. and Castle, R. L. *78 Battered Children: A Retrospective Study*. London: National Society for the Prevention of Cruelty to Children, 1969.

Smith, S. M. *The Battered Child Syndrome*. Boston: Butterworths, 1975.

Steele, B. F. and Pollock, C. B. A psychiatric study of parents who abuse infants and small children. In R. E. Helfer and V. H. Kempe (Eds.), *The Battered Child*. Chicago: University of Chicago Press, 1968.

Wasserman, S. The abused parent of the abused child. *Children*, 14:175-79, 1967.

8

Sexual assault
on children

This chapter reviews some of the commonly held assumptions and prejudices concerning children and adolescents who have been victims of sexual assault. Certain of these assumptions have resulted in young victims being treated as if they were the guilty persons rather than victims, and some sources of these unfortunate misconceptions are identified here. The first section describes how the trauma of a sexual assault can manifest itself in children's behavior, and is illustrated by two case studies, one concerning a five-year-old girl who was raped by a stranger, and the other concerning a nine-year-old girl who was molested by a neighbor.

This discussion is focused upon children, as opposed to teenagers or adolescents, although some principles that are referred to here are valid for young people in general. The section does not completely exclude the subject of incest, because so many sexual assaults on children are made by family members; but a clear distinction will be drawn between incestuous and non-incestuous types of assault. Confusing the symptoms of these two types can result in misinterpretation of the child's behavior and/or that of the child's family members. The classic father-daughter incest relationship will be described in the next chapter.

Many of the primitive prejudices that are commonly held about adult victims of sexual assault, which tend to ascribe guilt or blame to the victim rather than to the perpetrator, are also held about child victims (Hilberman, 1976). Many adults tend to think of children as either unreliable or naughty, and this stereotype often predisposes them to view a child as the "guilty party." Because of this tendency, many real incidents of sexual assault against children are dismissed as products of the imagination or as fabrication by a bad or difficult child. In fact, some writers on this subject have demonstrated more concern with the role of children in "bringing on" the assault, or whether or not children tell the truth, than with a victim's psychological well-being (e.g., Lipton and Roth, 1969). This predisposition to doubt that a child can actually be considered a victim is indefensible in the light of facts. For example, a study of 250 children who were known to have suffered sexual assault showed that 60 percent had been coerced by force or the threat of force (De Francis, 1969).

Adding insult to injury, many perpetrators of assault have defended themselves by claiming that the child was provocative, seductive, or extraordinarily mature (sexually) for his or her age; the adult thus attempts to shift responsibility for himself to the child. Meiselman (1978) has described in detail how some parents will place the blame for incestuous relationships on their children—by describing them as sexually mature and seductive when in fact the children were neither. Meiselman also pointed out how clinically important it is to stress that self-control is the responsibility of an adult, even if the child may be behaving in a sexually inappropriate manner.

Although children sometimes behave in a seductive way toward adults, their actions differ greatly from those characteristics of adult genital sexuality. Children who act out in this way are rarely comprehending of what could actually result from their sexual advances (Schultz and De Savage, 1975). When an interaction of this kind results in assault, the child can only feel shocked, confused, and betrayed. In most cases the child had been seeking recognition or affection from the adult and was not aware of the potential consequences of his or her behavior.

Because the details of incidents of sexual assault upon children are in many cases shocking and repulsive, many adults unconsciously prefer not to hear them or dismiss them as exaggerated fantasies. Peters (1976) clarified this issue very well when he wrote:

> In their aversion to what are often repulsive details psychotherapists allow and continue to allow their patients to repress emotionally significant pathogenic facts. They ascribe to childhood fantasy, which is a common developmental process, actual childhood assaults. As a result these childhood traumas were never brought forth for complete reconstruction, ventilation, and abreaction. In addition, it is important to note that because the reported offender was frequently the child's own father, in order to avoid the fact of incest our colleagues seized upon the easier assumption that the occurrences were oedipal fantasies. . . . Freud himself admitted to suppressing the fact of a father as the molester in two cases he reported in 1895 (p. 402).

Rather than being confronted with the details of assaults on children, it is understandable that many therapists would seek to ascribe the assaults themselves to the realm of childhood fantasy. Apparently even Freud, himself a father and already a controversial figure because of his "outrageous" theories about childhood sexuality, preferred to distort the facts of certain assaults upon children that he observed in his own practice.

At ETC, our findings in respect to children and adolescents who have been referred to the Center in acute crises confirm Peters' (1973) finding that a majority of the reports of sexual abuse of children are true. It is well known that young children cannot describe sexual behavior in a vivid way unless the child has been exposed to the type of sexuality involved. Further, from the Center's work with adults in psychological emergencies, we have learned that childhood sexual traumas, if treated improperly, may remain as unhealed wounds which reveal themselves years later and can cause serious problems in adolescent or adult life. Peters (1973) described childhood rape as an emotional time bomb that may explode at any time in the victim's future experience.

Children will be affected in one of two basic ways by molestation: 1)

There will be a delayed or "silent" reaction, which is usually depressive in nature (Burgess and Holmstrom, 1974a, b, and c; Peters, 1975a and b, 1976); or 2) there will be symptoms that manifest themselves immediately after the assault, including acute somatic symptoms such as gastrointestinal disturbances and sudden changes in normal toilet habits, sleep disturbances, and enuresis (in younger children). Child victims frequently withdraw from their accustomed activities and relationships, sometimes by refusing to play outside the home or by becoming school phobic. Burgess and Holmstrom (1974c) and De Francis (1969) noted in their studies that a majority of child victims had at least mild to acute post-trauma symptoms. Both Peters (1975a and b) and De Francis (1969) also observed that many parents tended to underestimate the degree of psychological trauma which their children had experienced as the result of an assault. Their underestimation was probably caused by the parents' wish that the horrible event had never happened. This kind of thinking can lead parents to believe that the child does not require treatment because he or she has been unharmed by the event. Thus, a wishful fantasy on the part of the parents can serve to prevent a child from obtaining needed treatment.

Another form that parental denial can take is pretending that, no matter what has happened, the child will just forget about it. This misguided attitude by parents can lay a foundation for more serious problems later, because the child *cannot* forget about it. Moreover, the parents' "let's keep it quiet" attitude implies that they are ashamed of the child.

If parents do not wish to subject their child to the trauma and publicity of a trial, they should at least clearly convey to the child that they feel he or she has done nothing wrong and that they want to protect him or her from future assaults. The importance of this parental reaffirmation of support and concern cannot be overstressed. And even if the parents do not wish their child to go through the experience of a trial, they should consider at least permitting the child to report this molestation to the police. The process of reporting the crime will help the child, in a symbolic way, to "work through" some of the trauma.

Because many child victims are often quiet and emotionally bland, they may be thought of as unaffected by the assault when, in fact, they are depressed. We have found (as did Peters, 1973) that a fairly lengthy period of play therapy sessions, in which the child is reassured that it is all right to express his or her feelings and to be angry with adults, is required before the child will be able to express anger toward the perpetrator. Often it is only after this outward expression of anger that the child's depression will begin to lift.

Some children find it particularly difficult to express their feelings toward adults. They may have been taught to obey adults and not to "talk back" to them. Considering the fact that 70 percent of molesters were previously known by the children whom they assaulted (De Francis, 1969), it is clear that molestation can often place a child in a double bind situation. The child was assaulted because of obeying an adult, but he or she cannot express angry feelings because speaking out against adults is forbidden. This kind of conflict can cause a child to suffer deep depression. The conflict may be further compounded if the parents react by severely restricting or excessively supervising their child after the molestation, which the child may perceive as a form of punishment for having been molested.

Because young children are still emotionally and physically dependent upon their parents for care and protection, they often reflect the parents' own feelings about something that has happened. As a result, it is vital that the mother and father of a child victim obtain the support and guidance they themselves may need, so that they will be able to respond appropriately to their child. In some cases it is difficult for parents to grasp what the assault has meant to their child in terms of the child's developmental level, and if they become involved in their own feelings, they may not be able to respond to the child on the child's terms. For example, parents may become angry with their child for having gotten into a car with a stranger or having gone to a neighbor's house in spite of having been told not to go there. As they become more involved in this anger, they may forget that the child has experienced a painful and terrifying ordeal. In reality the child *may have been* a curious (or even somewhat willing) participant in the event. He or she may have been flattered by the molesting adult's attention and may even have experienced some sexual pleasure through the initial stimulation. But when the parents, upon discovering the molestation, overreact and possibly misdirect their anger toward the child, the child may be prevented from expressing his or her true feelings about the event for fear of receiving added adult condemnation.

Our experience is consistent with that of Schultz and De Savage (1975) who wrote that the amount of psychological trauma a child suffers is usually correlated with the amount of violence or terror associated with the event, in addition to the degree of physical assault which a child has experienced. Landis (1956) found that children who were victims of rape were more severely emotionally damaged than were child victims of other types of sexual assault. The research of De Francis (1969) and Peters (1974) has shown that assaults on children by people whom they know are more traumatic than are assaults by strangers. It is well documented that the way in which parents, relatives, teachers, and other adults respond to the child will have a significant effect upon the child's recovery (De Francis, 1969; Peters, 1974, 1976). In simple terms, children whose parents respond in an understanding and loving manner show less trauma. In addition, the child's age is thought to be a significant factor in determining how traumatic an assault has been and how successful will be the child's recovery (Peters, 1974), i.e., a younger child is more vulnerable to trauma and more likely to be overwhelmed by the experience.

The literature contains considerable controversy concerning how lasting the effects of sexual assaults upon children are. The research of Bender (1965), which is frequently cited to prove that children can adjust satisfactorily after sexual assault, is less than convincing because the design did not include a control group. Also, in the retrospective studies of Gagnon (1956) and Landis (1956), a majority of the children studied had been victims of exhibitionism or petting, while fewer than five percent of them had been victims of rape. In fact, most of the major studies which have suggested that children suffer no lasting trauma from sexual assault have lacked control groups (of non-victims) and have incorporated a wide variety of types of sexual incidents (most of which were not physically violent). By contrast, there is a growing body of evidence which suggests that both prolonged trauma and later problems of adjustment result from childhood sexual assault (Bauer and Stein, 1973; De Francis, 1969; Finch, 1967, 1973; Katan, 1973; MacDonald, 1971; McCauldron, 1967; Peters, 1973, 1976; Price, 1975).

The psychological aftereffects of molestation depend upon the following variables, according to Katz and Mazur (1979):

1) Age of victim: younger children are more vulnerable than are older adolescents to permanent damage.

2) Emotional maturity of the victim: child victims who have had previous emotional problems may experience more subsequent problems, and those problems may be longer lasting.

3) Prior sexual experience: children who have had no prior sexual experience are more vulnerable.

4) Type of assault: the amount of violence experienced by the child is positively correlated with trauma.

5) Repeated assaults: repeated assaults cause more psychological damage than do isolated assaults.

6) Stranger versus known offender: rape by someone whom the child knows, in some cases, will cause more lasting damage than will rape by a stranger.

7) Reactions of others: negative reactions on the part of police, parents, teachers, friends, can contribute to permanent damage.

8) Therapy: as with adults, child victims of sexual assault who receive therapy are more likely to recover completely than are those who do not have treatment (Katz and Mazur, 1979, p. 247).

In conclusion, there are numerous factors which determine how traumatic a sexual assault upon a child will be. Our clinical experience strongly suggests that the most significant factor in how well a child recovers from sexual assault is the nature of the response on the part of his or her parents, as well as that of significant other people in the child's life.

The Case of Lisa

Lisa, aged five, was raped by a stranger on her way home from school. The policeman who responded to the initial call thought Lisa would feel safer if he talked with her when her parents were present. That was an unfortunate decision because the parents became extremely upset when they heard the details of the rape from their daughter, and ordered the policeman to leave their home. Before the policeman left, he suggested that the parents call the Emergency Treatment Center for some counseling or help in deciding what to do next.

Within an hour the Emergency Treatment Center therapist had arrived. She suggested that she would like to talk with the parents first, so that they could speak freely. The parents were extremely angry, and they displaced some of this anger by thoroughly questioning the therapist concerning her educational background and how much experience she had had with child rape victims. The therapist described her qualifications and experience, and attempted to reassure the parents. At first, she wanted them to ventilate some of their anger about what had happened to their daughter. Then she began trying to help the parents understand what the experience may have been like for Lisa, and to show them that Lisa might interpret their expression of angry feelings as anger directed toward her. The therapist explained that a child of Lisa's age could not fully understand the sexual aspects of what had happened to her. Instead, Lisa could only know that terror and pain had been inflicted upon her by an adult, while until that time she had trusted most adults.

The clinician explained to Lisa's parents that their child's primary need, at this moment, was to feel as protected and loved as possible. Further, they should be careful not to do or say anything to Lisa that she might misinterpret as anger or as blame. By the end of the session, the parents were able to admit that they had been so hurt and angry that they felt like striking out at everyone. They promised the therapist that from now on they would try to focus on Lisa's needs. Also, they decided to press charges against the rapist, with the thought of preventing the molestation of other children in future. As the intervention proceeded, the therapist said that, if Lisa felt comfortable with her, she would accompany Lisa to the police station when she had to go there for questioning. The parents were greatly relieved, and the father admitted that he would like to avoid hearing the details of the rape again, because he became too angry when he heard them.

When the ETC therapist asked if she could talk with Lisa, Lisa's mother brought her into the living room and introduced her to the therapist. Lisa was quite small and was fragile in appearance. She spoke softly and held on to her mother all the time. After the clinician had spent a while making light conversation with Lisa, she asked Lisa if she would show her her room, and Lisa agreed. The therapist played with her for about half an hour in her room, using Lisa's toys. Toward the end of this time the therapist asked Lisa if she would like to come to her office and play with the toys that were there, and Lisa said she would like to if her mother would bring her. During this initial meeting with Lisa, the therapist was very careful not to walk toward Lisa rapidly or to touch her unless Lisa initiated it. She allowed Lisa to set the pace and direction of this and subsequent play therapy sessions. The first office appointment was arranged for three days hence.

During the first three sessions, Lisa played out scenes in a doll's house involving a little girl doll. Each story involved a little girl who got hurt or was sick; she would have to go to the hospital and, later, her mother and father would have to take care of her. Throughout these sessions, Lisa appeared emotionally "flat" and depressed. She would narrate lengthy stories about the hurt little girl while remaining largely expressionless. Lisa brought some of her own toys with her to the third session, and it was then that she asked the clinician why she had not asked her about the "bad man." When the therapist replied that they could talk about the man if she wanted to, Lisa abruptly changed the subject.

Lisa brought some more toys from home to the fourth session. The therapist waited to see if Lisa would bring up the subject of the "bad man" but she didn't. Later on, the theme of play therapy changed, and the scene became a swimming pool. Before the next session the therapist learned, from Lisa's mother, that Lisa was still refusing to play outside the house because some older children had teased and frightened her. Four more sessions of play therapy involved elaborate feeding scenes, usually taking place near the fantasied swimming pool. After each feeding scene the children would be taken home by their mothers and put to bed.

Eventually the play therapy themes became more interactional, in that Lisa would create scenes of children playing together or watching television together. She then changed to scenes involving bedroom and toilet. The toilet scenes consisted of Lisa thoroughly examining both the male and female dolls and their going to the toilet. The clinician learned, when she spoke with Lisa's parents that same week, that Lisa was now willing to come home from school by herself, even though she would run the entire way home. To the next session Lisa brought a large doll who wore no panties, and when Lisa commented on this fact the therapist asked if the doll had left them at the hospital. Lisa replied with a definite "no." She buried the doll in the sandbox, but then suddenly uncovered it and picked it up. As the sand was falling from the doll's hair, Lisa quietly said "like rain."

The next session began with innocuous play, and then Lisa suddenly grabbed an adult male doll and began burying him angrily. She said that he was crying for help, but no one would help him because he was a bad man. Then, with obvious pleasure Lisa stuck the scary animals all around him. Pushing him under the sand, she triumphantly pronounced the man dead. After this she carefully removed the scary animals and put them away. Then she dug the man out, put him in a box and shut the lid, referring to the box as "his coffin." The therapist tried to show Lisa that she accepted this anger, and tried to reassure her that it was all right for her to be angry and to bury the man.

Following this session, Lisa's mood changed dramatically: Her manner became much more animated and her depressive symptoms began to lift. She continued to work through the anger that was still felt toward the man by repeatedly burying him or feeding him to ferocious animals. Slowly her anger began to subside and her play scenes became interactional again, in that she would once more create family scenes and scenes of children playing.

By then, the clinician had begun to believe that Lisa had confronted as much of the rape experience as possible for someone at her stage of psychological development, and thus decided to conclude the play therapy sessions. When meeting with Lisa's parents, the therapist explained that Lisa had worked through the rape experience as well as possible for the time being, adding that renewed therapy might be appropriate when Lisa became an adolescent and began to be attracted to boys.

The Case of Marie

The mother of eight-year-old Marie brought her to the local police department's Sex Investigation office because she thought Marie had been molested by a neighbor. The mother said that Marie had gone to visit the neighbor without her permission and had behaved like a completely different child when she returned. When she arrived home, Marie ran at once to the bathroom, locked the door, and would not answer her mother who could hear her crying inside. When she finally came out of the bathroom and was asked where she had gone that day, Marie answered, "I thought Mr. Smith was a daddy," and ran to her room, once more refusing to talk with her mother. From that moment, according to the mother, Marie's entire personality changed: A once well-behaved, friendly little girl, who loved to help her mother and had done very well in school, suddenly became moody and secretive and was afraid to leave the house—even to go to school. She withdrew from her father and brothers, with whom she had been very close. She also would have sudden, unexplainable tantrums and at times say odd things such as, "I thought only mommies and daddies did that," and run out of the room when her mother would try to question her. Marie had frequent nightmares as well, and often would wake up screaming.

In his questioning of Marie at the police station, the Sex Investigation Officer asked her what had happened at Mr. Smith's house. Marie looked away and said, "I forgot." The officer then asked Marie's mother to step outside so that he could talk with Marie alone; he then attempted to reassure Marie before asking her again what had happened. This time Marie began to tremble and cry, and her repeated answer was "I don't know. I can't remember." By this time the officer felt convinced that something had happened to Marie, but he was not sure exactly what. Thinking that a therapist who specialized in children might be of help, he suggested that the mother call the Emergency Treatment Center. He added that hypnosis might be worth trying if, in fact, Marie was blocking something from her mind.

An ETC therapist met with the officer, Marie, and her mother that same afternoon. After getting acquainted with Marie and her mother, the clinician decided to find out whether or not hypnosis could aid Marie in remembering what had happened. The counselor used a "guided-fantasy" technique in which Marie was asked to make a "journey" to a beautiful, safe, magic kingdom. In this kingdom she would be able to sit on a cuddly teddy-bear-policeman's lap and remember what had happened, because the teddy-bear-policeman loved little children and would protect her. Although Marie seemed comfortable in her trance and even appeared to be enjoying it, as soon as the subject of remembering Mr. Smith's house was brought up she began to tremble and big tears rolled down her cheeks. When Marie came out of the trance, the therapist asked her again what she remembered and Marie replied, "Nothing. I forgot. I can't remember." Then she began to cry once more.

At this point the clinician believed that Marie had suffered some traumatic experience on the day she visited Mr. Smith, but what it was remained a mystery. Further, she believed that Marie remembered what had happened but was afraid to tell. The therapist decided to ask Marie to return later on for play therapy. She explained to Marie's mother that the therapy would move forward at Marie's pace, and reassured Marie that she would not be forced to do or say anything she did not want to do or say.

During the next session, Marie and the therapist made drawings together. While Marie was engrossed in a drawing of her brother, she commented that "Mr. Smith only showed me pictures of naked people from here up," gesturing that she meant from the neck up. The therapist thanked Marie for sharing that with her, and added that she knew that what had happened to Marie must have been scary and embarrassing. But it was not Marie's fault, and no one would be angry with her if she told the rest. When Marie did not reply, the therapist dropped the subject and continued drawing with the girl.

Marie and the therapist began the next session by drawing pictures, but then Marie noticed a doll's house in the room and asked if she could play "mommie and daddy." While they were playing with the doll's house, the therapist asked, "What do mommies and daddies do?" In reply, Marie began enacting a very detailed scene in which daddy asked mommie to come inside and clean the house. As she continued with the fantasy of the mommie-doll cleaning the house, Marie became quite anxious; she abruptly stopped cleaning in the dining room and went back to drawing pictures.

Next time, Marie returned to the doll's house and began playing mommie and daddy again. But when the mommie-doll was in the dining room, the daddy-doll took off her pants and made her lie on the floor while he rubbed himself against her leg. As Marie played out this scene, she constantly looked toward the clinician to see what her reaction would be. Since the therpaist remained calm and accepting, Marie continued. She said, "He rolled her over and put his fingers up her bottom and it hurt." The therapist asked if that was what Mr. Smith had done to her. Marie began to sob and said yes; she added that she was pregnant and that her parents would send her away, because Mr. Smith had said that's what they do to bad little girls. The therapist reached out and held Marie close and assured her that Mr. Smith was a bad man and told lies. She explained that Marie could not be pregnant because she was too young, and that her parents would not send her away because of what had happened.

The therapist then went to find Marie's mother, and on the way back to the playroom explained that Marie had revealed what Mr. Smith had done to her. The therapist suggested that it was important for the mother to be very loving and supporting if Marie were to tell her about what had happened. When the mother entered the room, Marie—crying all the while—told her mother that Mr. Smith had asked her to come in and help him clean the house. He took her into the dining room and showed her some pictures of naked people, and then he told her to take her pants off. Marie had done what he said to do because she was so scared. Mr. Smith told her not to tell anyone because, if she did, her parents would send her away to be locked up because she was pregnant. Marie's mother reassured her that Mr. Smith was a liar and a bad man, and that she and Marie's father loved her very much and would never send her away.

The next day Marie and her parents returned to the police station and told the Sex Investigation Officer what had happened in the incident. When Smith was arrested, it was discovered that once before he had been convicted for molesting young children (in exactly the same manner) in another state. Later, when Smith was released on bail, Marie saw him from time to time in her neighborhood, and that frightened and confused her because she was afraid he would come back and "get" her. Because of this, Marie's parents felt it would be best for her if they moved to another city.

As in the case of Lisa, Marie's play therapy sessions during this phase of treatment usually involved sick or hurt children who had to "go away" to get better. After Marie's appearance in court, her play sessions revealed considerable anger: She had several tantrums during which she threw things around the playroom. Her drawings consisted of angry people fighting each other. With time, her anger slowly subsided and Marie began role-playing scenes involving her friends and her school. As therapy drew to a close, the clinician conducted several family sessions in which Marie's parents and brothers attempted to let her know they were proud of her for being brave. By the time therapy concluded, Marie had begun playing with her brothers again and felt at ease with her father once more.

The cases of Marie and Lisa serve to illustrate some typical behavior patterns of the sexually assaulted child. In our experience, a majority of these children appear at first to be emotionally bland or depressed. They need considerable support and reassurance before they will be able to express their feelings about the traumatic event. Unfortunately, adults often misinterpret the flat affect of the assaulted child as being that of a child who was undisturbed by the event. It has also been our experience that victims of childhood assault do not always need long-term therapy; instead, play therapy is recommended to assist the child in working through the trauma as it was experienced. Later on, a course of brief therapy will probably be useful during critical developmental stages, such as the beginning of adolescence.

THE ADOLESCENT VICTIM

Certain aspects of the experience of an adolescent rape victim are unique, and even though the general treatment principles are the same as for adult rape victims (see Chapter 11), the experience itself merits a brief description in this section.

Adolescence is a time of life when young people normally test limits and take risks—a vital, although vexing characteristic of this developmental stage. As a result of this kind of exploration or acting-out, a teenage girl may place herself in a vulnerable position and become the victim of rape. For example, she might think of hitchhiking as daring or adventurous and dismiss her parents' warning against it as stuffy or trivial. If she does become a rape victim as a result of disobeying her parents, she may tend to blame herself more intensely than would some adult victims. And this may lead her to hide the fact of the rape for fear of telling the parents.

Although, sadly, many adolescent victims do not tell their parents directly about the assault, the secret is often betrayed by their behavior. For example, sudden and inexplicable changes in the habitual behavior of a teenage girl may be a sign that the girl was the victim of a "silent rape" (Hilberman, 1977), namely one that was not immediately reported. These changes in behavior patterns may take one of several forms, i.e., a rapid drop in school attendance and/or school performance, flagrant and repetitive promiscuity, withdrawal from peers and peer groups, or obviously self-destructive behavior such as that of drug abuse. Any one of these changes can be the manifestation of a teenage girl's wish to keep secret the fact that she has been raped. Even so, this relatively sudden change in behavior on the part of the girl will call attention to itself eventually, and the secret may come out as a result. In retrospect, it can be said that the adolescent's rapidly changing behavior patterns represented a "cry for help."

A key to awareness in working with adolescent victims of assault is to realize that they have many of the same emotional needs as do children who have been molested or raped. This is especially true with respect to the need for nurturance and support on the part of parents. Even though an adolescent girl may have reached a similar stature to that of an adult and have attained the physical attributes of an adult, she is still in many respects a child. Her striving for independence from the parents may mislead an adult into thinking that she is more mature than is the case. Indeed, the parents themselves may be misled into the belief that their teenager needs less of their tender concern than she did when she was in elementary school.

Sometimes when an adolescent reports to her parents that she has been raped, they in their turn focus their attention on her risk-taking behavior and the poor judgment she may have shown. Some parents express their concern about the public scandal that might arise, i.e., "What will the neighbors think?" In this kind of shortsighted view, the parents lose sight of the fact that their daughter has suffered a terrible trauma and needs to feel loved. Above all, she needs to believe that she will be protected.

When parental concern "gets lost" and parental anger "spills over" onto the rape victim herself, it only serves to instill in her a sense of guilt or worthlessness that may lead to greater loss of self-esteem. Further, this too often becomes a motive for self-destructive acting-out on the part of the adolescent. While the parents may believe that they have done "what is right," in the process they may have contributed to exactly the kind of behavior they most fear.

An alternative form that these behavioral changes may take is that the girl may react by trying to avoid contact with boys as much as possible and for a considerable period of time. This kind of withdrawal should be respected at face value. A clinician should help the parents to realize that, because their daughter has been deeply and overwhelmingly frightened, they must let her find her own way back to a "social life." It is the mentality of "after a fall, put the rider right back on the horse" that needs to be prevented. A therapist must accept responsibility for helping the parents, siblings, and other important people in the girl's life to permit the wounds to heal and the fear to fade away with time.

There will be cases in a therapist's practice when he or she learns that an adolescent client has been a "silent rape" victim. When this happens, it is important to try not to react in a judgmental way. A clinician should focus immediately upon the girl's need for post-trauma care and protection—for example, should she have medical treatment and/or a pregnancy test? Next, the therapist should attempt to get her consent to inform the parents about what has happened. The fact that the rape was not previously reported suggests that the girl may welcome assistance in breaking the news to her parents. A therapist can let the girl know that she will not be forced to reveal the event, but that the therapist is ready to help when she is ready.

Even if an adolescent wishes to keep the rape secret from her parents, a clinician can encourage her to report it anonymously to the police. The therapist can say that he or she would like the person who committed rape to be punished and prevented from finding another victim. Most Sex Investigation Officers are well aware of the fact that many adolescents who are raped do not report the assault right away. But if the therapist has a concern about how this delay might affect the investigation of a particular assault, it will be a good idea to telephone the police department and make an inquiry without mentioning names or giving specific details. Another possible reason that the girl may not have reported being raped is that the rapist may have been an adolescent from her peer group, and she may have well-founded fears of ostracism by others in the group if she reports the assault.

In summary, while the case of an adolescent victim of sexual assault contains factors that are similar to cases of both adult and childhood assault, there are unique elements as well. In terms of psychosexual development, adolescence may be the most stressful phase of the entire life cycle, and an assault during this period can have a lifelong effect. While the authors do not believe that all parents will react to their daughter's trauma with insensitivity or indifference, we are convinced that how the adolescent's significant adults respond after the assault will be a key factor in her recovery.

Finally, it should be noted that in some cases of adolescent rape, being raped is the girl's first sexual experience. While most adults can clearly understand the difference between consensual sex and rape, an adolescent victim may have difficulty in making that distinction if she lacks prior experience. This is a subject that the therapist will need to explore with an adolescent victim, in order to help her unravel some of the possible misunderstandings about sex that may be part of the aftermath of rape.

REFERENCES

Bauer, R. and Stein, J. Sex counseling on campus: Short term treatment techniques. *American Journal of Orthopsychiatry*, 43:824-893, 1973.
Bender, L. Offended and offender children. In R. Slovenko (Ed.), *Sexual Behavior and the Law*. Springfield, IL: Charles C Thomas, 1965.
Burgess, A. W. and Holmstrom, L. L. Crisis and counseling requests of rape victims. *Nursing Research*, 23:196-202, 1974a.

Burgess, A. W. and Holmstrom, L. L. Rape trauma syndrome. *American Journal of Psychiatry*. 131: 9:981-986, 1974b.

Burgess, A. W. and Holmstrom, L. L. *Rape: Victims of Crisis*. Bowie, MD: Brady, 1974c.

De Francis, V. *Protecting the Child Victim of Sex Crimes Committed by Adults*. Pamphlet from the American Humane Assoc., Children's Division, Denver, Colorado, 1969.

Finch, S. M. Sexual activities of children with other children and adults. *Clinical Pediatrics*, 6:1-2 (Commentaries), 1967.

Finch, S. M. Adult seduction of the child: Effects on the child. *Medical Aspects of Human Sexuality*, 7:170-187, 1973.

Gagnon, J. H. Female child victims of sex offenses. *Social Problems*, 13, 176-192, 1956.

Hilberman, E. *The Rape Victim*. New York: Basic Books, 1976.

Hilberman, E. Rape: A crisis in silence. *Psychiatric Opinion*, 14, 5:32-38, 1977.

Katan, A. Children who were raped. *Psychoanalytic Study of the Child*, 28:208-224, 1973.

Katz, S. and Mazur, M. A. *Understanding the Rape Victim*. New York: John Wiley & Sons, 1979.

Landis, J. T. Experiences of 500 children with adult sexual deviation. *Psychiatric Quarterly Supplement*, 30:91-109, 1956.

Lipton, G. L. and Roth, E. I. Rape: A complex management problem in the pediatric emergency room. *The Journal of Pediatrics*, 75(5):859-866, 1969.

MacDonald, J. M. *Rape Offenders and Their Victims*. Springfield, IL: Charles C Thomas, 1971.

McCauldron, R. J. Rape. *Canadian Journal of Corrections*, 9:37-57, 1967.

Meiselman, K. C. *Incest*. San Francisco: Jossey-Bass, 1978.

Peters, J. J. Child rape: Defusing a psychological time bomb. *Hospital Physician*, 9:46-49, 1973.

Peters, J. J. The psychological effects of childhood rape. *World Journal of Psychosynthesis*, 6:11-14, 1974.

Peters, J. J. Social, legal and psychological effects of rape on the victim. *Pennsylvania Medicine*, 78, 2:34-36, 1975a.

Peters, J. J. Social psychiatric study of victims reporting rape. Study presented at the American Psychiatric Association, 128th Annual Meeting, Anaheim, California, 1975b.

Peters, J. J. Children who are victims of sexual assault and the psychology of offenders. *American Journal of Psychiatry*, 30:398-421, 1976.

Price, V. Rape victims—The invisible patients. *The Canadian Nurse*, 71:29-34, 1975.

Schultz, L. G. and De Savage, J. Rape and rape attitudes on a college campus. In L. G. Schultz (Ed.), *Rape Victimology*. Springfield, IL: Charles C Thomas, 1975.

9

The incestuous family

Incestuous impulses and fantasies have been experienced by nearly every person, and yet our society reserves its most powerful taboos and its most severe condemnation for incestuous acts. Impulses of this kind, when worked through in the ordinary course of maturation by the device of psychological fantasy, may lead to the person's being attracted to or marrying someone very similar to (or totally different from) their parent of the opposite sex. If these impulses cannot be kept in check appropriately by the parent because of poor impulse control, they may come crashing into the world of reality with more damaging effects than either parent or child could have imagined.

Since incest fantasies are such a deep and significant part of normal sexual development, there is a temptation to think of actual incest as potentially beneficial. Although this phenomenon may be exotic in the realm of dreams, it is not so in reality. For example, the French film, *Murmur of the Heart,* was a highly romanticized story of incest between a mother and son, but rarely does incest have anything like an ideal outcome. In reality the story is more likely that of a son and mother who are both very disturbed, often psychotic people (Medlicott, 1967; Shelton, 1975; Wahl, 1960). At best, the story is that of a young man who feels deeply betrayed and confused and who will have trouble in relating to women sexually—let alone trusting or being able to express love for a woman. In each of the rare cases of mother-son incest that the authors have encountered, the result was far from romantic. The theme of this chapter is that incest represents a tremendous breach in the basic trust relationships which together form the foundation of family life. Thus, the primary issue that a clinician must address in the treatment of incest is not sexuality, but rather this basic trust relationship between parent and child around which future love and trust relationships will be built.

The incest taboo, which is almost universal to cultures, has a purpose. It serves to protect the family structure and it assists in the healthy development of the human species. Although there are some exceptions to the incest taboo, closer examination of these exceptions reveals that, in most cases, specific limitations are placed upon what incestuous behavior is, in fact, permitted (Meiselman, 1978, p. 3). Socially accepted incestuous behavior is usually restricted to a special social class, e.g., royalty, or limited to specific religious rituals. The few cultures that do permit incest do not condone promiscuity among the privileged group, nor do they permit incestuous behavior outside of rigidly prescribed circumstances. Moreover, a majority of these cultures only sanction incestuous relationships between brother and sister, while prohibiting incest between parents and child. To exemplify how all-pervasive the incest taboo is, Murdock (1949) surveyed 250 primitive societies and found that each of those societies had strict sanctions against incest within the nuclear family.

Many theories have been put forth concerning the origin and purpose of the incest taboo. Despite Freud's explanation of the role played by incestuous fantasies in the development of the psyche, many critics believe that he failed to formulate a plausible theory of the origin of the taboo (e.g., Meiselman, 1978). One attempted formulation was the allegorical tale in *Totem and Taboo* (1913), in which Freud described a "primal herd" ruled by a cruel and tyrannical father who would not permit his sons to have access to women; because of this, the sons united in revolt against their father. When the sons had defeated the tyrannical father, they devoured him in a cannibalistic ritual. But afterward they were overcome with grief and guilt because they had also loved their father and realized that they would now be in competition among themselves for the women. Out of this conflict the sons "created" the incest taboo and agreed to practice exogamy. This theory has never enjoyed wide acceptance, and Freud himself was not pleased with it as a rationale for the taboo (Meiselman, 1978).

The anthropologist Malinowski (1927) advanced a theory which held that incest, if practiced, would destroy the structure of the family system by confusing family roles and generational boundaries. The intense emotional feelings that are produced by sexuality between parent and child would cause the balance of power within each family to collapse in such a way that the family could not function any longer as a social or economic system. More recently, the sociologist Parsons (1954) has pointed out that incestuous *fantasies*, on the part of the child, can be a positive motivating force in personality development. His thesis is that the erotic attachment between a parent and a child serves as a mechanism to draw the child through the sometimes difficult and painful stages of normal development.

There is very likely a biological basis for the incest taboo as well. Meiselman (1978) summarized the biological research that has been done on nuclear family incest, and although research on this subject is very difficult to carry out, two of the studies bear consideration here. Adams and Neel (1967) studied 18 children who were born as a result of nuclear family incest, by contrast with a matched control group. Each group was examined twice, at birth and at six months. At six months, only seven of the 13 surviving children of incest victims were considered to be normal and adoptable. (The children of five of these victims had been stillborn or had died very early in infancy.) In the control group, 15 children were considered to be normal at six months.

Another significant study was that of Seemanova in Czechoslovakia (1971): 161 children of nuclear family incest victims were studied over an eight-year period; these children of incest were contrasted with a control group of their half-siblings who were not the result of an incestuous union. Moderate to severe retardation was found in 25 percent of the children of incest, by contrast with no cases of retardation in the control group. In addition, 20 percent of the children of incest were found to have congenital malformations or at least one serious physical abnormality. Eighty-nine percent of the control group were considered to be normal children, by contrast with 41 percent of the children of nuclear family incest.

In review, the all-pervasive incest taboo likely has its roots in many essentially separate but intertwined human needs. The taboo serves a vital function in that it protects the structure and integrity of the family as the foundation stone of a social system. The taboo plays an important role in the process of psychosexual development and serves a biological function by advancing the healthy evolution of the species.

When beginning to contemplate the treatment of an incestuous family, it will be necessary to define the problem clearly. All too often an unsubstantiated or questionable claim of incest is simply dismissed as an "incest fantasy" or a story that has been fabricated by a "bad" or neurotic child. There is a growing body of evidence (Barry, 1965; Cowie et al., 1968; and Peters, 1976) which suggests that most reports of child molestation or incest are true. In this respect it is tragic that some clinicians look upon children as capable of lying unless proven innocent. A more kindly approach would be to assume that a report of incest is true unless proven false, an approach ably expressed by Geiser: "It is better to err on the side of believing the report than to shut off what may be a client's cry for help" (1979, p. 62).

If a child makes either a veiled hint of incest or a direct accusation of incest, each by itself is a serious matter. If the story turns out to be untrue, the child may be exhibiting hysterical symptoms or suffering from childhood schizophrenia. In another context, the false report might be a form of emotional blackmail. The following imaginary situation gives an example of this. A single-parent mother who has a teenage daughter remarries, hoping to bring authority and stability to the home. If the teenage daughter wants to get rid of this newcomer who is an intruder to her world, gives orders, and poses an emotional threat to her, one thing she can do is falsely accuse her new stepfather of incest, or behave in a sexually provocative manner toward him in front of her mother or other people. Thus, in beginning an intervention the therapist must weigh the relative contributions of reality and fantasy.

As a general rule, we have found that the younger the child the more credence can be given to the child's report of some kind of sexual advance toward him or her on the part of a parent. A small child is the more credible because he or she has probably had no prior opportunity to learn about adult sexuality. For example, when a child of five accurately describes an erection or ejaculation, the story may well be true because a child of this age would very likely have had to see something in order to give an accurate description. With an older child, the report should not be rejected out of hand, but more careful investigation will be needed because many other reasons may lie behind an accusation, or even a suggestion of incest.

Everyone knows that children are sensitive and have an uncanny ability to know when something unusual is happening or something has gone wrong. Because they may not know the right words, what they say about what they have sensed may sound as though an incestuous advance is being reported when, in fact, it is not. What the child may be feeling could be some sort of misdirected threat or tension in the family, and what the child describes (something that is half real, half fantasy) may be only a premonition. A classic example of a child's "knowledge" of a problem on the feeling level is the case in which parents say, "Yes, we are getting ready to separate and get divorced. We haven't told the children; they don't know anything about it." At the same time, the therapist may have observed that the children have been acting out and are showing other, deeply felt signs of anxiety. Children are quite often aware, on a feeling level, of basic family dynamics that the parents wish to avoid. A child may *feel* that there is something wrong or about to happen, but what that intuition means may be unknown to the child and beyond his or her ability to express in any way.

Another hidden reason for a child to accuse a parent of incest is that the child may be asking for protection from that parent because he or she senses either an impending sexual threat or a shifting of roles within the family. It has been found that many incestuous situations begin with the uninvolved parent as the *failed protector* (Weinberg, 1955). Usually the sexually involved parent is made out to be the monster/ villain, while the other parent is seen as an unknowing bystander. But in fact the uninvolved parent may play as important a role in the incestuous family system as does the sexually involved parent (Lustig et al., 1966; Meiselman, 1978). Too frequently, therapy is focused upon getting the ("perverted") sexually involved parent to change, or getting a ("perverted") brother to stop his assaultive behavior, and does not take into account the complicity of other members of a family system who may be helping to maintain this problem.

A wise approach in therapy is to view incest as a whole-family problem; and in this context a clinician should strive to do everything possible to reassure the child that it was not his or her fault. Often the sexually involved parent attempts to place blame upon a "seductive" or
malevolent child, but in therapy it is important to restore responsibility
for self-control to the parents (Meiselman, 1978). Treatment which is
focused upon a single victim and a single villain fails to acknowledge
that each family can be viewed as a system.

When incest has been reported by a child to an uninvolved parent
who has then ignored the accusation or dismissed the child as a liar or
"bad child" without further investigation, it is usual to find that this
parent is also an integral part of the incestuous situation. Imagine a
child of yours telling you that your spouse had had sexual relations
with him or her; reflect upon what your reaction would be. Now think
how desperately weak and terrified a parent would have to be in order
to ignore such an accusation. Too often an uninvolved parent will
condone or even try to protect this extremely pathological, symbiotic
relationship between an incestuous parent and a child.

Sometimes sheltering an incestuous relationship can serve to protect the uninvolved parent from adult sexual demands that he or she
cannot accept. A sad example of this was the case of a 13-year-old
who was a good student and a "nice" girl. When ETC responded to
her home, the therapist found that she had taken an overdose of pills.
The therapist called an ambulance to take her to the hospital and was
there with her when she began to regain consciousness. In a semicon-
scious state, the girl described five years of sadomasochistic sex that
had been inflicted upon her by her father. The Sex Investigation Officer of the local police department was notified, and the officer soon
verified that her story was true. The father was out of town but was
due to return in a few days, and because of what her father's return
meant to her, the girl had attempted suicide. During a subsequent visit
to the home, the girl's mother became enraged and asked the therapist to leave. Her parting words were, "How could she say that about
him? He gave her a stereo last Christmas." Generally, in a case in
which that kind of massive denial persists, we have found it prudent to
remove the child from the home. The mother's response was typical
of the signs which reveal that it may be impossible to work therapeuti-

cally with a family, because there are not enough strengths or resources within the family system to protect the child or children. The mother in question was presumably trapped in a deeply pathological relationship with the father, and had become so dependent upon him that she could not sustain a protective role on behalf of her children.

It is worth noting that the subject of incest introduces much more tension into a conversation than the concept of child abuse does. At the mere mention of the word "incest," many people become nervous or hostile. This is probably one reason why so many people prefer to ascribe an accusation of incest to the realm of fantasy. The phrase "child abuse" occupies a certain common ground of understanding, perhaps because nearly everyone can admit to having felt an impulse to strike an unruly child. While many people have had incestuous impulses, it is far less socially acceptable to admit them to another person.

Incest does not always mean that it is necessary or advisable to break up a family situation. An incestuous family will have a good chance to reconstruct itself if provided with essential treatment and a variety of support services. The prognosis, in cases of those incestuous families who are appropriate for treatment, is generally positive. In order to decide whether or not a particular family is appropriate for treatment—and, if so, what type of therapy should be provided—a thorough diagnostic evaluation will be required. This evaluation is important because one of the causal factors that might go undetected in an incest case is borderline psychosis or a paranoid personality disorder on the part of the sexually involved parent (Raphling et al. 1967). Careful diagnosis is especially relevant when the offending parent is fully adult and the victim is a quite young child (11 years or younger). If the sexually involved parent *is* schizophrenic, he or she may well be of the paranoid type. Or the parent may be borderline and appear superficially to be normal; but when he or she is intoxicated or under psychological stress the serious pathology may emerge.

Once a thorough pretreatment evaluation has been done, more pointed and realistic plans for treatment can be made. Another clinical issue that needs to be taken into account, when deciding upon a treatment plan, is the possibility of alcoholism as a confounding factor. In general there is a strong possibility that one (or more) family members is a chronic alcoholic (Marcuse, 1923; Gebhard et al., 1965; Kaufman et al., 1954). The sexually involved parent may be the sort of person who appears to be fine until he or she takes a drink. For such persons, the saying, "the superego is soluble in alcohol," may be relevant; and if so, serious pathology may lie beneath the surface.

The pathology (whether or not it includes alcoholism) in an incestuous family may be difficult to find, because one way in which an incestuous family system survives and protects itself is by unspoken family myths and rules of conduct. These methods of defense ensure privacy from an outside world that is sometimes perceived as hostile to (or wishing to destroy) the family. Because of this fear of outsiders and because of the potential for hidden pathology, a therapist will be wise to begin treatment with an incestuous family in a slow and systematic manner. Treatment should be preceded or swiftly accompanied by the diagnostic evaluation referred to above, as well as a thorough study of the home environment. As Meiselman wrote:

> The key to understanding the family's behavior is to realize that its members perceive themselves as being on the brink of disaster in the form of separation, public shame, loss of financial support, and possibly severe punishment for the perpetrator of incest. With occasional exceptions, the "collusive" family members have not demonstrated that incest is their preferred way of life by their uncooperativeness—they have only demonstrated that they are fearful of the alternatives to the status quo (1978, p. 338).

The following types of cases differ markedly in many respects: incest between a 40-year-old father and a three-year-old child; and between a 35-year-old stepfather and his 16-year-old stepdaughter in which the incest took place one drunken night. Yet according to law they are the same. A therapist will, of course, be required to report the suspicion (or evidence) of incest in both cases (and, for those who work primarily with children and adolescents, this need to make a report of incest will inevitably occur). Incest is one of the most underreported crimes in the United States: Meiselman (1978) suggested that for each reported incest case, three are not reported. It is vitally important

that clinicians who work in emergency services establish a good working relationship with the local juvenile probation department and with
the Juvenile Officer(s) and Sex Investigation Officer(s) of the local police
department. Once these relationships have been established and the
therapist has become known and trusted, he or she will have more
available options if incest is suspected in a family. For example, if recent or past incest has been discovered in the course of family therapy, and if one is known and trusted by the police or the juvenile probation department, one of those agencies may be willing to receive the
report. In turn, that agency may possibly decide not to take further
legal action if the prognosis for successful treatment is good. But if the
family drops out of treatment or renewed incidents of sexual assault
occur, the original report may be activated again at once. Even
though a convicted parent or sibling must go through the criminal justice system, if a clinician is known to that system the chances for the
person's being ordered by a court to receive psychotherapy (with probation instead of incarceration) will be much greater. Finally, when a
family comes in for treatment and the therapist feels that the accused
parent or sibling should be removed from the home and/or prose-
cuted, the therapist will be better able to assist remaining family members through the painful criminal-legal process as a result of being acquainted with people in the justice system.

The discovery of incest in a family may mean that a great deal of
pressure will be placed upon a therapist, by family members, not to report it to the authorities. It is not uncommon for a victim to recant his
or her story and try to convince the therapist to drop the entire subject.
Often there exists a kind of myth, in an incestuous family, the theme
of which is that if incest were revealed the family would be destroyed;
i.e., their "world" would dissolve and it would be the therapist's fault.
This kind of myth-making was ably described by Watzlawick et al.,
who wrote:

> There can be no doubt that a large part of the process of social-
> ization in any society consists in teaching the young that which
> they must *not* see, *not* hear, *not* think, feel or say (1974, p. 42).

A similar observation about family myths was made by Ferreira in
these words: "The individual family member may know, and often

does, that much of the [family] image is false and represents no more than a sort of official party line" (1963, p. 458).

One of the most important dynamics in incest families is the conspiracy of fear, as described above, by which some family systems sustain and protect themselves through secret coalitions. A therapist who permits himself or herself to join that kind of conspiracy, by agreeing not to report incest at the family's request, will surely be taking a dangerous step into the family's pathological *modus vivendi* and its complicated network of alliances. Keeping the secret would be a serious mistake for several reasons. By being honest with the family about a clinician's duty to report suspected cases of incest (see Chapter 13), the therapist will be role-playing for the family members a straightforward and healthy way to confront problems. The therapist will also be saying, "I am not going to enter your system; I am going to stay away from it. I am going to set up easily understood, aboveboard rules."

Both incestuous and abusive families are notorious for trying to avoid treatment. They tend to fear change, and they fear facing the insidious problems that they have kept so well hidden. Because of this tendency, it may be necessary to take advantage of the court's jurisdiction over the case in order to induce them to stay in treatment beyond the initial, frightening stages. There is considerable evidence to suggest that incest will not stop, even after it is reported, unless the family receives some form of treatment (Weinberg, 1955; Weiss et al., 1955).

Other important questions will have to be answered as the therapist continues to evaluate the situation and decides what action to take. Were there many incestuous incidents or only a single occurrence? If the child has reported just one (and only one) incestuous act to an adult or the uninvolved parent and something was done about it, a therapist could assume that there is less serious pathology in that family than if it had been going on for years. But is it possible that intercourse between one parent and his or her child could have occurred repeatedly for two or three years without the other parent suspecting something? It would not seem likely, but such a situation *did* actually take place, according to the mother of the family described in the following case.

The police were called to a home where incest had been reported.

An ETC clinician arrived shortly after the police had left, and one of the first things that the therapist noticed was that there were only three doors in the entire house—the front door, the back door, and the bathroom door; the other interior doors had been removed. Incest had been a part of this family's way of life for many years, as we learned later. The father was no longer with the family because he had been discovered to have been having sex regularly with his oldest daughter (now 17 years old) for about three years. Soon after this was revealed the wife filed for divorce, and the divorce had just become final.

Now it had been discovered that the 16-year-old son had been sodomizing his sister, aged 13; in addition, he had forced her to have oral sex with him when she was six years old, and had done so regularly through the ensuing seven years. The mother claimed that she had known nothing about it until the younger daughter had written her a note, reporting it, that morning. She also claimed that she had known nothing about the husband's incestuous behavior with the older daughter until the daughter had reported it to a school teacher. One of this mother's comments may add force to the assertion that great denial characterizes the uninvolved parent in these families: She told the clinician, with great relief in her voice, that she was grateful to God that it was only sodomy because her daughter was still a virgin.

In a case such as this, when incest has been occurring for a long time and should have been detected and reported years earlier, much psychological energy has probably been expended by more than one member of the family in order to keep the incestuous system going. In effect, when incest has been reported to a parent who denies the problem, who refuses to listen or to investigate whether or not the accusation was true, that "uninvolved" parent has become an *integral* part of the problem.

Incest can be conceptualized as an event (or series of events) which has the effect of radically revising generational boundary lines, i.e., the role of one parent changes in relation to one of the children (Figure 1). In many incestuous families, the mother is very immature and does not want to accept an adult sexual role (Kaufman et al., 1954). As a consequence, she gradually tends to push her child into adopting a simulated "adult" role. Thus, one predisposing factor in the development of an incestuous situation may be initiated when a mother tries to cajole her daughter out of the child's normal role in the family, because she herself wants to regress to being a child.

This type of mother's life script may read as follows. She is probably fearful of sex or is extremely inhibited sexually. She may have had highly romanticized fantasies about what "being married" meant. She may have thought she married someone who was "safe" in the way that a fairy-tale father/husband would be safe, but she may have found that the realities of an adult relationship are distasteful to her. In

NORMAL FAMILY

MOTHER   FATHER
GENERATIONAL AND SEXUAL BOUNDARY LINE
CHILD OR CHILDREN

FAMILY IN WHICH
INCESTUOUS THREATS OR ACTS
ARE OCCURRING

MOTHER	GENERATIONAL AND SEXUAL BOUNDARY LINE	FATHER
CHILD OR CHILDREN		CHILD OR CHILDREN

Figure 1

many cases, sexual relations have completely ceased between the parents in an incestuous family (Lustig et al., 1966; Maisch, 1972; Riemer, 1940; Weiner, 1962). Because of the wife's unrealistic expectations, the marriage has become a disappointment to her or, at best, it has become a "truce" relationship. The dirty dishes and diapers and responsibilities have dashed her unfulfilled wishes and dreams. Many of these women use denial as their primary defense mechanism (Kaufman et al., 1954; Machotka et al., 1967; Weiner, 1962). Denial is very important to the internal system of this kind of family and is often very difficult to break through, probably because denial is such a primitive defense mechanism. Moreover, instances in which a mother of this sort proves to be supportive of her daughter-victim are in the minority (Meiselman, 1978).

The incestuous father, as noted above, may be an alcoholic or may be suffering from a form of paranoid personality disorder. Many are openly obsessed with sexual concerns (Gebhard et al., 1965). This father is very likely neither sexually adept nor a sensitive person. Through reflection on how these kinds of marriage partners are likely to interact sexually, there unfolds a probable blueprint of how the incestuous family system is established. The husband's reaction to his wife's childishness and sexual inadequacy is, usually, hostility and increased ineptitude or insensitivity. He may not be able to recognize or to admit his anger toward his wife. This interpretation may seem confusing, because incestuous families can, outwardly, be those in which much mutual respect is professed and in which protecting the "home" is given great importance. However, while both the parents and the siblings will stress concern for family pride and security, beneath this facade can be tremendous anger and mistrust that the family takes great pains to deny. But when a father commits incest with his daughter, he has chosen the one sexual partner most calculated to punish and humiliate his wife. Thus, even though much family loyalty may be displayed superficially, under the surface lies tremendous resentment, rage, and shame.

Another product of this emphasis upon loyalty to the family is that a tremendous burden of guilt may be placed upon the child victim if she should permit the shared secret to escape the family setting. A case in point is that of a woman of about 34 years of age who had been involved in an incestuous relationship with her father from when she was seven until she was 13. As an adult she still felt tremendous guilt, because she believed that she had destroyed her parents' marriage. She sincerely felt that, at seven years of age, she had done something to seduce her father and that it was her fault because she was a bad, promiscuous child. She was convinced that if it had not been for her the parents would still be happily married, even though she knew that her father at that time had been, and continued to be, a hopeless alcholic. This weight of guilt is carried on into adulthood in too many cases and must not be ignored in therapy.

It is true that children are sexual. Even though they are not sexual in an adult-genital way, they have genuine sexual feelings and they seek affection. In turn, adult responsibility requires a measure of self-control, so that the child's need for affection will not be exploited. It is realistic to estimate, from the experience of the Emergency Treatment Center, that many childhood suicide attempts or psychotic episodes, particularly those incorporating bizarre sexual fantasies, had their origin in situations involving either incest or child molestation that were not discovered or reported. Geiser (1979) found that in a clinic population of disturbed children, 20 percent had been incest victims. ETC has been referred several cases of children who were severely psychotic, even though quite young, and who suffered from wild sexual delusions. After they had been hospitalized and were feeling safer, these children were able to reveal that they had been assaulted sexually. One boy had been molested by a homosexual stepfather; in his case, experiencing a psychotic break for a period of time was, in a certain sense, a healthy response and probably the only chance that the child had to work through what had happened to him.

How do incest cases first come to light? What are some of the "presenting problems" that may eventually reveal an incest situation? Incest may first surface with the case of a runaway adolescent, the suicide attempt of a child or adolescent, or an episode of sudden promiscuity. Alternatively, incest may be revealed when an adolescent girl first shows interest in boys and the father blatantly overreacts or behaves like a jealous lover. The child may have confided in an adult outside the family—although in our experience that is extremely rare. There follow a list of potential risk factors that include the experiences

of our Center as well as other researchers (i.e., Browning and Boatman, 1977; Meiselman, 1978, p. 334):

1) Alcoholic father.

2) Father who is unusually suspicious and/or puritanical.

3) Violent or authoritarian father.

4) Mother who is very passive, absent, or incapable of being a
   protective force in the family.

5) Daughter who plays the role of mother, assuming many of
   the mother's household functions.

6) Parents whose sexual relationship is troubled or nonexist-
   ent.

7) Situation in which the father must often be alone with the
   daughter.

8) Factors which may limit the self-control of the father, such
   as drug dependency, psychopathology, or limited intel-
   ligence.

9) Sudden onset of promiscuity on the part of a young girl.

10) A child who does not allow people to be close friends with
    her.

11) Parents who are reluctant (or refuse) to allow a clinician to
    talk with their child alone.

12) Hostile or paranoid attitude toward outsiders on the part of
    one or both parents, especially the father.

13) Previous incidents of incest in the nuclear family (families) of
    one or both parents.

14) Parents who had deprived childhoods in which there were
    inadequate role models.

15) Extreme jealousy displayed by the father in a case in which
    the daughter has recently reached puberty.

These warning signs of an incestuous situation are offered as guidelines for looking more closely for incestuous behavior within a family.

For example, a therapist may be working with a family when, suddenly, the therapist observes a change in the father-daughter relationship. Perhaps the daughter was once "daddy's little girl," but recently, now that boys have started looking at her, the father has become jealous in a way that is reminiscent of a lover. Soon excessive rules and restrictions are arbitrarily being placed upon the girl by her father. (In response to one emergency call, ETC staff members found the father marching about the house and yelling at his daughter, more like an angry boyfriend than a father.) That kind of clearly reactive behavior on the part of the father can be a cause for concern.

Another warning sign may possibly be observed in the context of an initial emergency home visit. For example, during such a visit, the ETC clinician often makes a point of talking briefly in private with each member of the family present, in turn. Whenever dad or mom says, "No, we can deal with this as a family," or when there is a reluctance to let us have a few minutes alone with each member of the family, we often become suspicious that some family secret lies buried. A case-in-point was referred to parenthetically in the previous paragraph. The father in that case was a rigidly controlled man and his very beautiful, 15-year-old daughter was quite socially mature for her age.

We were first called to the house because the daughter was supposedly beyond parental control. What we discovered was an angry, troubled (but to all intents and purposes normal) adolescent who was behaving with defiance toward her father. When she would defy him, he would become enraged and throw her against a wall or slap her repeatedly. It appeared that the father was placing limits on her that were more appropriate for an 11-year-old child: for example, she could only go out on one night each weekend, and she always had to be home by 9 p.m., never later; after she had gone out once, she could not leave the home again that same weekend. After talking with the whole family awhile, the clinician asked to talk with each family member alone. When each had agreed, the therapist talked with the two parents in turn. But when it was time to talk with the daughter alone, the father returned to the living room and said, "I'm going to work in the garden—excuse me." He proceeded to walk about just outside the sliding glass door, which he pointedly left open. He hovered there, usually about three feet from the door, and when the therapist got up and closed the door he reappeared, smiled, and opened it again; when the therapist closed it again he opened it once more, so that the daughter and clinician were within his hearing. There was no way that they could speak in private except for fleeting moments. While the therapist talked with the girl, she appeared angry but also seemed to be extraordinarily fearful of her father. Later, in family sessions, the therapist attempted to focus upon family communication and the establishment of more realistic rules for the daughter, as well as helping the father accept the fact that teenage girls do have dates with boys.

As time went on, ETC became increasingly concerned that some form of incest might be taking place in this home. For one thing, the girl simply could not form close relationships with anyone. She would keep friends for just a short time and then drop them or have fights with them and use the fight as an excuse to end the friendship. The ETC clinician discovered from the mother that the daughter had suddenly become extremely promiscuous, and the mother also confided that she simply could not understand her daughter's behavior. Whenever the daughter became hurt or angry, she would simply "pick up" the first boy that she could find. In fact, she would often choose boys who were rough with her and would abuse her physically. Finally, one night the daughter ran away from home and called the therapist. She was drunk, had taken some pills, and was very, very frightened. The therapist found her and brought her to the ETC office where, drinking coffee, they talked for several hours. The girl told a story of sexual abuse that began when the father first had intercourse with her when she was six; it continued until she was 13, when he began insisting that she perform oral sex. She begged the therapist not to make her go back home. The therapist reassured her that she would not have to return home and made arrangements for her to stay in the county's children's shelter. Later investigation proved that the girl's story was agonizingly true in every detail. Both parents then denounced her as a "tramp" who had betrayed and destroyed the family. The girl is currently living in a foster home and, following a period of "testing limits," is adjusting quite well. Her parents suddenly moved away to another state and broke off all contact with their daughter.

It is worth noting that incestuous intercourse between father and daughter may stop when the daughter becomes old enough to conceive a child. In many cases sexual activity then shifts to oral or anal copulation or to masturbation. Alternatively, the father may select a younger daughter.

Another tragic outcome of incest occurs when a child or adolescent confuses sexuality with anger, as when having sex and being hurt are confounded. By contrast, the more normal line of reasoning is as follows: "Sex and affection and 'being close' feel good, but when I am hurt or angry, I feel bad and I don't want to be close." Yet in many incestuous situations the reasoning becomes: "I was close to my parent and he (or she) used me sexually; I feel impossibly confused and uncontrollably angry." As a result of this confusion, many of the children of incest have acted promiscuously—in our experience—especially when they felt wounded or perplexed.

Much of the foundation supporting family life is the basic bond of trust between parent and child, i.e., "My parents will protect me," which provides the elementary lesson plan by which normal person-to-person attachment is taught. But the incestuous kind of family interaction implies a profound betrayal of that fundamental parent-child bond of trust. When basic trust is destroyed in a sexual way (quite often in a physically painful way), it is not hard to imagine the terrible perplexity that the child experiences. It is our observation that many children of incest cannot keep close friends. In many cases, when something bad happens, i.e., when they are hurt or unhappy, many will sleep with anyone who comes along. These adolescents tend to describe their behavior in terms epitomized by this young girl's statement: "Yeah, I don't know what it is, but something bad happens to me. I'm hurt and I go out and I want to get messed up. I want to party and I want to get it on with any guy. I just don't care—anybody."

One little girl, who had "gone through" 10 foster homes and was also a victim of incest, would immediately approach—in a very sexual way—any adult male in her current foster family, as a means of getting what she perceived as the inevitable sex "over with." It was as though she was saying: "Let's get it over with now because I'm not going to attach to you and then have you do the same thing to me that my father did." As soon as she moved to a foster home, she would express this totally inappropriate means of defense by sitting on the foster father's lap in a very provocative way, thereby infuriating the foster mother. For about a week she would seductively cater to her new foster father's every whim. Then, when the foster mother discovered her acting out sexually with boys in the neighborhood, that would be the "last straw" and the foster parents would ask to have her removed from their home. This behavior had been repeated many times before anyone became aware of what the problem was. Hence, a clinician who observes this type of promiscuousness would be well advised to investigate its origins. A clinician should be equally curious about an inability to "attach" or to let people get close without being seductive toward them.

Another example of this fear of attachment can be found in the case of a pleasant young woman who was being seen for individual psychotherapy. When a teenager, she had been sexually abused by her father for a period of about three years. By the time she began therapy she had had five or six fiancés. Each time she prepared to marry, she would unconsciously reflect that her future husband would possibly become a father, and she would suddenly find an excuse to end the relationship. Having a husband who would eventually be the father of her children was just too terrifying a thought for her. In this case, the memory of an incestuous experience had been deeply repressed, with extremely self-punitive results.

If a clinician suspects that incest is occurring with a two- or three-year-old child, the intervention should be quite thorough and aggressive, because serious psychopathology can be expected on the part of the sexually involved parent—with the attendant risk that this parent will lose control. A child of this age is desperately in need of protection. By contrast, when the suspected victim is a teenager, a therapist should intervene more cautiously, with a view to developing a trust relationship in which the therapist is seen as a person in whom the adolescent can confide. The therapist will want to establish at least the kind of relationship in which an adolescent will seek out the clinician in a moment of crisis or when he or she is in danger. It is not a good idea to push young people who may have been involved in incest unless it is absolutely necessary, because issues of trust are so essential in doing therapy with them. ETC has discovered that there are an amazing number of family emergencies in which incest (or incestuous impulses being confronted inappropriately) represents an important element of the family's problem.

When treating an incestuous family, it is useful to structure the therapy sessions according to the way in which the therapist would like to see the family change. For example, it is advisable to offer sessions for the entire family as well as sessions for the parents as a couple. Of course, individual sessions for the child victim are a vital component of treatment. During these individual sessions, the child may be encouraged to ventilate his or her private feelings, while in the family sessions the subjects discussed should be whole-family issues. Problems of the parents as adults, such as their sexual relationship, should be subjects of the couple sessions. In both the family and couple sessions, it may be useful to include a co-therapist of the opposite sex, because working with families can be emotionally exhausting and the support of another therapist will help, especially during the initial, emergency phase. It is also important for a therapist to be aware of his or her own limits and to guard against the intense feelings that incest arouses in every one of us.

It is generally recommended that the child victim be treated by a therapist of the same sex. Because in many cases the incestuous trauma has been a child's first sexual experience, much of therapy involves encouraging the boy or girl to describe his or her feelings, as well as providing appropriate information on sexual subjects. Moreover, a clinician should not be surprised or suspicious if the child's emotional reaction to incest appears, at first, to be emotionally bland (Peters, 1976). This reaction will pass when the child begins to feel safe with the therapist. Later on in treatment, it may be appropriate for the child to be seen by a therapist of the opposite sex. At first, a young girl may simply be unable to talk with a man, but after six months to a year of treatment it may be a good idea to refer her to a male therapist.

When working with the children of incest, it is vital to take into account how much they can or cannot accept. In many cases the first thing a therapist will want to do is reach out and reassure the child, but most children will be fearful and lacking in trust. Their trust has already been betrayed by an untrustworthy adult. This issue is a primary one, for in the process of establishing a relationship a child may "test the limits" of the therapist for a long time. Adolescents will break appointments or simply forget them and will find many ways to ask their most pressing question, "Do you really care about me?" With some clients a clinician does not permit evasive behavior; but with a victim of incest a clinician should expect considerable resistance or even provocation and be prepared to take action to ensure that the child remains in treatment.

How does a therapist bring up the subject of incest, or ask a child if it has occurred? If the child is 10, 11 or older, the therapist may say something like this:

> As you know, relationships between fathers and daughters [or mothers and sons] can be very close. In some ways, they can be difficult. I had feelings of love toward my own father [mother]. Everyone does. But some of the things that you told me gave me the feeling—and you can stop me if I am wrong because I am not always right—that something might have happened between you and your dad [mom] that hurt you or frightened you.

At a deeper level of inquiry, the therapist may say:

> What you told me is understandable. A lot of people think it is terrible, but even though it can be very frightening it happens in a lot of families, and it is not the end of the world. Just because it happened in the past doesn't mean it has to happen again, and I shall do everything I can to prevent it in the future. But I think it is important that I know the truth. Some things you said to me made me a little concerned that, maybe, one time your father [mother] put his [her] hands on you and frightened you, or maybe tried to have sex with you.

It is vital, at this moment, to be alert and watch the child's nonverbal behavior very closely, looking for sudden movement or averting of the eyes or rubbing the nose (when a person rubs his or her nose, it usually indicates that the other person has referred to something that has made him or her angry or uncomfortable). Also, it is useful to watch the child's feet—most people can control the nonverbal behavior of their facial musculature when they try to do so, but the feet may "leak" information about feelings (cf., Ekman and Friesen, 1969). When a foot is bobbed up and down suddenly, as though by reflex, the therapist can make a calculated guess that the inward emotion may not be matched by what is being said. By observing these indicators of stress through nonverbal behavior, the clinician may not have to pursue the subject of incest further with the child at this time. Instead, the therapist can merely note that the subject has proven to be a sensitive or painful one, at the same time letting the child know that no matter what he or she says it will be accepted, and that he or she is not the only person in the world to whom this may have happened.

When the proper moment arrives a therapist can establish a situation in which the child will feel at ease about telling his or her story. Having done the initial framing, the clinician can say something like this:

> I have worked with a lot of families before who have had this problem in which there has been a relationship between a father and a daughter [a mother and a son], and there are certain patterns and certain things that happen in these families. There seems to be a similarity between your family and that kind of family. Now I could be wrong, but. . . .

Here the child can be given an opportunity to get out of the situation, e.g.,

> I could be wrong, and please tell me if I am, but I have about an 80 percent hunch that this is happening in your family. I am not 100 percent sure. . . .

Then the therapist can proceed in this way: "Now it might not have been actual intercourse or sex, but . . .". At each step the therapist gives the child a chance to move toward the subject and a chance to test the therapist's reactions as well. "Maybe there was some petting" is another means of approach. By this procedure a child will be permitted to describe a little bit about the event, but is given the option to withdraw from the conversation if necessary.

In summary, incest is the culmination of a complex and pathological series of events which arise within the context of an entire family system. When a clinician first intervenes in a case of actual or suspected incest (by definition an emergency situation), there are several key issues to investigate fully. Was the incest a one-time event or did it occur repeatedly over a long period of time? Repetitive incest is rarely the result of only one family member's psychopathology, and is naturally more difficult to treat. Since the family has conspired to tolerate this problem for a long time, it may have depleted its internal strengths and may lack the necessary energy to accomplish changes in the system. While repetitive incest very likely involves the whole family, participation by some family members may take the form of "selective inattention," passive acceptance, or denial. Another important issue is the age difference between the sexually involved parent and the child victim. In most cases, the greater the age difference or the younger the child, the greater the likelihood of serious pathology on the part of the incestuous parent. Finally, a vital issue is whether or not a child has been able to tell someone about the incestuous events. If he or she did not tell the uninvolved parent, but instead went outside the family system for help, it may indicate that this family presently contains few sources of support or protection for the victimized child.

REFERENCES

Adams, M.S. and Neel, J. V. Children of Incest. *Pediatrics,* 40:1, 55–63, 1967.

Barry, M. J. Incest. In R. Slovenko (Ed.), *Sexual Behavior and the Law.* Springfield, IL: Charles C Thomas, 1965.

Browning, D. H. and Boatman, B. Incest: Children at risk. *American Journal of Psychiatry,* 134:69–72, 1977.

Cowie, J., Cowie, V. and Slater, E. *Delinquency in Girls.* Atlantic Highlands, N.J.: Humanities Press, 1968.

Ekman, P. and Friesen, W. V. Nonverbal leakage and clues to deception. *Psychiatry,* 32:88–106, 1969.

Ferreira, A. J. Family myth and homeostasis. *Archives of General Psychiatry,* 9:457–463, 1963.

Freud, S. *Totem and Taboo* (1913) (A. A. Brill, Trans.). New York: Vintage, 1946.

Gebhard, P. H., Gagnon, J. H., Pomeroy, W. B. and Christenson, C. V. *Sex Offenders.* New York: Harper and Row, 1965.

Geiser, R. L. *Hidden Victims: The Sexual Abuse of Children.* Boston: Beacon Press, 1979.

Kaufman, I., Peck, A. L. and Tagiuri, C. K. The family constellation and overt incestuous relations between father and daughter. *American Journal of Orthopsychiatry,* 24:266–277, 1954.

Lustig, N., Dresser, J. W., Spellman, S. W. and Murray, T. B. Incest: A family group survival pattern. *Archives of General Psychiatry,* 14:31–40, 1966.

Machotka, P. F., Pittman, F. S. and Flomenhaft, K. Incest as a family affair. *Family Process,* 6:98-116, 1967.

Maisch, H. *Incest* (C. Bearne, Trans.). New York: Stein & Day, 1972.

Malinowski, B. *Sex and Repression in Savage Society.* London: Routledge & Kegan Paul, 1927.

Marcuse, M. Incest. *American Journal of Urology and Sexology,* 16:273-281, 1923.

Medlicott, R. W. Parent-child incest. *Australia and New Zealand Journal of Psychiatry,* 1:180-187, 1967.

Meiselman, K. C. *Incest.* San Francisco: Jossey-Bass, 1978.

Murdock, G. P. *Social Structure.* New York: Macmillan, 1949.

Parsons, T. The incest taboo in relation to social structure and the socialization of the child. *British Journal of Sociology,* 5:101-117, 1954.

Peters, J. J. Children who are victims of sexual assault and the psychology of offenders. *American Journal of Psychotherapy,* 30:398-421, 1976.

Peters, J. J., Meyer, L. C., and Carroll, N. E. *The Philadelphia Assault Victim Study.* Bethesda, MD: Final Report from NIMH, ROIMH 21304, June 30, 1976.

Raphling, D. L., Carpenter, B. L. and Davis, A. Incest: A genealogical study. *Archives of General Psychiatry,* 16:505-511, 1967.

Riemer, S. A research note on incest. *American Journal of Sociology,* 45:566-575, 1940.

Seemanova, E. A study of children of incestuous matings. *Human Heredity,* 21:108-128, 1971.

Shelton, W. R. A study of incest. *International Journal of Offender Therapy and Comparative Criminology,* 19:139-153, 1975.

Wahl, C. W. The psychodynamics of consummated maternal incest: A report of two cases. *Archives of General Psychiatry,* 3:188-193, 1960.

Watzlawick, P., Weakland, J. H. and Fisch, R. *Change.* New York: W. W. Norton, 1974.

Weinberg, S. K. *Incest Behavior.* New York: Citadel, 1955.

Weiner, I. B. Father-daughter incest: A clinical report. *Psychiatric Quarterly,* 36:607-632, 1962.

Weiss, J., Rogers, E.; Darwin, M. and Dutton, C. E. A study of girl sex victims. *Psychiatric Quarterly,* 29:1-27, 1955.

10

Victims of violent crimes

Some of the varied psychological phenomena that are associated with the experience of being a victim are discussed in this section, and some of society's more typical responses to victims are described. When a person becomes a victim of a violent crime, he or she is psychologically "bombarded" by the acute reality of personal frailty, the seeming randomness of life events, and the inevitability of death. Most people arrive at such crossroads unsuspecting and unprepared. The experiences of few persons will have left them ready for the role of victim in violent crime. Few, if any, are capable of facing the enormity of such an event without considerable support from others.

As a result of victimization, the person goes through a "trauma response and recovery cycle," a process which serves to protect the ego during and after severely traumatic events. (This response and recovery cycle is fundamentally similar to the "grief response" that was identified and described by Lindemann [1944].) One of the primary roles of a psychotherapist in treating the victim of a violent crime is to assist and encourage the victim in proceeding through the trauma response and recovery cycle in a manner which will facilitate healthy, adaptive behavior. The purpose is to help the person recover from

163

"invisible" psychological wounds that, if left untended or untreated, may result in lifelong psychological problems.

It is not a simple task to treat the victim of a violent crime because he or she may resist participating in the emotional struggle that will lead to recovery. Moreover, social pressures can be strangely oppressive to victims, as Symonds (1975) aptly put it:

> . . . society has strange attitudes towards victims. There seems to be a marked reluctance and resistance to accept the innocence or accidental nature of victim behavior. . . . This general early response to victims stems from a basic need for all individuals to find a rational explanation for violent . . . crimes. Exposure to senseless, irrational, brutal behavior makes one feel vulnerable and helpless. . . . The community has other attitudes that block sympathetic response. . . . One is the primitive fear of contamination by the unlucky victim. The result of this primitive response of fear is to isolate or exclude the victim (pp. 19-20).

In many cases even the friends and family of the victim behave in an unsympathetic manner, which can make it difficult or impossible for a victim to work through the victimization experience. Others who are close to the person may choose to rationalize about why he or she was a victim, in this way convincing themselves that there was a specific reason for what happened to the other person. Further, they conclude that, because there was a reason, the same fate may not happen to them. When the unfortunate victim hears such rationalizations, they can only serve to reinforce his or her propensity for self-blame. Many who are victims feel responsible for what has happened, and this feeling may arise even at an early stage of the post-trauma period.

Victims typically spend hours dwelling on the "if I only" aspects of what has befallen them. If the victim's family members or friends or acquaintances indulge in the kind of thinking that shifts blame for a crime onto its victim, by their own efforts they may only serve to deepen the initial depression and retard recovery. This kind of thinking may also lead to the chilling answer, "It was your own fault," in reply to the victim's question, "Why did this happen to me?" Victims ask, of themselves and others, questions such as "why me?" for a long time following an assault. A similar mistake, often made by others, that will delay or prevent a victim's recovery is to say, for example, "Just forget about it," "Put it out of your mind," or "Pretend it didn't happen." These are examples of classic problem mismanagement, in the sense that belittling a problem may cause it to become more serious. A victim cannot simply put the traumatic event out of his or her mind, and such a comment may further alienate the victim at a time when he or she deeply needs understanding in full measure.

Those who are close to a victim can mismanage the situation and block the victim's recovery in another way: by overreacting in an hysterical or outraged manner. This can cause the victim to mask his or her feelings, because of being afraid of further upsetting a loved one. Within a short time after the event, many victims become hypersensitive to the anger or other strong emotional responses of those around them. Most are too depressed to express their own anger during this phase, and thus can be frightened by the anger of others. Beneath their fear lies the dread of another attack, in that many obsessively expect assaults from every quarter—even from people whom they know. Hence victims need to feel that the people around them are self-controlled and are capable of protecting them. Victims desperately need to regain a sense of order in their own environment, while attempting to cope with the chaos that the assault has brought to their lives. It is therefore part of the task of a therapist to treat not only the victim but also the significant other people in the person's life, in order that the others will not inadvertently say or do things which may block recovery.

The trauma response and recovery cycle is based upon the work of Bard and Sangrey (1980), Burgess and Holmstrom (1974), Lindemann (1944), and Sutherland and Scherl (1970). For the present discussion, these two distinctly different psychological phenomena will be described separately. First, a victim's response to the immediate situation following an assault is discussed, followed by discussion of the recovery cycle (which also starts when an assault ends). Each phase of this recovery cycle is described in detail, with suggested methods of treatment for each phase.

In most cases a victim will have been going about his or her daily life when the attack has come—in a totally unexpected way. The victim is overcome by disbelief, the mind reeling in a desperate attempt to cope with the situation. The sensation of disbelief occurs because the mind, in a primitive way, needs to dispel confusion by pretending that the event was not real. But when cold reality descends upon the victim, there often occurs a stage during which the person's affect becomes quite frozen or "flat." All cognitive functions are concentrated upon one issue: survival. In this state, referred to by Symonds (1980a) as "traumatic psychological infantilism" (p. 36), a victim will do practically anything that he or she believes will help him or her to survive. Most victims will be suspended in this "cognitive survival state" until the ordeal of victimization comes to an end.

It has been our experience that the intensity of psychological trauma is related to an interaction of several factors, the first of which is the degree to which the body was violated. Assaults in which the body has been penetrated in some way (e.g., rape, shooting, or stabbing) often prove to be more traumatic than when that has not happened. Another factor is the extent to which a person has feared being killed in an attack. Also, the victim's relationship to his or her attacker is an important factor. *Contrary to common belief,* an attack by someone known (and possibly trusted) by the victim usually raises more complex and serious psychological questions than does an attack by a stranger. In addition, the victim's past experiences and presently available coping skills are factors in the amount of trauma caused by victimization. Finally, the location of an assault can play a role in the degree of trauma experienced by a victim. People who, while safely sleeping in their own bed, are suddenly awakened by someone who holds a gun to their head and puts a knee to their throat are usually more traumatized than those who are attacked in a public place such as on a street at night (where they might have been somewhat prepared for trouble). In certain places people assume that they are safe and protected, and when one of those places is violated, it is a shattering experience. In fact, a victim will probably develop some form of phobic reaction to the site of the victimization, depending upon the contribution of other factors, such as those cited above. A woman who has been sexually assaulted in her bathroom at four o'clock in the afternoon will not experience a long, hot shower as being comfortable and relaxing for some time to come.

Directly after an assault, most victims enter a state of shock that will serve to insulate them from the experience to some extent. This state, with its characteristically dull affect, is often mistaken for a victim's not being upset about what just happened, or as being "all right." Shock can last from a few hours to several days, depending upon the severity of the trauma that has been suffered. After this stage many victims enter a depressed state, chiefly because very few are capable of expressing anger just after being assaulted. Toward the end of this depressed phase, a victim usually experiences severe mood swings. Moreover, during these early stages the person may feel considerable anxiety about his or her mental stability and whether he or she will ever be "normal" again. Throughout this period the clinician needs to reassure a victim that what is happening is part of a normal recovery process, which will pass more quickly if he or she tries not to resist it.

Following a depressive phase, the victim usually enters an actively angry phase, which can be quite destructive if the person who committed the assault has not yet been apprehended and forced to "pay" for what he or she did. This is a time when the victim may displace his or her anger onto some "safe" object such as a loved one or friend, and these significant others will need considerable help to understand why they are being attacked by the victim—especially since this phase usually occurs a while after the traumatic assault. Although this period of anger can be difficult, it should be welcomed by a therapist because it usually marks a turning point in the recovery cycle.

Following the angry phase, many victims enter a somewhat philosophical period in which they review what the event has meant to them. During this reflective phase, a victim realizes (if the rest of the cycle has occurred) that he or she is no longer the same person as before the assault, and reflects on what this will mean for the future.

Next, a victim moves into a period of "laying-to-rest," in which the experience is relegated to that of an ugly memory. In the process the person *accepts* that his or her life has changed because of the event. A victim of violence will never be able to forget what happened, and each will have lost some of the protective fantasies upon which we all rely. But if the person has gone through the entire recovery cycle, he or she is likely to be successful in putting the event in perspective.

Table 2

Trauma Response and Recovery Cycle of Victims in General

Trauma Response
• Shock

• Disbelief (attempt to deny reality of the event)

• Realization

• Nonaffective or cognitive survival state

Release or Escape

Recovery Cycle

• Shock (upon being released)

• Depression

• Mood Swings

• Anger

• Philosophical Reflection

• Laying-to-rest

Table 2 summarizes the principal stages of the trauma response and recovery cycle.

VICTIMS OF PROLONGED TERROR

In this section techniques are suggested for doing therapy with people who have been the victims of protracted terror and/or violence, such as those who are kidnapped, taken hostage, or held against their will in a lengthy robbery situation. Of course, many victims of rape and sexual assault fit within this category because they, too, have experienced prolonged violence and terror; in many cases they exhibit symptoms similar to those which are discussed in this section. Yet because of the complexity of rape and other forms of sexual assault in adulthood, those subjects will be discussed in greater detail in the next chapter.

A therapist who wishes to treat victims of prolonged terror and violence must be sensitive to the psychological forces that interact to create the sometimes strange and contradictory behavior of the victim. People in general have many fantasies about what they would or should do if they are attacked. Some believe that they would be able to run away or otherwise use their wits to escape the situation, but these common escape fantasies are seldom achieved in reality.

In most cases when people are attacked and held captive, there is no real prospect for escape. Few victims are capable of overpowering their attackers, lacking the strength or a weapon to do so; and even if they were capable, the reaction of most persons to an attack is one similar to shock. Bard and Sangrey (1980), Burgess and Holmstrom (1974), Sutherland and Scherl (1970), and Symonds (1980a) have referred to this kind of response as "frozen fright." During such moments a victim usually tries to undo the reality of the assault with thoughts such as, "This must be a dream," or "This could not really be happening." One victim of a bank robbery situation put this denial reaction into graphic terms by saying,

> When I saw the men coming into the bank with guns drawn, my first thoughts were that the men were police in plain clothes. Then I wondered why they had their guns drawn. It was only after the robbers forced me and the other people in the bank to lie face down on the floor that the fact this was a robbery came to my mind. And from then on the only thing that concerned me was how I was going to get out of this alive!

After this initial shock and disbelief pass, many victims enter into the psychological state called "traumatic psychological infantilism" (see above) in which, according to Symonds, "All recently learned behavior evaporates and only adaptive patterns from early childhood predominate" (1980a, p. 36). The person's affective state becomes frozen, and he or she adopts a false demeanor of calm. While the victim's behavior is outwardly quite cooperative, at the same time all cognitive functions have become channeled in the direction of survival.

It is this traumatic psychological infantilism that manifests itself as a key component of the phenomenon known as "identification with the aggressor" or as the "Stockholm syndrome." In this syndrome or state, a victim develops a pathological identification with, and attachment to, his or her captor or captors. Another component of the Stockholm syndrome is what Symonds called "pathological transference" (1980b, pp. 40-41), in which a person who has been kidnapped or taken hostage perceives that the captor had an opportunity to kill him or her but chose not to do so. Whether this was true or imagined, the effect is a powerful one and the person's appraisal of his or her captor may undergo a profound change: i.e., the captor may be seen as a protector who has "saved" the victim's life. Contrary to popular opinion, this kind of change in a victim's perception of his or her captor can occur within a matter of hours. Among the crucial factors that can bring about this perceptual transformation are the degree of perceived helplessness, the degree of physical vulnerability, and the closeness to death that a victim has experienced. Pathological transference of such magnitude can result when there are: 1) threats to the self; 2) a deluded view that the captor has spared his or her life; and 3) a distorted perception of the captor as the only one who is capable of saving the victim.

The concept of "failed protector" is equally useful to an understanding of the etiology of this type of pathological transference. A victim begins to view the captor as a "true" protector and the family, police, and community at large as failed protectors. In this misperception, the captor is seen as one who permits a victim to live, while the family or police are those who will kill the person or cause the person's death by their carelessness. This belief may be given impetus by the captor's own rationalizations about why the victim was captured.

Behind these distortions of reality lies a victim's anger (enhanced by the prevailing state of infantilism) toward those who are normally expected to provide protection—for permitting this terrible assault to occur. An example is the case of a person who was held hostage by a burglar and brutally assaulted for hours, who could later describe the assailant as being "kind" to him "at times"; the victim was subsequently angry at a neighbor who had called the police, and refused to see family members after being admitted to a hospital for treatment of severe injuries. Hence, within only a short time a sequence of events similar to those which led the kidnap victim, Patricia Hearst, into becoming a fugitive and a revolutionary can begin. Such seemingly paradoxical behavior can be more fully understood when viewed in the light of underlying dynamics, as outlined above. Once these dynamics are understood, a therapist can begin to take some of the following steps, in treatment, to help a victim of terror recover from the event.

First, it is vital that the clinician attempt to create a nurturing atmosphere in which the victim of prolonged violence can feel safe and protected. There are schools of psychotherapy which view defense mechanisms in a negative light, and use extremely confrontive and/or intrusive therapeutic methods to break down a client's defenses; the aim is to reach the "true feelings." This approach cannot be opposed too strongly for several reasons. Many victims have been through terrors that non-victims, in their worst nightmares, can only have imagined. During this ordeal their defense mechanisms served to insulate and shield them from disintegrating into madness. If a therapist attacks (or is perceived to attack) what a victim feels was a source of strength that protected him or her in an hour of deepest need, the person may well decide to leave the therapeutic relationship. A victim may feel that the therapist has assaulted him or her more violently than did the captor.

A therapist's task is to facilitate, in a nurturing way, the balance between a victim's defense mechanisms and what his or her ego can tolerate. In time, the goal will be for the victim to face and integrate the many facets of what has happened, and for the ego to heal its wounds. A clinician certainly should support healthy, adaptive defense mechanisms, while at the same time being careful to prevent the victim from acquiring destructive or maladaptive defense mechanisms.

After determining the pace at which a victim can comfortably proceed, the clinician needs to work on reversing those psychological factors which caused the states of traumatic infantilism and pathological transference. If at all possible, a therapist should try to work with the victim's family and loved ones, bringing them into the therapy process in order to assist the victim's recovery. It is wise to view the victim's family and loved ones as victims as well, because someone they care for has been hurt and they were helpless to do anything about it. After a victim's release from capture, these significant others are often bewildered recipients of the victim's displacement of anger —because they are safe objects. The anger that a victim is incapable of directing toward his or her captor may be directed toward them for being failed protectors. For this reason, most significant others need some therapeutic support to help them deal with their own feelings, in addition to guidance in dealing appropriately with the often paradoxical and confusing behavior of their loved ones. It has been our experience, as well as that of others (e.g., Fields, 1980), that when family members are involved in the treatment of a victim, recovery is almost invariably hastened.

Many family members make mistakes in judgment which, although well intended, can cause additional problems for the victim. An example of mistaken judgment is when a loved one's need to see the victim as "all right" interacts in a pathological way with the victim's "facade of competence." The latter is a residual of the victim's frozen affect just after the victimization. This need to perceive a victim as being "all right" causes a mistaken interpretation of the facade of competence, by means of which loved ones try to reassure themselves that the victim is, in fact, doing fine. This in turn influences the victim to avoid dealing with the trauma and makes it difficult or impossible for him or her to reveal—to these significant others—that he or she is having problems. Thus the facade will be maintained and a cycle begun which is hard to stop, in that it serves to seal the victim's trauma and leave it festering beneath the surface. Considering this sequence of events, it is not surprising to learn that many love relationships end soon after victimization. Victims too often break off close relationships and isolate themselves from those whom they love. Their isolation may be further compounded by the fact that many people tend to shy away from, and even ostracize, persons who have been victims, finding reasons to rationalize why it happened to someone else and not themselves. This reaction is very likely a primitive means to deny our vulnerability to seemingly random catastrophes.

Those who work in the helping professions should do their best not to cause what Symonds (1980a) called a "second injury," which can occur when professionals do not realize how vulnerable a person may be after victimization. In many cases the victim is unable to express his or her needs to a clinician even though, at the same time, he or she expects these needs to be met. This often places a therapist in the difficult position of having to guess about the victim's needs. It is vital to realize that most victims are not "all right," even though many cannot admit it, and that victims have enormous needs for nurturance and protection. The therapist can help to prevent a second injury by trying to create an environment in which the victim will feel safe to ask, eventually, for what he or she wants.

From the beginning of the therapeutic process, a clinician will strive to help a victim regain lost feelings of competence and control over his or her life. One cause of the loss of these feelings in the victim is an overwhelming sense of helplessness, which needs to be countered by giving the victim a measure of control over the therapy situation. Victims are extremely sensitive to any form of intrusiveness, insensitivity, or perceived coercion in their therapist's approach. Consequently, the wise clinician will be cognizant of the issues of power and authority in the transference relationship. As therapy evolves, a therapist acquires considerable authority in the relationship, and even if a therapist's intentions are totally benevolent and humanitarian, he or she must take care that a victim does not project (onto the therapist) aspects of the captor's *abuse* of authority. If this occurs, the victim will either develop a neurotic, dependent transference to his or her therapist or flee from the therapy experience. In effect, the usual limits concerning permissible levels of inquiry in therapy do not apply with victims of prolonged terror. A clinician needs to be extremely patient with the victim until a solid trust relationship can be established, and this process may take as long as several months in cases in which the person has suffered severe trauma.

During the initial phase of treatment, a therapist should help the victim to realize that he or she is not the only person who has been victimized and that his or her feelings and experiences are consistent with those of other victims. A clinician should be cautious not to demean the person inadvertently or to imply that his or her experience was any less traumatic or terrible than someone else's. Instead, a victim should be aided in understanding his or her behavior during and after the traumatic event. The person needs assurance that he or she was (and is) reacting normally to an abnormal situation, and many need frequent reassurance that they are acepted by their therapist. Even if others do not fully understand or accept what the victim had to do in order to survive, it is vital that the therapist does.

Many victims of terror need to review obsessively the events that occurred during their period of captivity, analyzing and working through their reactions and what they had done. In this phase, it will be helpful for a clinician to focus attention upon the concept of survival, i.e., that what was most important was that the victim survive the ordeal. It is also good to be aware that the person may eventually be interrogated by those who are trying to apprehend and prosecute the captor(s), and will very likely be cross-examined by the defense attorney. These people may be less than sensitive to the psychological trauma that results from prolonged victimization. Thus the victim may have additional doubts and questions about his or her thoughts and responses to the criminal-legal process.

During their captivity, victims may have done things which actually helped their captors, and sometimes much is made in a court case of this behavior. It is a therapist's role to help the victim put this kind of "second attack" into perspective, if it happens. Sometimes a victim may not reveal accusations by others of compliance, because of feelings of shame. The therapist may need to inquire tactfully from time to time whether or not significant others fully understand what he or she had done in order to survive being held captive. As stated above, the message that the victim did only what was necessary to survive may have to be repeated many times until it can be accepted.

Another subject which needs to be explored with a victim of prolonged terror (as with most victims) concerns the fantasies that they may have about why the capture occurred. It is very difficult for most people to accept the *randomness* of such a catastrophic event in their lives, and victims frequently have fantasies that they are being punished for past wrongs. This is a particularly relevant subject for exploration in cases in which there may have been some social or political motive connected with the victimization. While drawing out a victim's feelings on this subject, the clinician should be quite cautious concerning what he or she says about a captor, because the victim may still believe that he or she owes his or her life to the captor. It is wise to avoid using logical argument to contradict the victim about this misconception. In time this belief will fade, but first a victim needs considerable freedom to express his or her feelings about the captor, as well as angry feelings about failed protector(s).

During the first stages of treatment it is vital for a therapist to: 1) adopt a nonjudgmental approach in which the victim is permitted to express feelings freely; and 2) provide the victim with as much information as he or she can tolerate about the reality of what occurred, and the true roles and motives of various participants. In many cases the only information about what was taking place in the "outside world" was provided to a victim by his or her captor, who may have distorted the information to suit the captor's needs. During the recovery period, a therapist must help the victim assimilate and understand what had actually taken place. A victim needs this missing information, but only in a context that he or she can acknowledge and accept. If the information is presented too bluntly or too rapidly, a victim may become angry and defensive about his or her captor, believing that failed protectors are rationalizing in order to justify their own behavior.

In many cases there will be a direct relationship between the victim's ability to perceive the events of a traumatic situation accurately and the amount of control that has been regained over his or her life. Even in the recovery process following a crime of brief duration, considerable time may pass before the person will be capable of expressing anger at a perpetrator. But, as noted above, when the anger eventually is expressed, it should be welcomed as a significant turning point in the victim's recovery process. A victim needs to be encouraged to express his or her anger toward an attacker, and the clinician should provide reassurance that this anger will not bring on any revenge or reprisal.

In short, a therapist may view the treatment of a victim of prolonged terror as the process of welcoming back a friend (Symonds, 1980b), in which the therapist assists in guiding the person to a healthier perspective on his or her relationships with other people.

REFERENCES

Bard, M. and Sangrey, D. Things fall apart: Victims in crisis. *Evaluation and Change,* Special Issue: 28-35, 1980.

Burgess, A. W. and Holmstrom, L. L. *Rape: Victims of Crisis.* Bowie, Maryland: Robert J.

Brady Co., 1974.

Fields, R. Victims of terrorism: The effects of prolonged stress. *Evaluation and Change,* Special Issue: 76-83, 1980.

Lindemann, E. Symptomatology and management of acute grief. *American Journal of Psychiatry.* 101:141-148, 1944.

Sutherland, S. and Scherl, D. Patterns of response among victims of rape. *American Journal of Orthopsychiatry,* 40(3):503-511, April, 1970.

Symonds, M. Victims of violence: Psychological effects and aftereffects. *The American Journal of Psychoanalysis,* 35:19-26, 1975.

Symonds, M. The 'second injury' to victims. *Evaluation and Change,* Special Issue: 36-38, 1980a.

Symonds, M. Acute responses of victims to terror. *Evaluation and Change,* Special Issue: 39-41, 1980b.

11

The adult woman victim of rape

Rape is a severe and complex form of assault, and there are many elements of the problem to consider when planning treatment for a rape victim.* Too often therapists and counselors focus primarily upon the sexual aspect of an assault (Amir, 1971; Notman and Nadelson, 1976) and do not help the victim to work through other profound psychological questions which she may have had to confront during and after the assault. Being raped is a brutally destructive attack upon the victim's sense of personal integrity and competence, as well as her basic trust of others. Further, rape is an assault upon the victim's sense of territoriality, since the body is the person's "territory."

We are extremely territorial beings: Consider, for example, how it feels to be in an elevator crowded with strangers. We express and ex-

---

*There are many instances in which an adult male is raped by a man, and in fact the reported incidence of this crime increases yearly. That subject is not taken up in this chapter, except by analogy.

177

perience our sense of territoriality in myriad everyday situations, and it is so basic that we rarely think consciously of "territory" as such. People have a region of very private "space" around them, with a radius of about a foot-and-a-half to two feet. People in different cultures have differing critical areas of space; for example, Northern Europeans and North Americans generally tend to have a larger region of personal space than do Latin Americans. A profound source of trauma in sexual assault is the devastating breach, and temporary destruction, of the woman's basic feeling of territorial boundaries.

People who have been robbed experience a similar sort of territorial breach, but to a much lesser extent. An example is the case of a client whose apartment was broken into. While nothing of value was taken, she came home to find her clothes and other possessions strewn around the apartment, and for several weeks she felt uneasy in her own home. The apartment had become "violated" space, and it was much later before she felt safe about returning home in the evening. This feeling, compounded a hundred times, might describe the emotional state of someone who has been raped. For not only has something intruded into their space, but their very skin—the ultimate personal boundary—has also been invaded. There are only a few circumstances in which people's bodies are entered against their will, i.e., a stabbing, a shooting, or a rape.

A concept which is helpful in understanding rape and other forms of sexual assault is that the victim's sense of integrity is temporarily destroyed. Her basic feelings of wholeness, strength, and self-control are lost. And with them a person loses confidence in the ability to say no. Most of us are secure enough, within ourselves, to believe that if we say, "I don't want you to do that" or "Stop that," the other person will likely stop. We began to learn that when we were two years old, in the stage of discovering the word "no." Suddenly, as an adult, the woman's attempt to stop the attacker has not worked. She was powerless. For a rape victim, this feeling of powerlessness is devastating to her sense of being competent to interact with others and to have some measure of control over her life.

As mentioned above, sexual assault can greatly damage the victim's feelings of trust in others. These assumptions of trust are vital elements upon which personal relationships, as well as society itself, are based. Few of us are consciously aware of how much implicit trust we have in other people with whom we share social relationships. We assume that people will not intentionally harm us. Then, in one horrible moment, a victim realizes how vulnerable to others she has always been.

Although the assault is sexual, the most severe wounds that are inflicted upon a rape victim are not physical but invisible, psychological wounds. These psychological effects, combined with the physical assault, leave the victim in a profound state of shock. The present authors are of the opinion that it is instructive, from a clinical point of view, to make a sharp division between two major stages of the post-trauma process—hence, the usefulness of the trauma response and recovery cycle, which describes two distinct processes separated by the victim's release from his or her assailant (see Chapter 10, pp. 163-168).

Victims have a strong need to ask "Why?": i.e., "Why did this happen?", "Why me?", "What did I do wrong?" For example, even in a case such as that of a woman alone in her home, asleep in her bed, when someone has broken into her home and raped her at knife point, the woman is likely to ask why it happened to her. Human beings are basically rational and need to have some kind of plausible explanation for an event, especially one so traumatic as sexual assault. Most of us have some religious background and believe in at least a form of destiny or divine judgment, a fact that may explain a victim's asking "Why should I be punished?" or "What did I do to deserve this?"

If, as is often tragically the case, a victim may have done something prior to the attack that she feels guilty about or regrets, she may infer that the attack was some sort of punishment for a past deed. An example of that sort of misunderstanding is the following case of an adolescent rape victim. She was quite reluctant to see someone for treatment, but her parents insisted because of her unusual behavior. She had not wanted to report the rape herself, even though she had been badly beaten by the rapist. She seemed to be curiously resigned to the rape and was extremely uncooperative with the police once it had been reported by her parents. She refused to give a description of the rapist or to look at mug shots of suspects, despite having told her parents that she knew what he looked like. After the clinician had seen this girl for a while it was discovered that, until about a year before the rape, she had been through an acting-out period of nearly two-and-a-half years. During that time she had associated with the "wrong kind" of friends, had been sexually promiscuous, and had experimented with drugs. However, for the past year she had stopped seeing these "bad" friends and had stopped using drugs. Hence, following a period of time during which the girl had reformed her behavior, she had been brutally raped. But she intuitively believed that this was God's punishment for having once been a "bad girl." Once this secret belief had been discovered and discussed with her parents, she was able to work through the rape experience successfully by means of both individual and family therapy.

Each of us lives with problems and fears and sorrows, but usually there is an undercurrent of order and reason to our lives. Suddenly, an inexplicable, devastating event takes place, an event which occurs beyond the compass of our usual conceptual framework. Since many sexual assaults are committed by unknown assailants, they are (from the point of view of the victims) virtually random occurrences. In fact, they are typically "crimes of opportunity" (e.g., "The window was left open"; "She was walking down the street without suspecting any danger"; "She was driving, and when she stopped at a stop light with the passenger door unlocked, he jumped into the car with a weapon"). In the randomness of a moment like that, questions about destiny and injustice are inevitable.

Victims of rape, like other victims of violent crimes, experience a state that resembles acute grief, because of their severe psychological losses (Lindemann, 1944). They need to go through the recovery cycle of shock, depression, mood swings, anger, philosophizing and, finally, "laying to rest." The order of these phases may vary somewhat, but it is basically one unified process. What takes place in this cycle involves the same dynamic processes that function to reconstruct the ego after any personal tragedy or shattering trauma.

TREATMENT TECHNIQUES

When we begin working with a rape victim and her family, we usually take both a more directive and a more educational approach than is taken with most clients. The rationale for this approach is that the victim usually has a need for basic information, a need to have answers to questions about what she is experiencing, and a need to be reassured that she is not "going insane" and that her questions are reasonable ones. For example, many victims can be helped if one explains what ego defense mechanisms are, how these mechanisms are acquired, and how they work. Once the victim's shock wears off, she will probably be attempting to utilize certain of these mechanisms as vital components of the recovery cycle. The purpose of explanations such as these is that the woman gains some perspective on the total process, and the loved ones gain an understanding of what is going on inside the victim—even though she may not be able to explain it herself.

Many victims don't realize that they were in a state of shock while they were being raped or assaulted. Hence, they may feel some guilt or misunderstanding about their seemingly strange behavior. This doubt may find expression in questions such as, "Why didn't I fight?" Some victims describe the attack in terms such as these: "It was like I was under water"; "Everything was going in slow motion"; or "I couldn't even speak." Quite frequently a rape victim will say something like that and then describe feeling guilty for her inability to fight. A good way to resolve this guilt is to explain to the victim that, because she was in shock during the attack, she was incapable of fighting—or even of keeping track of time.

The following case will serve to illustrate how much support and information-giving is necessary, as well as to describe the problems that may arise if relevant explanations are not provided the victim. A young woman who had been raped by a man who broke into her apartment while she was asleep was referred to us by the police after a serious suicide attempt. She had previously been in therapy, for about a month, with a nondirective clinician who was competent but didn't have much training or knowledge about working with victims. During her course of nondirective therapy, the person would say things like, "I don't understand why, when I was raped, I couldn't fight; it was like everything was a bizarre nightmare." The therapist would respond by asking questions such as, "Well, why do you think you didn't fight?" What the therapist unwittingly had done was to put responsibility for the rape back upon the victim. Instead, a simple explanation of shock and how it affects a person's ability to respond would have resolved the issue.

By the end of a month of this sort of treatment the woman had attempted suicide because, as she put it, "If I knew why I didn't fight, I would have told him [the therapist]. I began to feel the rape was my fault. I felt so worthless I didn't want to live." A rape or violent assault is not the kind of event that the victim can reflect upon calmly or analyze logically. Instead, it is a totally irrational reign of terror in which the victim's primary goal is to survive (Burgess and Holmstrom, 1974; Sutherland and Scherl, 1970). A victim needs clarification of what has happened to her and why she reacted as she did.

As an initial intervention, our strategy is to explain shock to the victim, as well as the possibility that she may block out bits and pieces of what has happened. We also describe the basic defense mechanisms of repression, denial, projection, and displacement, in order to help her gain a perspective on what she is experiencing. Sometimes these mechanisms can be more easily explained to a victim by analogy to physical defenses: for example, "Just as your body has a defense against bacteria called 'antibodies,' so your mind has defenses against too much psychological pain; your mind uses these mechanisms to protect itself."

The clinician can continue by clarifying other aspects of the recovery cycle; for example,

> Each crucial event in our life carries a number of emotions with it that need to be expressed. Giving birth has a quantity of emotion attached to it, a birthday has feelings that go with it, a divorce has strong outpourings of emotion, and so has rape an intense emotional component. No matter what kind of event it is, the relevant emotions will need to be worked through.

Some of the personality changes that a victim will experience, such as fits of depression or anger or sudden bursts of exhilaration and energy, represent attempts of the psyche to cope with this recovery process and eventually put to rest the traumatic event. A victim should be encouraged not to fight these vital processes, but some will vigorously resist allowing their feelings about the attack to show for various reasons. For example, some rape victims have great difficulty in expressing the profound anger that they feel toward the rapist himself (Hilberman 1976, p. 47).

As mentioned in the previous chapter, many victims have a need to prove that they are "all right." For them to admit their feelings and the fact they are not all right would be, in the logic of magical thinking, a way of permitting their attacker to "know" how much he injured them. Another reason why many victims resist showing their feelings and working through their grief is that they are concerned about the possible reactions of friends and relatives (Silverman, 1978). In many cases there is also a strong desire on the part of a victim's family and friends to wish "the whole thing never happened" or to think, "Let's just put it out of our minds." People can be very sympathetic and understanding when it comes to a person's need to talk about physical wounds, but they are often impatient or unsympathetic (or even cruel) with a victim's invisible, psychological wounds. The woman's family members may also be obsessively concerned about a social stigma or "what the neighbors will think"; because of this they may be insensitive toward her. The concept of the invisible psychological wound is too complex for many people to understand, but that kind of wound can be more serious and long-lasting than a physical one. It, too, requires a healing process.

When a rape victim begins the angry phase of the recovery cycle (see Table 2, Chapter 10, p. 168), she may benefit from an explanation of the defense of displacement, in which anger is vented upon another, "safe" object. A clinician could explain this defense by telling the victim that she may not wish to be "nice" toward men—or even want to be close to them—for a while, because she has been so terribly hurt by a man. Some version of this comment may prove helpful: "You have a right to be angry about what happened, and some of your anger may be projected onto your father, your brother, a male friend, or some person who is equally 'safe'." It is well to remember that the victim may also harbor unconscious resentment toward her husband or father for not "being there" to protect her. A therapist must help the woman balance her need to ventilate anger against the necessity of preserving the most significant male relationships in her life. In addition, a therapist should explain to these significant other(s) (father, husband, lover, uncle, or brother) that the victim may displace anger upon them as a part of the recovery process and that this understandable reaction, if dealt with appropriately, will subside and pass away. It is a good idea to present this concept to each significant other in a separate session when the woman is not present, so that each may give vent to some of his own feelings (Silverman, 1978).

After a rape, it may take from six months to a year and a half of therapy before the victim will begin to work through the trauma and recover her confidence and self-esteem. The typical length of time required for treatment varies from six to 10 months. In this connection, it is worth noting that the unfortunate assumption is often made that a victim of sexual assault is a person who has few other problems and will necessarily be cooperative in treatment. It is possible that a victim may have had serious personal difficulties before the assault took place, e.g., she may be a member of a dysfunctional, unhappy family or she may have been experiencing a miserable marriage relationship. A sexual assault may interact with and exaggerate these kinds of existing problems (Silverman, 1978). Also, there is emerging evidence that women who are going through life crises may be more susceptible to being chosen as victims of rape, for the reason that their thoughts may be more directly focused upon internal problems than upon external safety (Hilberman, 1976, p. 63).

The family of a rape victim can be of enormous help as a tangible source of support, or it can contribute additional problems. Moreover, it is important to be aware of the social system in which a victim lives and to draw as much support as possible from that system. Both relatives and friends can assist in the recovery process, or they can cause the assault to be a lingering illness that never heals and is never discussed. The family must understand that *a victim needs to talk, but should not be pushed to talk.* One reason why those who are close to the woman should accept this wish to talk is that their characteristic impulse is to avoid listening to the grim details over and over again. But if they can see the importance of letting her tell about the assault many times, she may perceive them as more understanding. Sometimes a victim needs to tell her loved ones the most gruesome details, because in a symbolic way she is asking a loved one to reassure her that, despite what was done to her, she can still be loved. Other victims, by contrast, do not want loved ones to know any details of the assault. In either case it is the task of a therapist to discover and respect the woman's wishes.

When therapy with a victim begins, it is helpful to refrain from asking about details of the rape; this recommendation applies especially to male therapists. The woman has already been asked to tell her story too often, to too many people. Eventually, when she trusts the therapist, she will tell about the assault, usually in great detail; indeed, as mentioned above, some rape victims need to repeat the description of what happened again and again. A clinician can say something such as this to the victim: "I don't need to know any details of what was done to you, but we can talk about it if you want to. Whenever you want to talk about it, that's all right with me . . . but I don't want to push you to talk about anything prematurely, or get you to tell me something that you would feel uncomfortable to talk about."

It is important to try not to coax the victim into doing or saying anything she does not want to do or say, but rather to convey the message that a therapist's first role is to help her recover and to regain a sense of personal integrity and independence. This advice may seem to contradict previous suggestions about being directive, but there is a difference between being directive and supportive (while giving a clear explanation of the psychological processes that a victim is experiencing), by contrast with pushing the person to deal with thoughts she may not be ready to confront. Because victims of sex crimes have been forced to commit acts against their will, it is vital that similar coercion does not occur in therapy, so that a strong trust relationship can be established. What the woman needs above all is to regain a feeling of control over her life. Thus, in therapy it is important that she work at her own pace (not the therapist's) as a means to establishing some control within the context of the therapeutic relationship. Many assertive interventions that a therapist would make with other clients are simply out of place when working with a rape victim.

In psychotherapy it is sometimes necessary to "confront" a client, but this should be avoided with a rape victim. A therapist may say, for example, "I think you need to face the possibility that you are holding back some feelings you should try to express, but I am not going to force you to do so." An event that actually occurred in counseling a victim will make these points clear. The woman was being seen as a psychotherapy client and some hypnosis sessions had been conducted as well to help her make an identification of the man who had raped her.

On the day before a scheduled third therapy session, she called the office and asked to see the therapist right away. When the woman arrived, she was obviously deeply shaken and, when asked what had happened, began crying uncontrollably. Haltingly through the hour, she told the following story. A few days before, a friend had called and asked her to accompany him to a weekend encounter group. The client didn't want to tell this friend about the rape, so she just said, "No, thank you," adding that she didn't feel like going out on the weekend, and said "goodbye." Later on that same evening the friend called again and repeated his invitation. This time he was more forceful, insisting that the group experience would be good for her and arguing that she should change her mind and go. When she said no again and he continued to badger her, she finally put down the phone. The woman said that she was sincere in not wanting to tell her friend about the rape (in fact, she did not feel comfortable in talking about it with anyone other than the therapist at this time). Finally, the friend called a third time, at about 12:30 a.m. He was very aggressive and said that she was a coward and a chicken for not wanting to go with him. This time she was half-asleep and blurted out, "Leave me alone; I have just been raped." Then she put the phone down sharply.

After that incident, she felt as though she had been raped a second time. She was sobbing as she ended her story: "I didn't want to tell him . . . he kept after me, and after me, and made me tell him. It was like being raped all over again . . . .. Have I lost control over everything? I can't say no to anything!" This example serves to emphasize how important it is for victims to reestablish the ability to say no again, and to feel that they have control over their lives once more.

Some resistant rape victims may need to leave therapy for a period of time, even though they have not completely worked through their trauma. The clinician can deal with this by saying, for example, "I really don't think you have come to terms completely with your feelings about what has happened. And I think there are more issues that you need to work through. But if you want to stop for now, that's all right. If you decide to come back in a while, that will be okay too, but I'm not going to insist." The woman will appreciate it if a therapist respects her decision in this regard. Most will return to treatment, usually within two or three months.

An example of this was the case of a young woman who tried to go to work the day after she had been brutally beaten, raped, and sodomized. She arrived at work but immediately felt compelled to run to the women's room, hide for about 20 minutes, and then go home. She had felt a great need to prove to herself—and everyone else—that she was all right. She refused to cry or to show any negative emotions, believing that if she allowed herself to show how badly she was hurt she would be permitting the rapist the satisfaction of knowing, in some symbolic way, how much he hurt her. She resisted expressing her feelings in therapy for a considerable time and finally decided to leave treatment. When discussing this decision, the therapist told her that she was resisting working through some feelings and that she would be welcome to return at any time.

When she resumed treatment approximately four months later, in the first session she said that she was now ready to work on her feelings. During the first series of visits, she revealed that she had been struggling terribly just to survive from day to day. If she had been forced to express her feelings, which the therapist could have accomplished very easily, she would have run out of the office and never returned because she would have considered it another form of assault. She remained in therapy for about five months on this occasion and successfully resolved the emotional and sexual conflicts that once she had refused to acknowledge.

SEXUAL FACTORS IN RAPE

It is important to be aware that rape is not a sexual encounter in the usual sense. Instead, it is an event in which one person hurts another *by means of sex*. Thus, in essence it is an assault. Of course, in most cases the rapist is sexually aroused when committing rape, but what motivates him is not sexual desire but the impulse to hurt a victim. The desire to humiliate or destroy is that which produces arousal. Quite frequently, habitual rapists become increasingly more violent from one rape to the next, getting as much involved in the attack on the woman as in the sexual act. Moreover, it is not unusual for a rapist to have difficulty producing an erection until he actually hurts the victim or forces her to do something bizarre or humiliating, i.e., when the rapist sees his victim's face distorted with pain or disgust.

In some cases a victim who has been forced to do extremely degrading acts will be reluctant to tell anyone, including the police, the details of what happened. For instance, a victim may have been questioned repeatedly by both the investigating officer and a district attorney, yet not until she is on the witness stand, under oath, will she reveal having been forced to commit oral sex or having been sodomized. A possible cause of this reluctance to provide details of vital importance to the criminal case is that the woman may not yet have encountered a nonthreatening person to whom she could tell her story candidly. In many cases, what a victim is willing to say at first differs markedly from what she will say later on when she feels safe and accepted by her therapist. In fact, a clinician may discover that many things other than being raped were done to her. Unfortunately, the formal legal process tends to discourage rape victims from revealing the full details of what was done, especially because the woman will be questioned repetitiously by what may seem an endless parade of strangers. However, police attitudes have changed considerably in recent years, mainly because officers have learned that through more sensitive questioning of victims they will get more cooperation and will be able to solve more cases.

In this discussion of sexual factors in the rape assault, it will be useful to clarify two key concepts: 1) the "rape fantasy"; and 2) the mistaken notion that rape victims must admit their "enjoyment" or "pleasure" in respect to the rape and thus their consequent feelings of guilt (a view unfortunately held by Whitlock, 1978). To begin with, fantasies about being forced into having sex are created and controlled by the woman who has the fantasy (Notman and Nadelson, 1976); that is, the person who is having the fantasy decides who is going to commit rape, where the rape will occur, and specifically what sexual acts will take place. The important consideration is that the woman who has such a fantasy has decided that *she* wants to be raped in this particular fantasy. In an actual rape, the rapist is probably an exact opposite of the person in the woman's fantasy and in every respect as repugnant as a creature from the most terrible nightmare. In an actual rape, there is real fear and real violence, not the kind of romanticized force that a woman may include in her controlled fantasy. Hence rape bears the least possible resemblance to rape in fantasy, because the purpose of the former is to cause physical and psychological pain. Instead of seeking physical pleasure or sexual gratification, the rapist's primary motive is to inflict harm.

Another misconception that is related to this rape fantasy concept is the view, shared by some, that women enjoy being "taken by force." This belief is a consequence of the passive social roles that women have been trained to adopt. For example, some rapes have occurred because the woman has simply done what the rapist told her to do, instead of running or screaming for help. Moreover, many sexual misunderstandings occur between men and women because the woman, when a child, was not taught to make clear that "no" means what it says. When a man believes that "no" does not always mean no, he will question its meaning even though he hears it repeated a second or third time.

One plausible reason for the view that a victim of sexual assault may have desired or enjoyed the experience can be found in the typical behavior of rape victims, as described above. A victim, by asking questions such as "Why did this happen to me?" and "Am I being punished for something that I did in the past?" may foster this kind of suspicion unwittingly, while in fact she is just trying to sort out her thoughts and restore some balance to her image of herself. Many of the same women who interpret being raped as a punishment often have an accepting or passive nature that may easily be misunderstood by the observer. In our work, we have interviewed or conducted therapy with more than a hundred victims of sexual assault, and not one of these women enjoyed a single moment of the experience in any way.

THE CRIMINAL JUSTICE PROCESS

Although the decision of whether or not to report a rape is left to the victim, we usually encourage the woman to report it for several reasons. Above all, we know that few rapists rape only once. They will rape again and again in the future, and there is a likelihood that subsequent rapes may be progressively more violent. Each new case presents the logical possibility that this rapist has raped in the past, and any evidence provided by a current victim may be information that is useful in apprehending the rapist or strengthening an existing but weak case against a suspect. In addition, there is a certain symbolic value in the victim's making a report of the rape to the police and asking society for justice. The potential significance of reporting to the recovery process should not be overlooked, even though many of us tend to forget the significance of symbolic or ritualistic behavior in our own lives. In the case of sexual assault, even if a rapist is not caught or slips through the criminal justice system by some means, the woman will know that what she did could right the wrong that was done to her. Finally, if the woman can witness the man who raped her being brought to justice, the experience may aid in her recovery and help her to regain a sense of reason in her life.

Often, victims who have just been raped will seek some form of clinical support before calling the police if, for example, they know a therapist already or know of a local crisis clinic. The clinician should be aware that it is not wise to go to the scene of the assault alone because the rapist may still be nearby. It is a good idea for a therapist to call the police before leaving, to make sure that they are responding to the scene—for safety's sake. After meeting and talking with the victim, the therapist should advise her not to wash herself or her clothing. Most victims have an understandable urge to cleanse themselves and their clothing as soon as possible, but if they are going through the criminal justice process, they may accidentally destroy physical evidence by bathing or by washing their clothes. Tragically, many rapists have escaped justice because vital evidence was lost in this manner.

In most cases the police will take a victim to the nearest hospital or medical clinic for an examination, for the collection of physical evidence, and for treatment to prevent venereal disease and pregnancy. A clinician should advise the woman to take a change of clothes to the hospital, because the clothing in which she was assaulted must be held as evidence. Questioning by the police may take place either at the scene or in the hospital emergency room. The police officer will make a tape recording of her statement, and while it is being spoken, the therapist will be able to provide much emotional support by being there.

On the following day, in many cases, the woman will be questioned by a Sex Investigation Officer or detective. The officer will have to ask her many intimate questions which are necessary to the investigation of a rape. Answers to these questions are important because each rapist acts differently from every other, and the way in which a man rapes is often an identifier as distinctive as a fingerprint or a signature. Some rapists tie their victims in a unique way; some say or do things to each victim in a certain order; and some have a special way of stalking or surprising their victims. Indeed, one case was solved because the victim was able to describe a type of knot that the rapist had used in tying her up, as well as certain details of a speech pattern that proved to be unique to a certain suspect. The therapist may be able to prepare a victim for this questioning, and his or her very presence may encourage the woman to be more frank about details. In addition, a clinician's skills in communication and counseling may assist the officer in obtaining necessary information, with less risk of added trauma for the victim. During this interview session, an investigator will review the tape recording of the victim's original statement and ask her if there is anything that she wishes to change or to add. Most sex investigators are aware that the original statement will have been given when the woman was in a state of shock and thus may contain some omissions or incorrect information.

There may be subsequent meetings with the investigator to clarify details of the incident as certain leads are followed to a conclusion. A victim will also be asked to assist in making a composite picture of her attacker's face, by means of an Identikit. (As used by the investigator, this kit contains specimen drawings of parts of the face from which a victim selects those features which most resemble the attacker's.) She may also be asked to look at pictures of suspects and, probably, to witness a line-up (usually through a one-way vision screen) which will contain one of the suspects. Going to the line-up can be a frightening and even traumatic event for the person in many ways—some direct and some symbolic. A potential source of trauma is that this may be the first time she will see again the person who attacked her. That can be a powerful and painful moment.

Victims often have a feeling that an attacker is omnipotent while they are helpless. In some cases a clinician will be called upon to reassure the woman that a rapist cannot escape from the line-up and attack her again because she has reported the rape to the police. A victim needs to be reminded frequently that plenty of people will be around to protect her and that she will never be left alone during this necessary procedure. (In fact, it would not be wise to leave the victim alone at all during these police investigation procedures.)

It is also worth noting that a victim should not be accompanied to the room where the line-up will take place by a husband, lover, or parent, because her emotional reaction to seeing the attacker again may well be quite strong. This reaction could be misunderstood by the loved one and lead to more complications. For example, a victim may have tried to be brave and to maintain her pride in front of the family, and yet when she sees the rapist she may be obviously shaken or hysterical. Should a loved one see this, he or she may become upset; in turn, when the woman realizes how much she has upset her loved one, she may become even more distraught. A therapist will find that victims usually want family members to be nearby, but not actually present with them during that possible "encounter" with the assailant. Seldom are we turned down by a victim when we offer to accompany her to the line-up in place of a loved one. While some may not accept the offer, it is well worth making. On occasion a woman has expressed relief that we offered to go with her, because she was too afraid or embarrassed to invite us instead of a family member.

After the police line-up, it is a good idea to schedule some time to be alone with the victim. Or, if the therapist has not accompanied her to the line-up, it may be wise to arrange an appointment that same day or evening. Key issues will probably arise in this session—for example, if the rapist was not present in the line-up, a victim will probably be depressed that he wasn't there. Memories of the attack will surface again, and her fears of an attacker's omnipotence will be renewed because the police have not been able to catch him. In fact, there may be recurring fantasies about the rapist's returning for revenge because the woman has called in the police. Conversely, if the attacker *was* in the line-up, another issue may arise that will require help—namely, now that she has identified him, will he be able to get out of jail and will he try to murder her or assault her again for revenge? Victims sometimes ask, even though they have just seen their assailant in a jail uniform and in handcuffs, questions such as, "Are you sure there isn't some way he can get out and get us as we are leaving?" Sometimes this kind of question is stated in an embarrassed, half-joking manner, but in fact the person is not making a joke at all. It takes considerable time (in some cases long after conviction) before many victims feel safe from revenge in the form of another attack by the same rapist.

If the person who committed rape is never apprehended, or is found but for some reason not convicted (a frequent state of affairs), the fears described above will persist even longer. It is difficult for a woman to comprehend that what was such a terrible personal affront and wounded her so deeply could have been a totally impersonal incident to her assailant. Even so, whether the attacker is apprehended or not, a therapist will do well to devote a significant amount of time to helping the woman reestablish a basic feeling of personal security and protection. For example, the clinician may suggest that she ask a police Community Relations Officer (or the person in charge of crime prevention in the local police department) to inspect her home and give advice about how to make it as secure as possible. Most departments are willing to provide this service, which includes instruction about which locks are the best for certain purposes.

There are groups that sponsor personal safety and self-defense courses for victims of assault, and these can have clinical value in helping the woman to realize that she does not have to be passive; in addition, she will learn that, if attacked again, there are methods she can use to escape. Many such seminars are effective in teaching a victim to "think defensively," so that she will try to avoid certain high-risk situations in the future.

Another suggestion (which may seem trivial but has proven useful if the woman is fearful of the dark or has trouble sleeping) is that she buy a little night-light of the sort that fits into a wall plug. Many will remember these lights from childhood; they reminded us that we were safe in our parents' home, and also gave just enough illumination to make it possible to survey the room if suddenly awakened from a nightmare. Leaving a radio on, or playing a hypnosis or relaxation tape once she is tucked into bed can be helpful to the victim as well.

If a victim has been successful in identifying the person who assaulted her, the assailant will be formally arrested and charged. Later the suspect will be arraigned, i.e., he will appear before a judge and plead guilty or not guilty to the charges which have been brought against him. At the arraignment, a date for the preliminary hearing of the evidence will be set. A defendant has the right to have this hearing within 10 days of arraignment, but he may waive the right if he chooses. A victim's next participation in the court process will occur at this preliminary hearing of the evidence, and the required waiting period is likely to be filled with disquieting fears and concerns about what will happen at the hearing. During this time in therapy, strengthening assertiveness skills and role-playing of potential situations and questions can be most helpful to the woman. It is advisable to make sure she is aware that the hearing is not a trial, but instead a review of evidence that will enable the judge to decide whether or not an actual trial should take place.

At the hearing, a victim will be asked in detail and under oath about what took place during the assault. A therapist can assure the woman that the defense lawyer will not be permitted (in most states) to ask personal questions about her past life history or about her sexual orientation. A lawyer may try to do this, but such questions will usually be objected to and disallowed. The woman can prepare for this first court experience by means of role-playing in which she learns to answer questions slowly, thus permitting the District Attorney enough time to object if necessary. In general, the purpose of the hearing in a case of rape is to establish: 1) that there was force or fear of force involved, as well as penetration of the victim's body by the attacker; 2) that the rapist was not the woman's spouse (except in states which have enacted spousal rape laws); and 3) that the victim can identify the person who raped her. During this hearing, the judge will also examine any medical evidence and question any other witnesses pertaining to the case. The woman's therapist is the most suitable person to help her become as ready as possible, psychologically, for the hearing. If she is psychologically prepared and given support through this first phase, the actual trial will in most cases be easier for her because she has been somewhat desensitized to the distressing court process.

The preliminary hearing and the trial, as with the previously discussed line-up, are situations in which the presence of relatives and loved ones should be carefully thought through. No matter how well prepared the person is, a court appearance in a case of sexual assault is never a benign experience. Once more the victim will have to see her (alleged) assailant, and this time without the shield of one-way glass through which she viewed the line-up. Moreover, both she and her loved ones will find themselves in close proximity to the accused for an hour or more. So when considering whether or not a parent, husband, or lover should be present during a hearing or trial, it is wise to reflect on the following: This person will have to be fairly close to a man who may have violated or beaten or threatened to kill someone whom he loves. The woman must be present meanwhile, and she will be expected to keep her composure and behave calmly and rationally. The family members themselves will be required to keep their emotions in check while they listen to a graphic description of exactly what was done to their loved one. Also, both they and the victim may face harassment by the defense lawyer, the defendant himself, his own family, or friends.

Even though a victim's spouse or children or parents or other relatives may believe that they can provide "moral support" by being in the courtroom with her, it is unlikely that they will be able to accomplish this aim. It is more helpful if the friends and family members wait outside the courtroom while her therapist (or victim advocate) accompanies the woman. Should she feel awkward about telling her relatives or friends to wait outside, she can ask the district attorney to request that the judge close the court. This means that the proceedings will be made more private in that the woman can be accompanied by no more than one person. (While this court procedure applies especially to cases in which a juvenile is the victim, many sensitive judges will make use of it in adult cases if asked to do so.)

Following the preliminary hearing, should proof against the defendant be compelling, the District Attorney and the defense lawyer may conduct plea bargaining. In this procedure, a defendant may plead guilty to some of the charges. Most enlightened district attorneys will discuss that kind of maneuver with a victim before accepting any bargain which has been offered. If the defendant does not plead guilty to some charge at this time, another waiting period will ensue before the trial occurs. Most trials for sexual assault last from three days to two weeks; the duration varies according to how difficult jury selec-

tion is, the number of witnesses who are called, and how straightforward the case may be.

Usually a rape victim is on the witness stand from one to two hours,
but her questioning may take longer in more complex cases, and she
may be called back. Being on a witness stand is difficult in the best of
circumstances, but it is far more painful when the victim has experienced a crime of an intensely personal nature and now must reveal
disgusting, humiliating details in a room filled with strangers. The worst
part is that she must be face-to-face with the person who assaulted her.
A victim should be prepared for the fact that the rapist may attempt
to upset and confuse her by smiling, licking his lips, grimacing,
or making gestures toward her while she is testifying. To help a victim
get ready for the trial psychologically, a clinician may wish to plan
some relaxation-type exercises that she can repeat before taking the
witness stand. These will differ according to the psychological needs
of the woman, and they may range from breathing and muscle relaxation exercises to fantasies of the attacker being sentenced to jail, or
pleasant scenes such as walking through a meadow or sitting in front
of a cozy fireplace. The therapist may let her know that if she needs
time to regain her composure when on the stand, she can ask for a
drink of water or to be excused for a moment to go to the restroom or
because she feels ill.

If their assailant is convicted, most victims will experience a feeling
of great relief and a sense of "closure." When a trial is successful, it
may represent an important symbolic event that will assist the recon-
structive, therapeutic process on many levels. It amounts to a clear
demonstration that there are social factors which will protect and
avenge people who have been violently attacked (without their having to take revenge themselves). Above all, the woman will have
done battle with her attacker and won. Most rape victims with whom
we have worked, especially those who have had strong support systems, later reported that the court process was worth going through—
providing the assailant was tried and convicted. Also worth noting is
the fact that those who work in the criminal justice system (e.g., district attorneys, police officers, and judges) are beginning to recognize
the value of providing support services to victims. These professionals
realize that one possible benefit of such programs is that they may ob-

tain a higher percentage of convictions. As a by-product of this changing view of a victim's key role in the prosecution of crimes of violence,
the Police Officers' Association (a trade union) in one Northern California city has voted to contribute to a fund that will provide aid for victims of sexual assault.

What happens when an accused assailant is not convicted? This
distinct possibility exists and must be confronted realistically. Yet even
though there is no conviction on the charge of rape, there may be instead a conviction on another count, such as assault with a deadly
weapon. In many cases this kind of lesser punishment does provide
some solace to the woman, especially if it enables her to overcome the
helpless, passive role that many victims drift into almost inadvertently. Even if the accused person is not convicted of anything, the
clinician can reaffirm that the woman took a step toward regaining
control over her life by attempting to right a wrong. Finally, it cannot
be emphasized too much that persons who commit assault rarely stop
after a single offense. The present case may provide significant evidence toward a later case that will lead to the ultimate conviction of
the assailant in question.

If the person who committed the rape is neither caught nor convicted, a victim's entire recovery cycle will be prolonged; as such, it
may be accompanied by recurrent nightmares and strong fears of being alone, as well as fears of the rapist returning to attack her once
more. During this period of anxiety and fear it is wise for a clinician, at
least initially, to recognize the woman's needs not to be alone and try
to strengthen her support network. In therapy it will be a good idea to
proceed slowly in a structured, stepwise manner, encouraging the
victim to attempt to do more and more on her own. Meanwhile, the
clinician can persuade her to explore practical tasks that she can perform in order to ensure her personal safety and to make her home
secure.

THE SUPPORT NETWORK

If the rape victim has a "significant other," such as a husband or
lover, it is advisable for the therapist to schedule at least one visit alone
with that person. Too often the feelings and needs of these important

people have been overlooked during the initial shock after the attack. Because of their pain and feelings of helplessness at seeing someone they love so dreadfully hurt, they may blurt out questions such as, "How could you have let him do it to you?" or "Why didn't you lock your car door?" An unthinking outburst of this sort can serve to deepen the woman's misguided sense of guilt and intensify her feelings of self-doubt (Silverman, 1978, p. 167). In addition, an accusatory question of that type, in a moment of psychological crisis, can create an irreparable tear in the fabric of the relationship. Few love relationships can withstand the trauma of sexual assault. According to a representative of Women Against Rape in Santa Clara County, California, in about half the cases of rape the woman's primary love relationship or marriage comes to an end. Yet many of these relationships could have been saved by providing the loved one with counseling and support at the time of the emergency, as well as during the recovery period. Ideally, a clinician would arrange two or more sessions with the victim's loved one and at least four sessions with both persons jointly.

During individual sessions with a loved one, it is important to give the man plenty of time to express his feelings of hurt and anger about the event; he may not have been able to show these feelings in the presence of the victim (Silverman, 1978, p. 167). A therapist should try to give him some insight into what is happening to the woman psychologically, explaining the recovery cycle that a victim needs to experience in order to heal after having been raped, and why the woman may be behaving in what appears to be a paradoxical manner. A therapist may also discuss the importance of not pushing the woman to talk about the assault, because even though she may need to talk, she must be permitted to do so at her own pace. Although the woman feels intense anger or even rage, she may not be able to express these feelings for some time to come. This apparent lack of angry feelings in the victim can cause unfortunate suspicion (or at least confusion) to arise on the part of a significant other. A clinician can explain to the loved one that she may not be capable of expressing anger at this time because her defense mechanisms (psychological healing processes) are completely engaged in reconstructing her crushed ego.

During these sessions with a significant other, the therapist can help him resolve some of his stereotyped misconceptions concerning rape victims such as, "Only bad women (or women who are looking for it) get raped," or chauvinistic thoughts such as, "Did she enjoy it?" In these individual sessions, a loved one can learn to express and work through his anger toward the victim for not having been "more careful." The next step is to help a loved one look beyond the sexual factors in rape itself and come to terms with some of the larger issues that the woman is struggling with—for example, those of personal worth and integrity. In this respect, it is a good idea to dissuade the loved one from making sexual advances toward the victim—in a misguided attempt to "undo" the attack too soon after it occurred. He should be counseled to let the woman indicate when she is ready to resume sexual activity. Even when she makes that indication, the loved one should proceed slowly and gently.

If a rape victim is planning to follow through with the entire criminal justice process, a clinician will do well to prepare the significant other(s) for this process as well as herself. During some stages of this process, such as the preliminary hearing and the trial, a woman may wish her loved one to be nearby but not actually in the courtroom. It is important to her case that she describe the details of humiliating or bizarre events candidly and precisely, and the presence of a parent, husband, or lover may inhibit her testimony. Some of these events may be difficult to reveal to a loved one even when they are alone together. Further, when she is on the witness stand it is vital that the woman keep her composure, because the defense will take advantage of it if she appears to falter or become confused; it could be devastating for her to see a loved one express shock, pain, or disgust about what she has described. Family members and loved ones should also be prepared for the possibility that the courtroom experience may stimulate what victims have described as "flashbacks," during which the woman experiences (visually as well as kinesthetically) a terrifying memory of the actual rape. Of course, after the court process has concluded, a victim will need the continued concern and protection of her loved ones.

Family members and others who are made to feel a part of these proceedings and are helped to understand what the victim is going through, what her needs are, and what the duration of the recovery cycle may be, will be less likely to do destructive things such as counseling the woman to "forget about it" or striking out with useless violence against the assailant. Friends and loved ones are more likely to behave inappropriately under the following circumstances: 1) when they do not understand what is going on, i.e., if they have not been educated about the recovery process; or 2) when they are overlooked or not given time to talk with a counselor or therapist for the purpose of expressing feelings. In many cases a loved one will be able to express anger before the victim herself is able to do so (Hilberman, 1976, p. 38). Because of this, the woman and her loved one may be recovering emotionally from the assault (and subsequent events) at differing rates. A clinician should be aware of this possibility, so that he or she can help clarify the behavior of the victim and the loved one to each other.

Although it is easy to understand why a loved one may wish to act out violently against the rapist, it is vitally important that he does not. He must permit the criminal justice system to perform its function, a function which may become a positive factor in the victim's recovery. When the judicial process serves to avenge a woman, it gives her a message that life is not totally beyond order, reason: i.e., there are forces that will protect her if someone hurts her. In this sense, the woman is being encouraged to feel that she has recaptured a measure of control of her being.

REFERENCES

Amir, M. Patterns of Forcible Rape. Chicago: University of Chicago Press, 1971.
Burgess, A. W. and Holmstrom, L. L. Rape trauma syndrome. American Journal of Psychiatry, 131(9):981-986, September 1974.
Hilberman, E. The Rape Victim. New York: Basic Books, 1976.
Lindemann, E. Symptomatology and management of acute grief. American Journal of Psychiatry, 101:141-148, 1944.
Notman, M. T. and Nadelson, C. C. The rape victim: Psychodynamic considerations. American Journal of Psychiatry, 133(4):408-413, 1976.
Silverman, D. C. Sharing the crisis of rape: Counseling the mates and families of victims. American Journal of Orthopsychiatry, 48(1):166-173, 1978.
Sutherland, S. and Scherl, D. Patterns of response among victims of rape. American Journal of Orthopsychiatry, 40(3):503-511, 1970.
Whitlock, G. E. Understanding and Coping with Real Life Crises. Monterey: Brooks/Cole, 1978.

12

Suicide

Psychological emergencies often engender suicidal thoughts, and most therapists will be called upon to work with many suicide threateners and attempters during their careers. This chapter traces the causal forces that can lead a person to suicidal impulses, and suggests certain techniques which can prevent threats and attempts from becoming suicidal acts.

By way of circumscribing the limits of this chapter, it may be useful to begin with a full accounting of the types of suicide which are *not* discussed here. First, this discussion does not pertain to the suicidal thoughts of the person who is dying from an incurable disease, e.g., a person who says to himself or herself, "In a few days I shall be dead, so why shouldn't I take my own life?" Second, the discussion does not pertain to the fugitive from justice or the murderer who has been caught and will surely be convicted and put to death, e.g., a person who says to himself or herself, "I shall be executed for what I have done." Third, no attempt is made to discuss causal factors in the suicide of hallucinatory or fanatical religious origin, e.g., a person who says to himself or herself, "The voices command me to take my own life" or "It is God's will that I end my life this way." Fourth, no attempt is made to discuss causal factors in the case of a person whose value system gives positive significance to self-mutilation or self-sacrifice, e.g., a person who feels "I shall bring honor to myself by taking my own life," as in the notable case of the Japanese kamikaze pilots dur-

201

ing World War II. Finally, this discussion does not pertain to those whose conviction that there is eternal life leads them to look upon worldly death as a painful, but necessary, transition into the pleasures of life everlasting, i.e., the case of a person who says to himself or herself, "I shall kill myself in order to be reborn in the hereafter" lies outside the scope of this discussion.

The various types of suicidal ideation referred to above are not uncommon but are seen as encompassing a full range of exceptions to the concepts advanced below. For the most part, they represent various forms of *involuntary* suicidal thinking, in which the person having such thoughts may be seen as acquiescing to a higher force that transcends his or her limits of control. By contrast, the theory presented here concentrates upon *voluntary* suicidal motivation, in effect the case in which a person desires his or her own destruction and takes action as an expression of personal will.

For many years prevailing theories of the etiology of suicide have been linked with the standard view of the effects of clinical depression. In this view, despair which reaches pathological proportions is thought to be a sufficient causal factor of suicidal behavior. The theory holds that when a depressive state is permitted to worsen, thoughts may arise for which the only solution is a suicidal act. The traditional view suggests a continuum of pathology in which suicide is a possible extension of the severely depressive state, i.e.:

DEPRESSIVE   SUICIDAL
STATE $\longrightarrow$ IDEATION

When this paradigm is expanded to take into account the bipolar character of the manic-depressive affective state, suicide is seen as a deviant by-product of an extreme shift in the direction of depression. If the pendulum of mood swings too far toward depression, the person's ego will be in a perilous position, as follows:

MANIC $\longleftarrow$ STATE OF $\longrightarrow$ DEPRESSIVE $\longrightarrow$ SUICIDAL
STATE   WELL-BEING   STATE   IDEATION

These dynamics have become well-entrenched both in clinical explanations and in lay thinking on the problem of suicide. When a clinician warns a ward technician that a hospitalized person has "suicide potential," the warning is usually justified on the grounds that the person is "extremely depressed." The accompanying treatment will probably include one or more of the "mood elevating" drugs. Similarly, most lay people, upon learning that a person has killed himself, will ask, "Was he depressed?" And most newspaper accounts of a suicidal death will include some comment such as, "He [or she] was believed to have been despondent in recent weeks over . . . ."

The origins of this prevailing view of the dynamics of suicide have deep theoretical roots. Freud subscribed to a theory, first advanced by Stekel (1910, reported by Friedman, 1967), that suicidal impulses are based upon guilty feelings which emanate from the superego. Stekel proposed that the ancient "law of talion" ("an eye for an eye and a tooth for a tooth") can serve to explain the pathological thinking of a suicidal person. Stekel reasoned that the law of talion applies in roughly this way:

1) The person (later to become suicidal) forms a wish that another person should be dead;

2) The wish has no means of expression;

3) A murderous wish is a "crime," and "the punishment must fit the crime";

4) The person who formed the wish must bear guilt for having conceived such a wish;

5) Guilt can only be expiated through the person's own death (eye for an eye), a death that can only be self-inflicted.

In graphic terms, this process occurs in Stekel's theory:

MURDEROUS
WISH   IMPULSE
TOWARD——→ REPRESSED——→ FEELINGS→SELF-
ANOTHER   BY SUPEREGO   OF GUILT   DESTRUCTION

The conceptual framework that was proposed by Stekel had such appeal for Freud that he incorporated it whole (without credit) within the larger context of *Mourning and Melancholia* (1917). The sole embellishment provided by Freud was to add the concept of "melancholia" as an intervening variable between guilt and the self-destructive act, i.e.:

FEELINGS
OF $\longrightarrow$ MELANCHOLIC $\longrightarrow$ SELF-
GUILT   STATE   DESTRUCTION

This conceptual schema has formed the basis for most etiological explanations of suicide for decades past.

From a clinical standpoint, it is difficult to take seriously a theoretical view whose cornerstone is melancholia, chiefly because that concept has little diagnostic relevance today. From a logical standpoint, any causal theory that can eliminate an intervening variable such as melancholia is preferred, because the simpler of two explanations is more likely to be the correct one. Moreover, the existence of a depressive state (melancholia) may represent a necessary but not sufficient condition for the occurrence of suicidal thinking; if that is the case, some other, more direct causal factor must be sought.

Does a person have to be depressed before he or she contemplates suicide? In the case of any death known to be suicidal, was a depressive state one of the predisposing factors? Was it the major factor? Does a completed suicide represent the outcome of greater depression than does a suicide attempt, and does an attempt represent the outcome of more depression than a suicidal gesture or threat? In effect, is the depressive emotional state a motivating force for suicide? These are key questions for an understanding of the nature of the relationship between suicide and depression.

A crucial dynamic in the depressive syndrome is the force of anger turned inward against the self. Aggressive impulses are turned back because they cannot be directed openly toward the person or persons for whom they are meant. The depressed person is prevented from attacking the object of his or her anger, and that same anger must be given masochistic expression: i.e., the angry person believes himself or herself to be worthless. The depressed person cries with pointless rage and moans repetitively, "I am no good." The force behind that statement is the failure (or perceived failure) to express anger outwardly. In fact, electroconvulsive shock—still the treatment of choice for depression in many parts of the world—is considered by some to be a symbolic punishment for the perceived "crimes" of the person receiving the treatment. Few would disagree that anger is the primary affective source of depression. Yet two questions remain: 1) Is suicidal behavior merely an exaggeration of the depressive state? and 2) What is the relationship of anger to suicide? Even though for most of this century suicidal behavior and depression have been inextricably linked, this chapter challenges that widely accepted view and presents a sharply contrasting concept of the source of self-destruction.

In 1938 Karl Menninger published a thoughtful essay on suicide, *Man Against Himself*, in which he looked beyond the axiom that depression causes suicide and saw other possible explanations. Menninger advanced three major causes of suicidal behavior, namely: 1) the "wish to die"; 2) the "wish to be killed"; and 3) the "wish to kill." The first is tautological, the second essentially a remnant of the thinking of Stekel and Freud, but the third, "wish to kill," was a truly innovative concept. Menninger wrote:

> . . . persons prone to suicide . . . masking with their conscious positive attachments large and scarcely mastered quantities of unconscious hostility (the wish to kill) [allow] the murderous impulse, now freed, to expend upon the person of its origin as a substitute object, thus accomplishing a displaced murder (pp. 32, 50).

The theoretical construct of "displaced murder" lay unused to all intents and purposes for many years, chiefly because much clinical thinking about pathology originated in the intrapsychic formulae of orthodox psychoanalysis. But recently therapists have begun to look for the causes of emotional disorders in a more interactional context. This new movement in the theory of psychopathology was introduced by Bateson et al., in their pioneering work, "Toward a Theory of Schizophrenia" (1956).

Following the contribution of Menninger, there were essentially no major developments in the field of suicidology until the emergence of the work of Shneidman and associates. There is an echo of Menninger's concept of the "wish to kill" in this description by Shneidman (1969) of a type of suicide called "dyadic":

> . . . in which the death relates primarily to the deep unfulfilled needs and wishes pertaining to the significant partner in the victim's life. These suicides are primarily . . . *social* and relational in their nature . . . the dyadic suicide is essentially an interpersonal event. . . . Most suicides are dyadic; they are primarily transactional in nature (pp. 14–15).

From these new formulations came a view of suicide—perhaps the most personal among acts of violence—as another species of relationship between people.

AN INTERACTIONAL VIEW

Breaking free from the tendency to look for a depressive (or other intrapsychic) "state" as a precursor of the suicidal act makes it possible to see both suicide and depression in new contexts, as follows. Anger which has no object and which finds no outlet in sublimation may well be turned against the self. Logically, no other means of expression is possible. It is true that through masochistic acts and processes, such as psychosomatic disorders and accident-proneness, a person may hurt himself or herself. Or, the person may permit to occur the debilitation and verbal self-deprecation which are characteristic of acute depressive states. Yet even this masochism is an outlet for feelings and a means to give those feelings overt expression. A masochistic act or symptom can be seen as a "display" mechanism which operates in an interpersonal context. The tears of the depressed person and the puffy skin of the urticaria sufferer can be considered as public "performances"; in the same category is the scarred wrist of the chronic suicide attempter. These self-negating acts and others like them are performed in order to make a statement—to send a message to another person. What appears to be an autistic gesture becomes a pathetic attempt at communication.

When anger directed outward is observed in an interactional context, it can be seen that a relationship is formed between the one who acts out and the one who receives anger. And because an interaction is conducted on many levels, from the verbal to physical, the two interactants will portray their roles in the giving and taking of anger with as much subtlety as they have established for their relationship in general. Each person possesses multiple methods to convey the sentiment, "I wish you were dead," and the form chosen is the more direct or indirect according to guidelines already operating within the relationship. These kinds of messages, as conveyed by one partner in a marriage to the other, are exemplified by a case described at the end of this chapter in "A Serious Attempt."

The wish for the death of another—an issue that is central to the talion principle—has a solid basis in psychological reality. Yet a paradox can be found in the incompatibility of that wish with suicidal thinking: Why would a person take his or her own life in a situation that patently calls for homicide? The following diagram shows this paradox in graphic form:

THE PARADOX OF TALION

I wish to kill X $\quad\mid\quad$ I shall kill myself

The paradox becomes resolved in this way: A suicidal person reaches the conclusion that, by killing himself or herself, the murder of X can best be accomplished by symbolic means.

From the premise that suicide occurs in an interactional context, these premises follow:

1) Suicide is an event which is intended to send a message from one person to another;

2) There is one specific person who is expected to receive the message of suicide; for that person, above all, the suicidal act is performed; and,

3) The primary content of the message being conveyed is anger.

In effect, this theory of suicidal etiology holds that suicide is committed *toward* at least one other person, for the purpose of conveying information to that person. In the "ideal" case, a person who receives

this information will be forced to reflect upon it and to draw conclusions from it. The ultimate impact upon the other person is that he
or she must contemplate, understand, and react to what has happened. The symbolic representation of a completed suicide is the
"death," or "living death," of a surviving person. This significant other
is assigned the role of the one who survives but, by proxy, has been
murdered. Hence two deaths are intended by a single act—one an actual death and the other a symbolic death.

In summary, a suicidal person progresses through these stages: 1)
wishing the death of another; 2) being prevented from actualizing that
wish; and 3) "killing" the survivor by means of the effective technique
of killing him/herself. The survivor is forced to live on, and the life that
he or she lives will be marked by an indelible brush.

In many instances of suicide, a process of "marking the victim" is
accomplished by means of symbolic behavior on the part of the suicidal person, behavior which is no less brutal for being subtly done.
An example is the case of a young man in his twenties who killed himself less than a year after his first child, a boy, was born. The young
man had not been able to find work since the birth of his son, but his
wife had found a good job and had become the family breadwinner.
One day when she was at work and the child was at a baby-sitter's
house, the young man hanged himself with a necktie on a rod which
held up the shower curtain in his bathroom. He died alone in the apartment. This man could not have been sure who the most likely person
to find his body would be, and the method he chose to hang himself
was especially cruel. He selected a necktie that had been a gift from
his wife on the previous Christmas, and one which bore a poignant
significance because it was the only gift for him that she could afford.
She was the "intended victim."

The purpose of the symbolic murder that is carried out by suicide is
to ensure that a survivor must live with the constant contemplation
of tragedy and must bear responsibility for it. The survivor is con-
demned, in memory, to life imprisonment. If the death of another
person "diminishes me" (in the words of the poet, John Donne), it
follows that the death of a loved one will diminish me profoundly, and
the death of a loved one by his or her own hand will diminish me totally and without recompense.

The dynamic processes referred to above are based upon evidence that is beginning to emerge through a process called "psychological autopsy" (see Shneidman, 1979, p. 161). Ironically, the salient facts which are revealed through the autopsy process provide more information about the *survivors* of suicide than about the thoughts or feelings of a suicidal person before the act was committed. For example, Whitis (1968), in "The Legacy of a Child's Suicide," studied the aftermath of the death of a 13-year-old child, by hanging, upon other members of his family. Whitis (1968) wrote:

> The act of dying by suicide is difficult for the surviving family members to comprehend and its pathologic emotional sequelae may be enduring for the survivors. . . . Suicide, seemingly an intensely personal act, has come to be seen as an act with interpersonal dimensions. One of the relatively unexplored areas is the response of persons intimately affected by the suicidal act (p. 159).

The response in question was described succinctly by Shneidman (1979) in these words:

> The cold sociological truth is that some modes of death are more stigmatizing to the survivors than are other modes of death, and that, generally speaking, suicide imposes the greatest stigma of all upon its survivors (pp. 150, 151).

The placing of a stigma upon one person by another person is a direct, deliberate, and hostile act.

The autopsy approach to research in suicidology was carried forward by S. E. Wallace, who studied 12 women whose husbands had committed suicide. In *After Suicide,* Wallace (1973) drew this conclusion:

> *The suicide of a conjugant is a life-threatening action,* and it produces the most intense grief of any type of death. Some researchers call it "complicated" and others term it "acute" grief, but by any name its intensity is searing (p. 229) [italics added].

The description presented above may be clarified by substituting "blame" for the word "grief," as follows:

•The suicide of a conjugant is a life-threatening action, and it produces the most intense *blame* of any type of death.

•Some researchers call it "complicated" and others term it "acute" *blame,* but by any name its intensity is searing.

In describing the 12 widows, Wallace (1973) made these observations:

To the living death is loss, and our three types of widows suffered different kinds of losses. For the conjugants who were socially dying from each other's lives, the loss of one life from another . . . was desired, willed through decisions that at least the widow and probably both had made. . . . The cost of suicide to these . . . women was being joined by death from that which they were already fleeing in life. The fact that the physical death followed the social one they desired made them fear they were also responsible for the suicide, and in a way the tougher-minded knew they were (p. 230).

Summarizing his knowledge of this research sample of women who became survivors of the deaths of their husbands, Wallace (1973) concluded:

. . . a relationship, a status, and a way of being are . . . lost when someone goes out of our lives. The . . . person lost also takes with him or her that part of our self that they alone maintained— our self which was a son, our self which was a mother, our self which was a spouse (p. 231).

What is significant in these accounts of the retrospective thoughts of widows, and the observations made of their common predicament, is that each woman was herself *diminished* by the suicidal death of her husband.

The theory presented by this chapter amends the talion principle by changing its dynamic basis from an internal mechanism to a process of coming to terms with external reality. The internalized guilt feelings that were previously attributed to a suicidal person—and were considered a motivating force—are differently interpreted. Guilt is made actual and is transferred from one partner in an interaction to the other partner. The one who lives on is palpably and blatantly implicated in the death of the person who has killed himself. This transferred guilt is made public without a trial, and will serve to color the survivor's relationships with others who recognize the guilt and who represent both jury and sentencing judge. The survivor-victim is forced to become vividly aware of his or her own mortality, and the remainder of the person's life will be preoccupied with resolving an enigma. The dénouement of a suicidal act is an involuntary reversal of roles of the following character: The secret murder of suicide creates, for a survivor, the mythic role of murderer.

In a thoughtful essay called "My Own Suicide," Arnold Bernstein (1976) contemplated why he was still alive, and in the process tried to find among his own thoughts the rationale of a seeker of death:

> Since the person who succeeds at suicide ceases to exist, the only persons upon whom his suicide can possibly have an impact
> . . . are those who survive and have been in contact with him. It is to them that suicide has meaning. Our analysis of suicide must thus be shifted from an examination of the dead to analysis of the living. The difficulty I have in allowing others I am involved with to freely commit suicide—means that I do not want them to kill themselves because of the effect of their suicide upon me! (p. 99)

And from the perspective of a person who did kill himself are these words from the grave—a suicide note, left by a 13-year-old boy, ended as follows:

> I am not going to kill her because I want her to see my body and realize that because she has possessed me and shut me and her in glass cases, I am dead. I want her shown up for what she is, a maniac (reported by Randall, 1966).

The boy referred to his mother.

The murderer "dies" and the suicide "kills." That theme in the form of paradox permeates the work of Albert Camus, whose play "Caligula" (1958) was the story, in Camus' description, of "a superior suicide." The Emperor Caligula was many times a murderer. As the tragedy reaches its conclusion, Caligula forces others to plot his assassination, thus choosing to create his own death. In the final scene, Caligula is attacked and stabbed repeatedly. As the stage darkens he is heard shouting, in the final words of the play, "I'm still alive." Yet by the excesses of his murderous life, his spirit had died long before. The allegory of Camus shows the interpenetration of life with death, of dying with living. And the creation of death, whether that of the self or of another, is a willful process.

In summary, both murder in the first degree and self-murder occur by design—i.e., with premeditation. The motive for each emerges from the relationship that one shares with another person, and in that respect both homicide and suicide are events which write the epitaph of an interpersonal system. The nature of the system determines the form taken by the final encounter, and the content of that encounter can best be described as rage. A life will be taken, whether one's own or the life of the other person. An horrific tragedy in which three lives were lost is described at the end of this chapter, in "Anatomy of a Suicide."

It was Camus who wrote, "There is but one serious philosophic problem and that is suicide" (1955, p. 3). The rationale is that it calls into question the meaning of life. Yet for psychology the problem of suicide is equally compelling because it epitomizes the most intimate form of violence. By contrast, the act of homicide is absurdly impersonal. It signifies that "life is cheap," and murder brings that message inescapably to public attention. A very different purpose is served by suicide, which is a private message, intended for a private audience, and encoded in a private language. It signifies "life is precious" and implies "look what you have made me lose." This message is no less treacherous for being simple and direct. It is no less venomous for being private and personal.

The energy that motivates suicide is as intense as any force generated by the human spirit. This intensity can be felt in the following note that was written by a 23-year-old woman some weeks before she killed herself by hanging (in the note, "her" is the woman's mother):

> . . . I hate her and all the people who couldn't love me just for
> me. They would just begin to love me and then they would meet

her and the love for me would stop almost immediately. I am never going to let her take anyone from me again. I will do anything however wrong to prevent this—however drastic. I will stop at nothing (reported by Shneidman, 1980, p. 74).

That statement is not the description of an internal state, nor of a fire that smolders inwardly. As with a homicidal impulse, the passion is directed outward and has a distinct object. The wellspring of suicide is hate.

In conclusion, the authors believe that the presence of depression is an insufficient cause of suicidal behavior. In effect, depression may or may not be the antecedent of a suicidal act. While an intrapsychic process is of course a factor in suicidal motivation, the source of the impulse is more likely to be found in one or more of the person's relationships with other people. In order to prevent this impulse from being converted into action, a therapist is advised to concentrate upon the significant relationships of the suicidal client. A touchstone of this approach is identification of the intended "victim" of suicide, as introduced in the section to follow.

METHODS OF PREVENTION

For a clinician, the merest suspicion of suicidal motivation is a serious matter, and whenever this subject arises in the course of crisis intervention or any other therapeutic mode, a definite emergency exists. Thus the therapist or counselor (or indeed an investigating police officer or welfare worker or inquisitive bartender or perceptive motel-keeper) has an obligation to err on the side of caution in these matters. Even so, prevailing laws in the United States do not permit the concerned observer of suicidal behavior much flexibility for taking appropriate action. The legal status of a potentially suicidal person is such that, very likely, nothing whatever will be done to provide help or protection. For some obscure historical reason, a suicidal threat is equated, in many states, with psychotic behavior. Thus the only action which can be taken by law enforcement officers (or, for that matter, by the clinician) is to have the suicidal person admitted to a psychiatric hospital.

The fact is that many suicidal people exhibit no symptoms in any way resembling those of psychosis; moreover, they seldom act in an unusual way and rarely will have threatened harm to anyone else. For those reasons, these people do not fit the description of someone who is "gravely disabled," and few resemble someone who is "dangerous to others." The only remaining category that will entitle them to intensive mental health care (i.e., 24-hour hospitalization) is that of "dangerous to self," and it is extremely difficult to substantiate that label with concrete evidence. As a consequence, many suicidal persons who have been taken to an inpatient ward by a police officer, ambulance driver, or mental health professional are refused admittance and hence are denied treatment for their problems.

The point is not that suicidal people are "crazy" and should be admitted to psychiatric hospitals on the slightest suspicion of trouble or at the whim of any practitioner who is worried about them. In fact, most inpatient wards have little to offer a person who is contemplating suicide, except perhaps for round-the-clock surveillance. The reality is that a potentially suicidal person is only "disabled" in a metaphorical sense, and is only "dangerous" in a sense that is addressed specifically by the theory presented in this chapter.

We do not mean to imply that suicidal persons are not extremely needful or that their pathology is only a mild variety of illness. Instead, these persons are acutely vulnerable, and they are capable of doing immense psychological damage to others as well. Such a case requires immediate intervention by a therapist or, in fact, anyone who can act to save their lives. But because hospitalization is likely to be little more than a "holding action," the medical-model approach to treating symptoms instead of interpersonal relationships may prove to be the least effective mode. For this reason, the issue of whether or not a therapist can persuade the nearest inpatient ward to admit the person may be a futile exercise. It is a shame that some courses of psychotherapy continue for years before the therapist asks a question such as, "Have you ever thought of killing yourself?", a fact which reflects both the strong societal taboo against suicidal behavior and the considerable threat that suicidal thinking poses to therapy of the psychoanalytic type, in which transference is so vital a component of success.

For the foregoing reasons, the first recommendation to be advanced here may seem trivial, but it is of primary importance:

• Do not presume that a client has no thought of suicide; when in doubt, ask; the earlier in treatment this question is asked, the better the client will be served.

When a person spontaneously reports suicidal thoughts or fantasies, it is well to take them seriously. Even though chronic threateners and attempters are more difficult to work with than most clients, it should be recalled that few persons who kill themselves have not made at least one prior threat or attempt (Litman, 1976). In effect, a suicide threat or attempt made during the course of therapy is a vital part of the therapeutic process, and therapy can seldom proceed until this part of the process has been confronted and resolved in some way.

Of paramount importance when a suicidal fantasy appears in a therapeutic context is the effect that such an intrusion makes upon the *therapist-client relationship*. For if suicidal thinking is relationship-bound, one must be careful to protect the therapist-client interaction from becoming distorted by that kind of thinking. In effect, it is important that the clinician does not become a surrogate for the suicidal person's originally intended victim. This recommendation follows:

• Try not to be thrust into the position of survivor-victim, the one who is chosen for punishment by the suicidal death; this will involve asking questions, showing concern, and taking the fantasies seriously; it will also require some distance and detachment, as well as acceptance without being accusatory or judgmental.

Just because immediate steps need to be taken in the case of a client who is suicidal does not mean that the clinician should permit himself or herself to be drawn into the client's "system," and under no circumstances should a therapist become a symbolic "actor" in the drama.

A decisive step toward intervening with the aim of preventing suicide is to find out who is the client's intended victim. Since the pathological process that a therapist wishes to interrupt and restructure is taking place within the context of an interpersonal relationship, it is crucial to identify which of the client's relationships is central to the suicidal fantasy. In short, the task of the therapist is to *find* a certain person who is marked for potential tragedy.

In many cases when a suicidal threat is made, the therapist will know at once who the intended victim is. In other cases, it will not be so obvious and it will be necessary to search for clues by asking subtle questions. It is not advisable to ask a client, point blank, who will probably suffer most as a result of his or her death. Because of the powerful taboo against suicide, the client may be the least likely person to provide a clinician with candid details of his or her murderous intent. While a therapist may assume that the most likely candidate for survivor-victim is one of a client's significant others of the moment, that line of investigation may lead to a false trail. The suicidal ideation may involve even a remembered person, or a fantasy version of some relationship either remembered or invented. This intended "victim" out of the past (or this creature of imagination) may or may not be represented or embodied by some person who now plays a part in the person's real life. In effect, the intended victim may be a ghost or figment or specter or dream. It may be the suicidal person's father who has been dead for 20 years. Or it may be a celebrated person whom the client has never met. The chief criterion is that potential suicide and potential victim are locked into a relationship, however illusory.

This search for the person who is a partner, however unwittingly, in the suicidal plan is a principal task of therapy once suicidal ideation has been introduced. And for the search to succeed, confrontation of the suicidal threat—as recommended above—will be of considerable usefulness. It is necessary to draw the person out until he or she has revealed enough of the suicidal fantasy that it becomes clear who is to be the recipient of the secret message. This recommendation follows:

●Search among the client's relationships, past and present, until it becomes clear who (or the memory of whom) has been chosen to bear responsibility for the threatener's death; look for proxy victims and other substitute objects of anger.

When an intended victim has been identified, the next course of action will be to focus the full attention of therapy upon this pathological relationship and attempt to defuse the rage that has heated the relationship to a lethal intensity. It may be possible to do that within the context of a course of individual therapy which is already well established with the client. Or it may be useful to bring into therapy, at least temporarily, the most likely survivor-victim if that person is available and willing to be of help.

Often the most significant other person in a client's life is the one who is most reluctant to help at this critical moment, but when potential suicide is involved this kind of resistance must be dealt with firmly. The next recommendation has obvious relevance:

• Treat the pathological relationship, which may be an existing one or one which was left unresolved in the distant past; involve the intended victim or proxy as directly as possible in the intervention.

Two pathological processes that need to be resolved in working with the suicidal client are: 1) formless, nameless hatred that is directed toward another person with no wish for diversion or dilution; and 2) the lack of means to express one iota of this anger toward its intended object. This latter dynamic of futility, aimlessness, and foreclosed opportunity is the most deeply entrenched site of infection in suicidal thinking. The suicidal person lives in an emotional cage from which there is no rational escape nor any channel of communication to the jailer/oppressor. Confronting the object of anger is to choose one of only two possible doors: insanity or death.

It is worth noting that very few persons who kill themselves are schizophrenic at the time when they take their own lives. They may have been suffering from either acute or chronic psychosis at some time prior to making a serious attempt, but few are in a full-blown dissociative state at the moment of truth (e.g., while someone is trying to talk them out of jumping from a great height just prior to their leap). By contrast, people who have killed themselves are often described as calm or even euphoric by those who have last seen them alive. But "euphoria" can be a misleading term in this context because it conveys just the wrong kind of emotional state. A person who has come to the final deciding-point on the way to suicide is an effigy of his or her true self. The correct metaphor is that of a person whose image has been carved into a statue of glowing metal, forged by the white heat of rage.

As suicidal ideation grows more sharply focused and the malignant

hatred of another spreads throughout a person's ego, he or she becomes more resolute and single-minded in the obsessional striving.
The gaze is more penetrating and the smile more fixed. The general
mood is one of distractedness—to the observer—because a suicidal
person is deeply rooted within his or her own thoughts, the better to
concentrate upon the *means* and to prepare for the *moment*. This
recommendation follows:

> •Beware of an effort on the part of a person who has threat-
> ened suicide to retract that threat or to deny that it has been
> made—especially after therapy has begun to probe its implica-
> tions; beware of an apparently bland or nonemotional period
> in which a client attempts to brush aside or belittle the subject of
> suicidal feelings.

The person who has made a serious suicide attempt is at considerable
risk of making another potentially more lethal attempt in future, and
the defense of denial (or even reaction-formation) can be strong in
many cases. A wise clinician will be on the alert for these defenses and
will make use of therapy to put them into perspective. It will be necessary to ensure that none of the reasons for a previous suicide attempt
still apply.

While the mere subject is distasteful to the sensibilities (and offen-
sive to the moral code) of most psychotherapists, a suicidal threat can
have some positive utility for therapy. First, suicidal ideation may be
the most pathological type of thinking to emerge in the course of outpatient psychotherapy, and in that sense it may hold high potential for
yielding fresh insights into previously hidden personality dynamics.
The client may be giving a sign that a symptom once reported was a
"screen" behind which his or her most distressing fears and confusions lay masked. In a sense the client may be forcing the clinician to
abandon a misleading or fruitless line of investigation, and may have
chosen a dramatic means to focus attention elsewhere. In fact, this
threat of suicide may represent a covert challenge to the therapist,
i.e., a test of his or her sensitivity to the client's needs and a sounding
device to measure the depth of the therapist's concern. To the extent
that a threat is a "cry for help," it is surely one that a clinician, above

all, is obliged to hear and from whom a most sensitive response is expected.

Finally, the maelstrom of fantasy may yield an important clue to a client's more highly cathected relationships, present and past. The clinician should remember that beneath suicidal thinking is a molten core of anger, and its target is a principal in the person's spectrum of relationships. Often a therapist will find that the nature of a relationship thus discovered will lead to the source of other pathology that he or she seeks to excise or heal. In short, a suicidal threat may represent the kind of life-threatening psychological emergency that ultimately reaches a beneficial outcome. The threat itself may signal a readiness for psychological growth, and when dealt with properly this emergency can very likely be converted into a life-enhancing event.

A SERIOUS ATTEMPT

One night at about 10 o'clock, ETC received a call from the wife of a motel manager. The message was that there was a suicidal woman with a gun in the motel, which was located in a town about five miles away. The manager's wife was vague; she wouldn't give much information and repeated the phrase, "I don't want no trouble." Because of the lack of information and the fact that the caller had said there was a weapon involved, we decided it would be wise to have the police meet us at the motel entrance.

When the two therapists arrived they preceded the police by a few minutes. They found a young woman in her middle twenties, unconscious, lying sprawled on the bed in her room. The color of her face was bluish-white. The loaded pistol lay at her side on the bed. The motel manager said that he had seen her in her car in the parking lot, slumped over the wheel, since about one o'clock that afternoon. At first he thought that the woman was drunk, but later he became concerned when the woman did not regain consciousness. It was nearly nine o'clock when the manager carried the woman to her room and placed the gun, which he had found on the seat of the car, beside her. When reflecting on what he had seen, he became fearful and called the police, who suggested a call to ETC.

Because the young woman was very cold, pale, and barely breathing, the therapists asked the police officer to call for an ambulance immediately. Then we began searching through the woman's belongings to find out what drug she had taken, and soon two prescription bottles with the labels partially torn off were discovered. Fortunately, the name of a local hospital pharmacy remained on one label and we placed a call to the hospital at once. When prescriptions were found, it was learned that the woman had taken approximately 15 Seconals and 10 Valiums. This information was telephoned ahead to the hospital where the woman would be taken by ambulance. The ambulance arrived and the woman known to the motel manager only as "Cheryl Moore" was taken away, still unconscious. The police officer took the gun and left to return to patrol.

The therapists stayed at the motel in order to get more information about what led up to Cheryl's suicide attempt. The manager said that Cheryl had arrived there from another state just three days ago; during that period she seldom left her room. The manager's wife said that Cheryl had revealed that her husband called her the day before to tell her he wanted a divorce. From the conversation with the motel manager and his wife, it became clear that Cheryl had exhibited many of the warning signs of a potentially suicidal person. Later, when the manager saw her slumped over in her car, his reason for not calling the police was that he did not wish to become "involved."

In the search of Cheryl's belongings an address book was found which contained the name and telephone number of Cheryl's husband; the telephone number was that of a nearby military base. The therapists tried, without success, to reach the husband, and then went to the hospital to check on Cheryl's condition. The physician said that she was in serious condition and probably would not regain consciousness for a day or two. We asked him to leave instructions for the nurse on duty to call us as soon as Cheryl regained consciousness. The next morning several more unsuccessful attempts were made to reach Cheryl's husband, who was finally located late that day. George Moore was very concerned about Cheryl and he agreed to come in to talk as soon as he could leave his job.

One of the therapists who responded to the initial emergency met with Cheryl's husband for about an hour and a half on the second night of the incident. George made it clear from the beginning of the interview that while he would do whatever he could do to help Cheryl, he had no intention of returning to their marriage. As far as George was concerned, the marriage was absolutely finished. The therapist assured him that we had no intention of pressuring him into returning to Cheryl. In fact, the therapist cautioned George to be very careful, in his attempts to help Cheryl, that he not do anything she might misunderstand as a gesture of reconciliation.

George said that he and Cheryl had separated about six months ago and that he applied for a transfer to his present base in the hope that the separation would be easier for her. He added that Cheryl had suffered several terrible shocks in the months since the separation occurred. First, Cheryl's mother, a chronic alcoholic, attempted suicide by ingesting sleeping pills; second, her brother, with whom she was extremely close, separated from his wife; and third, she had just found out that her father was dying of cancer. George said that he thought all these shocks, experienced in so short a time, were simply too much for Cheryl to handle because she was not a very resilient person. The husband described Cheryl as a woman who had enormous difficulty in adapting to change of any kind. She was a woman who could not forget her troubles nor forgive anyone whom she felt had wronged her. Each time they had had a fight (or even an argument), she would recall and describe in detail all the "bad things" he had done to her since she first met him. In fact, he said, her habit of not forgiving "anything" was one of the problems that finally drove him away. When George left, he thanked the therapist for his concern and said that he would do whatever he could to help Cheryl. While the therapist believed that George was genuinely worried about what might happen, he thought it better if George were to see her as little as possible.

The other therapist was at the hospital when Cheryl began to regain consciousness. As she grew aware of where she was, she became enraged and ripped out the tracheal tube and intravenous needle before the nurse could stop her. She kept repeating, "Damn you, damn you; why did you bastards interfere?" Cheryl was still very suicidal, but because she was still under sedation, she soon went back to sleep.

The same therapist returned to see Cheryl the next morning and found her to be fully awake. Although she had a great deal of difficulty in speaking, she made it clear that she was very angry about our intervention. Her original suicide plan had been to drive her car to the entrance of her husband's base and die there of the overdose. The purpose of having the gun was to shoot anyone who tried to "save" her. The intense resentment that Cheryl felt toward her husband emerged in clear perspective. In addition, the therapist soon became aware of what a stubborn and fiercely competitive woman Cheryl was. A decision was made to mobilize these qualities in an effort to rekindle her desire for living. The therapist redefined "suicide" as quitting, and "staying alive" as fighting back—i.e., showing her husband that he was not as important as he thought he was. Since Cheryl placed a high value on being tough and strong, much of the session became focused upon this theme: People who survive are tough and those who quit are weak. She appeared to hear what was being said, and finally agreed to talk with the therapist again on the following day.

The therapist made five follow-up visits to Cheryl in the hospital. While there, Cheryl decided to return to her home state, so that she could be close to her parents and family and resume her career as an accountant. She also realized that the best way to "fix" her husband or take her revenge was not to die but, instead, to create for herself a successful life. The therapist arranged for a referral in her home town and made two subsequent telephone calls to that clinician, in order to make sure that Cheryl had followed through with the referral.

ANATOMY OF A SUICIDE

On September 17, 1979, there appeared an article in the newspaper of a large city in France whose headline read "An Atrocious Drama" (Luchesi, 1979a). This article, which occupied half of one page and included a large photograph of ambulance attendants lifting a cot covered by a sheet, was followed by another, the next day, headlined "The Drama" (Luchesi, 1979b). These articles told the story of a father who had killed his only children—two daughters aged six and three-and-a-half—and then killed himself.

It was a Sunday afternoon when Lucien Sardou, a 40-year-old plumber, loaded six shells into a 12-gauge shotgun and went to the room where one of his daughters was taking a nap. He shot her at point-blank range and then went to the room where his other daughter was sleeping and shot her—also at point-blank range. By then five shells had been fired. He took each dead child to his bedroom and placed them on the bed, lay down between their bodies, and shot himself with the final shell. A Medean drama had reached its curtain fall. What were the forces that called forth this tragedy and how were the date, the hour, and the instant preordained? The following is a reconstruction, in the manner of a psychological autopsy, of the suicidal sequence of events.

Lucien Sardou and his wife Nicole, 39, had enjoyed some happy years together and their two children, Helene and Anne-Marie, were healthy and obedient little girls. Their father was so fond of them, according to a friend, that he "coddled" and "brooded over" them when they were infants. It was said that when they were little he "occupied himself with them" as though he were "a nanny, perhaps even better"; in fact, he wouldn't hesitate to do much of the housework so that the mother would have more time for their care. It was also said that, for Lucien, "they were the center of the world."

About a year before, he and Nicole began to have problems in their relationship. Nicole, who had quit her job as a typist-stenographer in order to have babies and raise them properly, decided to return to her job on a full-time basis. Separation occurred soon after, when she moved to an apartment across town and took the daughters with her. (Later, she would say that the reason she left was because he had repeatedly threatened her life.) With the help of an attorney they had worked out an "amicable" agreement in which the girls would live with Nicole, but in which Lucien would have liberal rights of visitation. It was in the context of this arrangement that Helene and Anne-Marie were visiting with their father on the day they were killed.

For Lucien, the future held an action for divorce that Nicole would soon file against him, accompanied by a custody decree in which Nicole would keep the children and control his access to them. As Lucien had once expressed his deepest dread to a friend, "The idea that these little ones could be raised . . . that they would live under another roof and under the eventual influence of another man; that, to me, is unbearable." With these thoughts coursing through his mind, Lucien Sardou was transformed from a generous, self-sacrificing father into a broken, self-loathing "protector of honor" and defender of parental rights. Somehow he had failed the children, but only because their mother—his wife—had failed him. It became possible for Lucien to project his anger onto a source beyond himself and beyond the children themselves. His rage could be concentrated, in its full lethal passion, upon their mother and his wife.

In 1976, the business which had employed Lucien went into bankruptcy, and some said this event had a bad effect upon his morale. These worries plus his increasing marital difficulties combined, in the words of an acquaintance, to "swing him into a depression," and he was hospitalized in a psychiatric ward for approximately four months. Lucien wrote letters that chronicled his recurring thoughts of suicide, but no one believed this apparently doting father and docile spouse. After the event, a neighbor was to offer these comments: "We knew that Sardou had great problems and that he had often spoken of suicide, but in general people thought that the raising of his children, to which he devoted nearly all of his available time, would dissuade him from this terrible plan." As far as the neighbors were concerned, while Lucien Sardou "still deeply loved his wife," he continued to be a "model parent," and with respect to the children he was "the person who loved them most in the world."

There came a day when these expectations, desires, hopes, and promises were reduced to ashes and silence. The six-year-old Helene looked forward to Sunday's visit with her father, because she had just passed a difficult test in reading achievement and was now qualified to enter the first grade of school. She had wanted to tell him the good news and insisted that their mother let them visit the father's apartment. At noon on the day in question, Lucien Sardou invited his next-door neighbors to join him in his apartment for a drink. According to this couple, who considered themselves to be good friends of Lucien, he appeared to be relatively "relaxed," and when they tried to find out about his current state of mind, he appeared to have regained "hope" by announcing that he planned to consult an attorney on the following day to get advice about the court battle that lay ahead.

Three hours after they left Lucien's apartment, these neighbors were astonished to find on their doorstep a piece of paper containing a cryptic note. It had been written by Lucien and said only that he, Lucien, was planning to call two telephone numbers on the following morning. Puzzled and anxious for reasons they did not understand, they went back and rang the doorbell. There followed a long silence. The door was not locked; in fact, the keys were lying on the floor just inside the doorstep. Cautiously they entered the impeccably tidy home, and when they saw the three bodies lying on the bed, their horror was inexpressible.

The police were not able to find Nicole Sardou, but toward evening she returned to the apartment to fetch her children, and when she learned what had happened she was prostrated by grief. In the article that appeared the following day she was quoted as having said: "I had a terrible premonition, but I didn't think that anything like this would happen, especially not to the children." The fact that Lucien had left behind a note in his apartment was duly recorded in the newspaper account, but the note merely described what was going to happen and did; even so, it is unlikely that anything he wrote would have clarified the ineffable.

The newspaper reporter concluded his grim task with sensibility, showing that he thought only of the children: "Two lives were sacrificed as the price of a conflict between adults, of which they were already the indirect victims" (Luchesi, 1979b, p. 8). In the balance, that seems the most important lesson to be learned.

What caused Lucien Sardou to take his own life? He wanted to kill his wife. Why did he kill both of his children? The answer is the same as before. Why did he carry their bodies to his bed and lie down between them before shooting himself? He wanted his wife to walk in upon that scene. In the last few days before it happened, could he have been helped by admission to a psychiatric hospital? That may have delayed the event and possibly altered some of the circumstances, but the benefits would only have been temporary and thus no "help" would have been given in a real sense. Was he crazy? No, he was obsessed. He was no more mad than was Van Gogh when he painted sunflowers swirling in a darkling sky. When he came to his savage night of the sun, Lucien Sardou was as sane as ice.

REFERENCES

Bateson, G., Jackson, D. D., Haley, J., and Weakland, J. Toward a theory of schizophrenia. *Behaviorial Science*, 1:251-264, 1956.

Bernstein, A. My own suicide. In B. B. Wolman, (Ed.), *Between Survival and Suicide*. New York: Gardner Press, 1976, 95-102.

Camus, A. *The Myth of Sisyphus*. New York: Vintage Books, 1955.

Camus, A. *Caligula and Three Other Plays*. New York: Alfred A. Knopf, 1958.

Freud, S. Mourning and melancholia (1917). In *Standard Edition*, 14:237-259. London: Hogarth Press, 1957.

Litman, R. E. A management of suicidal patients in medical practice (Chapter 27). In E. S. Shneidman, N. L. Farberow, and R. E. Litman (Eds.), *The Psychology of Suicide*. New York: Jason Aronson, 1976, pp. 450-451.

Luchesi, A. Le drame atroce de Nice. *Nice-Matin*, 17 September, 1979a.

Luchesi, A. Le drame de Nice. *Nice-Matin*, 18 September, 1979b.

Menninger, K. A. *Man Against Himself*. New York: Harcourt, Brace, 1938.

Randall, K. An unusual suicide in a 13-year-old boy. *Med. Sci., & Law*, 6:45-46, 1966.

Shneidman, E. S. Prologue: Fifty-eight years. In E. S. Shneidman (Ed.): *On the Nature of Suicide*. San Francisco: Jossey-Bass, 1969.

Shneidman, E. S. An overview: Personality, motivation, and behavior theories. In L. D. Hankoff, and B. Einsidler, *Suicide: Theory and Clinical Aspects*. Littleton, Mass: PSG Publishing Company, 1979.

Shneidman, E. *Voices of Death*. New York: Harper & Row, 1980.

Stekel, W. Presentation (1910). In P. Friedman (Ed.), *On Suicide*. New York: International Universities Press, 1967.

Wallace, S. E. *After Suicide*. New York: John Wiley & Sons, 1973.

Whitis, P. R. The legacy of a child's suicide. *Family Process*, 7:159-169, 1968.

13

Clinical ethics
and legal
responsibilities

GENERAL PRINCIPLES

Clinicians bring to their work a certain measure of authority over their clients, but they owe a debt of responsibility to them in respect to the client-therapist relationship. The profession sets certain standards of rectitude that no clinician can ignore, and society regulates the work that a clinician does by a network of conventions and laws.* For these reasons, therapists must constantly be aware of their social and professional obligations, and it is wise for them to consider this task a lifelong program of continuing education. If therapists do not know what is required of them to conduct themselves ethically

The thoughtful comments and suggestions of Richard J. Kohlman, Attorney at Law, were especially helpful in the writing of this chapter.

*The authors are licensed in, and practice in, California, and for that reason have first-hand knowledge only of legal requirements pertaining to that state. They have read extensively in literature that pertains to both nationwide requirements and those which differ in spirit from state to state. In this chapter an attempt is made to describe and interpret general principles of conduct that are appropriate in any setting. Some discrepancies between what is set forth here and the most recent laws applying in certain regions are inevitable, and we recommend caution on the part of the reader.

and legally in their professional work, they will serve themselves poorly and their clients not at all.

In order for clinicians to keep current with the laws and regulations governing their profession, two actions are necessary: 1) becoming aware of the basic national requirements with respect to their duties to warn, to report, etc.; and 2) becoming aware of the specific requirements that are placed upon their profession in the state where they practice. Another recommendation is to follow developments in this two-layered structure as it is modified and transformed by new laws, by new interpretations set forth in "case law," by the prevailing ethical rules of therapists' professional organizations, and in the thinking of their peers on these matters.

A few well-chosen sources of information that exist on these subjects have been placed in a bibliography at the end of this chapter. These publications and committees generally recognize an obligation to keep their membership or readership well informed about the most recent developments in this complicated and volatile field of concern.

A clinician who specializes in emergency work can expect to encounter certain conditions that are unique to his or her calling, as a function of the unique characteristics of the clients who are served. Because the family in general or at least one family member is undergoing a crisis, special circumstances prevail. The fabric of family life is frayed, family members are distraught or desperate, and rational thinking may be in short supply. Under these conditions, one fundamental requirement for ethical conduct on the part of a psychotherapist—namely obtaining informed consent for treatment—may be difficult or nearly impossible to meet. This example will be discussed in detail later on in this chapter, for it serves to epitomize many problems that a clinician faces in this type of work.

The chapter is organized in the following way:

1) A distinction is drawn between the issue of client privacy and the issue of client confidentiality;

2) a Duty of Care is examined as a guiding principle of clinical practice;

3) three specific duties of clinicians, namely the Duty to Hospi-

talize, the Duty to Warn, and the Duty to Report, are addressed as separate issues.

Within the context of each, the special circumstances prevailing in psychological emergencies are described.

While the subjects of privacy and confidentiality are often regarded as two sides of a coin, they require examination as differing entities. The distinction between them was recently drawn by Everstine et al. (1980), as follows:

- Confidentiality is a subset of the larger concept of privacy.

- "Privacy" can be defined as a conceptual space or "domain" which pertains to the person as well as to the person's identity and security. As such it is a symbolic region that each person occupies and whose right it is to control. There are certain situations in which a clinician must breach the privacy rights of a person or of a family, and these will be described below.

- "Confidentiality" can be defined as the informational component of the concept of privacy; further, information concerning a person is like property in that it belongs to the person to whom the information pertains. The fundamental issue concerning personal information is how, and to what extent, access to that information will be controlled by the person who is the subject of the information. There are certain situations in which a clinician must reveal confidential information, and these will be described below.

Before examining the specific requirements of confidentiality and privacy, it is worthwhile to outline the general legal status of psychotherapy. In many states, and indeed throughout the nation, psychotherapy is not strictly regulated by a comprehensive code of statutory law. This situation can be expected to change with time, but for the present it can be said that the actual practice of mental health treatment is only loosely regulated by law. (Of course, this observation applies more to the private than to the public sector of our profession.) That status has positive aspects as well as negative, advantages and disadvantages simultaneously.

In the absence of rigidly binding statutes governing therapeutic practice, other forces come into play. These are the forces of *common law*, a set of unlegislated—and to some extent unwritten—rules of our society, many of which were inherited from British common law. For the most part, common law operates on the principle that a rule does not exist until it is broken. An example would be that of a man and woman living together as husband and wife but being unmarried. Between them exists a bond that may not have been formalized in writing, and in fact may not have been stated or acknowledged by either party. But common law recognizes that there is an *implied* contract between two people who enter into such a relationship, and thus there may be contractual obligations between the two. Should one party claim that the other has broken the contract or has not lived up to it properly, such a claim can be taken to a court of law for judgment. It is circumstances such as these upon which many lawsuits are based.

As far as the law is concerned, psychotherapy is a form of service that one person renders to another. This view is drawn from the legal view of medicine (Shea, 1978), but subsequently it has been much modified from its basic starting point. Hence there are similarities in the legal requirements which govern medicine and psychotherapy, but there are also marked differences that this chapter will examine.

Both psychotherapy and medicine are expected to perform a common-law Duty of Care. That is, a physician or therapist must demonstrate or exercise care toward his or her client or patient. In the reality of this common-law stricture, "care" is loosely defined if at all. There can be many degrees and levels and qualities of care, naturally, so that what is required along these lines is usually left to the provider to determine for himself or herself. In practice, most clinicians leave the judgment of what is "reasonable care" to one or more of the professional organizations of which they are members. And most professional organizations have, in fact, established standards for reasonable care. If a clinician is unlucky enough to be the object of a civil law suit (e.g., for malpractice), it is indeed likely that these standards (of the profession) will be used by the court to determine whether or not a therapist has sufficiently performed his or her Duty of Care. In most instances, malpractice is interpreted as a failure to provide the client with reasonable care. It should be emphasized, by way of bringing this overview to a conclusion, that the burden of proof in a malpractice suit lies with those who claim that proper care was not given. There will be few instances in which a clinician will be unable to demonstrate that the Duty of Care was discharged faithfully. Most therapists are genuinely concerned about the welfare of their clients, and most do all they can to alleviate the problems for which the client has sought help through therapy.*

DUTY TO HOSPITALIZE

In most states at least an implied duty exists for a therapist to take action in the case of a client who needs to be hospitalized. Precisely what action is called for and under what circumstances it must be performed (i.e., what definition is given the phrase "need to be hospitalized") is subject to change and regional variation. At best, some general guidelines can be supplied here.

It should be emphasized that this is a controversial subject because there are few statutory requirements which regulate how or when a therapist *must* hospitalize someone. Since it would be inappropriate for the law to dictate this or any other aspect of clinical judgment, it is well that we remain free of legal requirements of this kind. Even so, there may be an *obligation* for a therapist to hospitalize someone under certain conditions and, if there is, that obligation may someday be tested in a court of law. In effect, a lawsuit may be brought in which a therapist is accused of having been negligent in failing to hospitalize someone, with the result that a judgment is handed down against the therapist for malpractice. Such a situation might arise, for example, in a case of this kind: A person is not confined to a mental institution, even though family members have asked the clinician to hospitalize their relative; later, the person becomes distracted by hallucinations and is killed by a car while crossing a street; the driver of the car is absolved of any responsibility, and the victim's surviving family members bring a suit against the therapist for failure to discharge a com-

---

*The Duty of Care, since it suggests what must be done, has certain positive connotations. Conversely, there is an equally compelling prohibition against making the client's problems worse. It has been said, for example, that the most fundamental rule of medicine is *primum non nocere*, meaning, "Above all, do no harm."

mon-law duty. Should this claim be upheld by the courts, a new de-
mand would have been placed upon therapists by virture of case law,
and the standards required would be no less compelling than if they
had been imposed by statutory law.

What must a responsible clinician observe, on the part of a client, in
order to make the correct decision concerning whether or not to hospitalize (or recommend hospitalization)?* By way of review, at least
one of the following criteria should be met:

1) The client is believed to be dangerous to other people;

2) The client is believed to be dangerous to himself or herself;

3) The client is believed to be "gravely disabled."

In each criterion, the phrase "believed to be" signifies that a clinician is
given considerable latitude in making his or her decision. This does
not at all imply that the decision can be made frivolously, or on the basis of hearsay or secondhand evidence. To some extent, a hospitalized person has been deprived of his or her liberty, property, and
other civil rights—rights that many of us take for granted. A decision
of that gravity concerning another person must be taken seriously and
fairly, and must be based upon carefully reasoned judgment.

The three criteria noted above contain other, more subtle, elements of subjectivity. For example, is it always clear whether or not a
particular person may be dangerous to another person? If that were
the case, fewer unsolved murders would be recorded in police files.
This dilemma will be discussed in more detail below. With respect to
the second criterion above, namely the belief that a client is dangerous
to himself or herself, is it easy to tell when a person has decided to
commit suicide? Many people threaten suicide repeatedly over the
years and yet die of old age. Many people make repeated suicidal gestures and attempts without seriously harming themselves. Even so,
some people hide their lethal intentions quite cleverly before actually

---

*The steps and techniques recommended for arranging hospitalization were addressed
earlier in this book (see Chapter 4, "Hospitalizing Persons in Crisis"). The present discussion
concerns only the relevant ethical and legal issues.

killing themselves. What this amounts to is that prediction of suicide is an exceedingly uncertain form of prophesy. In practical terms, judging whether or not a person is dangerous-to-self is a highly subjective process, with many components of intuition and other chance-laden decision rules. To conclude that a person should be hospitalized because of self-destructive tendencies is at best a "working hunch" that may yield a fair number of "false positives" (i.e., instances in which persons are hospitalized needlessly).

The "gravely disabled" category is one that carries as many meanings as there are therapists. The decision rules are totally subjective and, in application, are often contracted or expanded to fit the case at hand. Does "disabled" mean relative to what the person had been formerly, or does it mean relative to what any person could be if he or she were "able"? In general, the category is a catchall that is often used to hospitalize clients with whom their therapists can no longer cope on an outpatient basis. This is not meant to suggest that clinicians use the category unwisely or with negligence; instead, the intent is to show that imprecise definition of the phrase "gravely disabled" makes nearly any usage acceptable. And when language as vague as this is used to justify a serious judgment such as whether or not to hospitalize, some people may suffer as a result. Persons who need hospitalization may be denied admittance on a whim, or someone who is able to care properly for himself or herself may be forced to enter for an equally questionable reason.

Returning to the first criterion for deciding to hospitalize a client, namely the belief that a client is dangerous to other people, it will be useful to identify what special circumstances prevail. In a sense, "dangerous to others" is the most salient of the three criteria because it represents a more readily observable (if not objectively measurable) category of proof. In many cases dangerousness is suspected because of a specific threat against a person, type of person, or persons in general. Each threat should, of course, be weighed against other evidence, much of it from knowledge of the client's recent and past history of violence. In the absence of a specific threat, this kind of knowledge will be of paramount importance. In any event, a heavy burden will be placed upon the therapist's personal judgment in these matters. For while a person who is brandishing a gun may be exhibiting sufficiently dangerous behavior for a policeman to decide that he should be disarmed, a therapist must often base the decision to hospitalize on a word or a tone of voice.

A larger controversy has recently surfaced over problems in prediction of dangerous: i.e., detection of violent tendencies (see Megargee, 1976; Monahan, 1975; Shah, 1981). For some reason, a general belief has arisen to the effect that psychotherapists are in possession of special knowledge or skill in deciding who is potentially violent and who is not. Certainly some clinicians have fostered this belief, especially those who frequently offer their services to testify as "expert" witnesses in murder trials, parole hearings, and related forensic proceedings. Even so, not all therapists claim to be able to predict dangerousness, and even those who do should request that their judgment be granted a wide margin for error.

It was in the case of *Tarasoff v. Regents of the University of California* (1976) that these issues were first made the subject of debate at a high judicial level. In the next section of this chapter on the Duty to Warn, relevant questions will be confronted directly. In the present discussion of the Duty to Hospitalize, prediction of dangerousness has the following significance: If a clinician has reason to believe that his or her client (or nonclient whom he or she has had an opportunity to observe) is presently, or may soon become, dangerous to someone (anyone), the therapist has a professional obligation to make an attempt to hospitalize that person. This does not mean that a therapist is expected to subdue a dangerous person by force (the standard does not require heroism), drag the person through a hospital door, or personally close the bolt of a lock (a therapist is not an officer of the law). Instead, the intent of most legal requirements in most states is for the clinician to *make an effort* to intervene between the person who is dangerous and someone who might become the victim of that dangerous tendency. One way to accomplish this purpose is to hospitalize the person; or, if a therapist lacks authority to do so, an equally valid solution is to *make an effort* to persuade someone else who does have that authority to carry forward the procedure in the therapist's stead.

The foregoing should be considered in the light of a recent U.S. Supreme Court ruling on the decision to hospitalize. In *Addington v. Texas* (1979), a case was brought by a citizen against the state for hospitalization without due cause. Prior to this case being heard before the high court, the standard for commitment to a hospital, as established by precedent and in wide usage, was that "the preponderance of competent evidence" was sufficient grounds for a person to be committed to a public institution for involuntary treatment. With its decision in *Addington,* the court struck down this standard and replaced it with one of its own making. From now on, the commitment of a person to a public institution for involuntary treatment must be based upon "clear and convincing" proof of the need for hospitalization. This difference in language may appear subtle, but its significance is profound. It means that the ultimate judicial authority has decreed that hospitalization will now be justified by markedly more compelling evidence than was formerly the case. The larger implication is: The Justices believed that more persons were being committed than should be. The decision surely portends that relatively fewer persons will be committed than formerly.

Here, then, is a dilemma. A clinician is bound by his or her Duty to Hospitalize, but that task itself has become more difficult to accomplish. Where these conflicting currents will lead is not foreseeable at present, and in the absence of a guideline the wise therapist will proceed with alertness and caution.

DUTY TO WARN

The key situation in which Duty to Warn pertains is one in which a client has told a clinician that he or she intends to commit bodily harm (or worse) toward another person. Such a case clearly invokes a need for the therapist to make a prediction of dangerousness, and the next step is to decide how serious the threat is. For the sake of this discussion, the reader may assume that a therapist believes the threat to be genuine. When that is the case, there are essentially two possible courses of action:

1) Since the client's behavior fits one of three basic criteria for hospitalization, a therapist may decide to exercise the Duty to Hospitalize and take steps to have his or her client admitted. In the best of circumstances an effort to persuade the client to

enter voluntarily would succeed; failing that, at least some form of temporary commitment will be worth trying.

2) If the client refuses to enter a hospital voluntarily, or for some reason a temporary commitment cannot be arranged (e.g., the hospital does not have room to admit anyone, or someone in authority decides that the reasons given for hospitalization do not meet the "clear and convincing" standard of proof), the Duty to Warn becomes a guiding principle of immense proportions. As long as a therapist has reason to believe that the client's threat is still genuine, his or her repeated but unsuccessful efforts to arrange hospitalization will not suffice by themselves. The clinician must *make an effort* to warn a prospective victim of the threat that was conveyed by his or her client.

The latter requirement was made legally binding by the decision of the California Supreme Court in *Tarasoff* (1976). Details of the case and decision were presented by Everstine et al. (1980). What is most relevant here is that the *Tarasoff* ruling was predicated upon a common-law principle, namely that a person has a responsibility to act on behalf of the welfare of the community. Even though the persons in question were therapists, as such they were accorded no immunity from the common-law principle. But *Tarasoff* was the more significant because the negligent therapists in that case:

1) Had accurately predicted that their client was dangerous (to a specific person); and

2) Had made an effort to exercise their Duty to Hospitalize, however unsuccessfully. *

What the therapists had not done was to take the additional step of performing their common-law Duty to Warn.

---

*It is worth noting that the defendants in Tarasoff (i.e., the clinicians) were *not* held liable for failing to hospitalize someone. This unusual situation arose out of a technicality in the law by which those therapists were immune from liability for failure to hospitalize because they were government employees, i.e., employees of the state by virtue of the fact that they worked for a state university. In effect, they were the beneficiaries of a kind of bureaucratic security that most clinicians do not enjoy.

A more recent case has broadened and toughened the precedent established by *Tarasoff*. In *McIntosh v. Milano* (1979), a New Jersey Superior Court advanced an opinion which contains these major points:

1) A psychotherapist *can*, in fact, predict dangerous behavior and should do so by (for example) carrying out the Duty to Warn.

2) The welfare of the community and, in particular, individual members of that community (such as an intended victim) may require more attention on the part of a therapist than does the therapist's own client, albeit only under certain circumstances.

3) It is the obligation of a clinician to know what his or her duties toward the community consist of, and to discharge them faithfully even when to do so may *not* be in the obvious best interests of a client.

In a related but somewhat contradictory case, the *Tarasoff* ruling was both narrowed and weakened. The case of *Thompson v. the County of Alameda* (1980) was taken up by the same California Supreme Court which had produced the original *Tarasoff* landmark. The court's decision in *Thompson* held that:

1. While a therapist *can* predict that a client is potentially dangerous toward a particular other person, it may not be possible to predict that the client is dangerous toward people in general (e.g., when a sniper shoots people at random);

2) The clinician does not have a Duty to Warn the public at large or even a certain group within society (e.g., residents of a neighborhood) about the dangerous tendencies of his or her client;

3) In the absence of a clear-cut Duty to Warn, the therapist will be expected to preserve client confidentiality.

A useful summary of the implications of the *Thompson* decision was given by Kazan (1981).

The issues addressed above pertain to situations in which either client privacy or confidentiality must be breached. For example, when a person is hospitalized against his or her will, personal *privacy* has in many respects been lost. While this invasion of privacy is considered to be for the good of the client (when that person is dangerous-to-self or gravely disabled) or for the good of the community (when the person is dangerous to others), under different circumstances it would have been an illegal, or at least unethical, intrusion upon personal freedom. By contrast, breach of *confidentiality* is characteristic of the situation in which Duty to Warn must be invoked, because when a therapist warns a potential victim of a threat by a client, the identity of the person making the threat, as well as the fact that the person is a client in therapy, will sooner or later be revealed. Both types of breach may be necessary for the clinician who specializes in emergency work, especially because so many of the clients whom one encounters in this work are potentially violent, markedly suicidal, or poised on the brink of a break with reality. Special considerations that pertain to emergencies are discussed in the last section of this chapter.

It is worth noting that many psychotherapists will never be called upon to carry out the Duty to Warn. Nevertheless, most will at one time or another have necessity to hospitalize a client, and nearly every therapist will be called upon to exercise the Duty to Report that is described below in the next section of this chapter. All clinicians will do their best to meet these requirements, and it is important for each to accept that client privacy and confidentiality are not immutable rights. In effect, when a client seeks treatment certain of those rights, which might otherwise be cherished by the person and kept under his or her control, may have to be surrendered in the course of receiving psychotherapy.

When a person enters into treatment with a therapist, at least an implicit contractual arrangement is joined. Whether or not this contract is written or spoken, it nevertheless exists, and to some extent it binds each party to implied responsibilities. Since there are definite legal requirements which a clinician must meet, it is only fair that these conditions be made clear to a client early in the course of treatment. For example, the Duty to Warn implies a duty, on the part of the therapist, to warn a client that the Duty to Warn exists (Everstine et al., 1980, p. 839). The client has a right to know, in advance, that if he or she should threaten another person with bodily harm, the therapist may be constrained to notify an intended victim that a threat was uttered and give the client's name.

A Duty to Hospitalize presents similar obligations for disclosure. It is only fair to warn a client that certain kinds of behavior may lead the clinician to try to persuade him or her to enter a hospital; or, a therapist may make arrangements for the client to enter a hospital against his or her will. Finally, the Duty to Report (see below) is another therapist responsibility that should be disclosed to a client early in treatment. In each of these contexts, the intention is that a clinician freely disclose what his or her legal and ethical requirements are. The client should be aware of what kinds of information will require a therapist to assume a different role—for example, as the protector of a threatened victim or as the guardian of community welfare. Certain observers have argued that a comprehensive, *written* contract should be drawn up between client and therapist at the outset of their relationship (e.g., Coyne and Widiger, 1978). While we do not endorse that view, we are of the opinion that each clinician should be aware of the issues that such a contract would address. Primary among these are the therapist's responsibilities to society, the community, the profession that he or she represents, and his or her common-law obligations as a citizen and human being.

DUTY TO REPORT

Our profession is increasingly becoming a part of the public domain after many years of dwelling in a realm of shadow and mystery. Surely this is a beneficial trend both for psychotherapy and for the community at large. For, as the demystification of therapy has proceeded rapidly in recent years, so too have the contributions of the mental health profession become more appreciated. And as psychotherapists have gained in public acceptance, our society has come to expect of them a more active role in the maintenance of social order.

With the development of this trend over the past 20 years or so, a similar trend has emerged toward the revelation of more and more

pathological aspects of modern culture. Revelation of these pathologies is the result of more frequent identification and reporting of behavior long branded simply as "outrages against humanity." Now a
concerted effort is being made to discover these crimes as they occur,
punish those who commit them, offer help to their victims, and act to
prevent them from occurring as frequently in the future. Among these
pathological behaviors, child abuse, child neglect, child molestation,
and incest are the most prominent. Only in the past 10 or 15 years has
our profession engaged itself actively in ameliorating these deplorable
social conditions, and led the way toward governmental recognition
of the need for broad social reform and public education as preventive
measures.

Several chapters of this book have described in detail the traumas
that are suffered by victims of these crimes, as well as methods to les-
sen the force of the traumas and to help victims in regaining a sense of
well-being. In this chapter, only the requirements that clinicians must
meet in reporting their knowledge of these events are discussed. By
design, each requirement is presented in its broadest possible con-
struction—i.e., conservatively, so that possible therapist error will be
minimized.

Child Abuse

Within three years after the publication of Dr. Henry Kempe's
groundbreaking article on the battered child syndrome (1962), each
state had drafted and passed legislation requiring the reporting of
child abuse. A compelling account of the legal implications of these
statutes was provided by a California attorney, Richard J. Kohlman
(1974). In order that the reader appreciate the full scope of this reporting requirement, a definition of "child abuse" from a legal standpoint is called for. In general, it refers to any nonaccidental harm that
is done to a person under the age of 18, whether that is done by the
child's parents or other relative, by a guardian or caretaker, or by a
total stranger. This definition includes the full range of possibilities, but
it is well to bear in mind that each state defines "child abuse" differently (Fraser, 1978, p. 218). A therapist should follow the cautionary
procedure of checking each point raised here with the statutes and

case-law decisions that currently pertain to his or her jurisdiction. There are good reasons for reporting child abuse—quite apart from the legal requirement. Kohlman has noted that treatment of the victim of child abuse often begins promptly and is successful, but "the principle problem is *finding* the victim" (1974, p. 245). Moreover, there is reason to *search for* cases of child abuse, as Schmitt (1978a) has made clear:

> There are approximately 2,000 deaths per year . . . in the United States. This represents a major cause of death in children. The overall mortality rate is approximately 3 percent nationally. In areas where there is early detection and intervention, the death rate is less than 1 percent. In areas where the case finding is inadequate, the death rate may climb to 10 percent (p. 1.)

The data speak for themselves. By our efforts in case-finding we may be able to reduce a 10 percent death rate to one percent.

As far as the duty of a therapist is concerned, these are the facts: "Every state has a law which mandates certain persons or certain groups of persons to report suspected incidences of child abuse" (Fraser, 1978, p. 208.) Those "persons or groups of persons" vary from state to state, but perhaps the most comprehensive list is the one that applies in California, namely:

> *Medical Practitioners.* Physicians and surgeons, psychiatrists, psychologists,* dentists, residents, interns, podiatrists, chiropractors, licensed nurses, dental hygienists, et al.
>
> *Child Care Custodians.* Teachers, administrative officers, supervisors of child welfare and attendance, or certificated pupil personnel employees of any public or private schools; administrators of public or private day camps; licensed day care workers; administrators of community care facilities licensed to care for children; head start teachers; public assistance workers; employees of child care institutions including, but not limited to,

---

*In California, clinical psychologists are examined by, and licensed by, the Board of Medical Quality Assurance and, as such, are included in the "Medical Practitioners" category.

foster parents, group home personnel and personnel of residential care facilities; social workers and probation officers.

Nonmedical Practitioners. State or county public health employees who treat minors for venereal disease or any other condition; coroners; paramedics; marriage, family, and child counselors; religious practitioners who diagnose, examine, or treat children.

Child Protective Agencies. Police or sheriff's departments, county probation departments, or county welfare departments (State of California Penal Code, Revised 1981).

It is worth noting that this list was first revised in 1978, and again in 1980 (taking effect on 1/1/81), by the addition of many more professional groups than were previously listed; in the future, the numbers of groups or agencies can be expected to expand.

To whom must this report of suspected abuse be made? There are state-by-state variations in this respect, too, but Fraser (1978, p. 208) has given us a brief list of relevant agencies:

- •Department of Social Services

- •Department of Protective Services

- •Department of Family Services

- •Social and Rehabilitative Services

In California, a "child protective agency" must be notified, namely: 1) the local police; 2) the juvenile probation department; or 3) the county welfare department. Differing combinations of the types of agencies referred to above will be the appropriate recipients of reports of abuse in other states.

The subject of this legally mandated report is, for the most part, that some evidence of abuse (as defined in each state) has appeared to the clinician or other practitioner who does the reporting. Much is left to the discretion of the person who reports in this respect. Generally, these kinds of events are those upon which a therapist will decide that evidence of abuse appears to exist:

1) When the child says so: according to Schmitt (1978b, p. 40), "When a child readily indicates that a particular adult hurt him, it is almost always true."

2) When a person makes an admission of having committed child abuse: Schmitt (1978b, p. 40) added, "A confession by either parent [is] diagnostically important, but rarely available."

3) The report of an eyewitness can be a basis for action, but the clinician should weigh the veracity of each witness carefully, and should probably seek additional evidence.

4) Direct observation of an incident (in which nonaccidental harm was inflicted on a child in the clinician's presence).

5) A therapist's own *reasonable suspicion,* usually based upon physical criteria such as those presented in detail in Chapter 7. Again the clinician is given wide latitude for his or her suspicions.

A most startling development in respect to child-abuse reporting occurred recently when a strict revision of California law was enacted. Legislation that took effect on the first day of 1981 requires that a report must be made when a therapist "has knowledge of or observes a child . . . whom he or she reasonably suspects has been the victim of child abuse" (State of California Penal Code, Revised 1981). The phrase "knowledge of or observes" implies a distinction between the two, thus meaning that knowledge could be gained without benefit of observation. Many practitioners have interpreted the letter of the law to indicate that one is required to report abuse even though he or she might never have seen the child in question. Although this inference has yet to be confirmed or denied in a test case, it may be that the merest suspicion (however "reasonable") of abuse should be reported. In fact, it may be necessary to act solely upon intuition in these matters— while refusing to heed hearsay, gossip, or rumor. Even so, in the prevailing climate of public opinion, clinicians would be well advised to report their speculations concerning abuse, rather than to err on the side of timidity.

In what form must reporting take place? Probably the most strin-
gent statute is the one in force in California, which requires that a
report be made both by telephone and in writing to a "child protective
agency" (see above), within 36 hours of the incident in which
evidence first appeared. What will happen to a therapist who fails to
report his or her evidence of abuse? In nearly every state, the person
who does not report will be charged with a misdemeanor. The person, if convicted, could be required to pay a fine and might have to go
to jail for as long as six months. And it may be that the clinician will be
sued for a civil liability (i.e., malpractice) for not reporting well-founded
suspicions. In effect, a therapist would be accused of not adequately
performing his or her Duty of Care toward the abused child. Every clinician should be informed of this prospect, and a most valuable document is the seminal paper by Kohlman (1974), in which a lawyer ad-
vises other lawyers concerning how to prepare a malpractice case on
these grounds.

What happens if a therapist *does* report a suspicion of abuse? Unless
the report was falsely made, "Civil and criminal immunity is accorded
those who report" (Kohlman, 1974, p. 248). That means a person
cannot be sued for reporting (in good faith), nor be charged with a
misdemeanor for doing so. It also means that the existence of evidence concerning child abuse immediately nullifies the "client-therapist confidentiality privilege." This privilege, which normally pertains
to the content of conversations between a therapist and a client, tapes
of therapy sessions, and/or therapist notes or test results, becomes
invalid when information concerning child abuse is being exchanged
or is being recorded in some way. When abuse is a factor in the case,
any information pertaining to the case can be handed over to an agency of law enforcement or of the judicial system; in addition, it can be
provided to other professionals who may have some legitimate interest in the case. Moreover,

> Many states have no requirement that a family be notified . . .
> that a child-abuse report has been filed. This means that a state
> agency may be in the process of investigating a family without the
> family's knowledge of the report or investigation. Even those
> states that notify families often do not provide any procedure

whereby a child or a parent may challenge the report (Garinger et al., 1976, p. 174).

These developments may imply that our legislators have chosen to set aside certain civil liberties in their zeal to combat child abuse, and who will say that their cause is unjust?

Child Neglect and Emotional Abuse

By now a majority of states have expanded their statutory provisions on child abuse to include the category of neglect. A relevant example is a law that was enacted in Massachusetts, where "neglect" was defined as when a child is found to be:

> . . . without necessary and proper physical, educational or moral care and discipline, or is growing up under conditions or circumstances damaging to a child's sound character development, or who lacks proper attention of parent, guardian with care and custody, or custodian, and whose parents or guardian are unwilling, incompetent, or unavailable to provide such care . . . (State of Massachusetts, as quoted by Garinger et al., 1976, p. 177).

The forms of abuse referred to in that definition can be subdivided even further and finer distinctions drawn. For example, California law separates "physical neglect" from "emotional deprivation," as follows:

> Physical neglect is essentially the failure of a parent or caretaker to provide a child with adequate food, shelter, clothing, protection, supervision, and medical and dental care (California Department of Justice, 1978, p. 9).
> Robert M. Mulford, a member of the National Advisory Committee of the Children's Division, American Humane Association, defines emotional deprivation as "the deprivation suffered by children when their parents do not provide the normal experiences producing feelings of being loved, wanted, secure and worthy" (California Department of Justice, 1978, p. 8).

Then, to expand the scope of this law even further, a category labeled "emotional abuse" is identified, referring to any assault upon a child's ego of the kind and degree that may evoke one or more symptoms of distress. Elsewhere in a document which explains the intent of this law, the term "emotional cruelty" is used synonymously.

The foregoing fine points of law were included in this discussion in order to show that this house has many mansions. The informed clinician should find out if the law pertaining to his or her own jurisdiction contains concepts similar to these. If the law is comparable, a therapist should be aware that:

1) These psychological (i.e., nonphysical) forms of abuse, in addition to "physical neglect," are crimes.

2) A clinician is bound by the same Duty to Report his or her reasonable suspicion of mental suffering as is the case with physical abuse.

3) A clinician is granted the same form of legal immunity for making such a report.

4) A clinician is liable to suffer the same penalities if he or she *does not* make this report.

Naturally, in cases of emotional deprivation, neglect or cruelty, the opinion of a mental health professional will be taken quite seriously, and for that reason the therapist's judgment should be governed by judicious restraint.

Sexual Abuse

Most states have laws for the reporting of sexual forms of abuse which are parallel to those described above. Two major categories of sexual abuse that are universally recognized are incest and molestation; these terms are best defined (respectively) as familial and nonfamilial tampering with a child's sexual feelings and needs. Suggested treatment methods for the clinician endeavoring to help victims of these forms of abuse were presented in Chapter 8 and Chapter 9. An additional category that has been a target of legislation in California concerns the exploitation of children for prostitution and/or pornography (California Department of Justice, 1978, pp. 13-16).

As far as reporting requirements are concerned, the guiding principle for a therapist is much the same: When reasonable suspicions arise, report your suspicions. Since sexual abuse against children is a form of assault, it is a crime, just as child-battering and emotional cruelty are crimes. The clinician's report should be made to the same type of agency and in essentially the same format. There are no exceptions to this rule.

Rape and Wife-beating

These sordid examples of man's inhumanity to women have been addressed elsewhere (Chapters 6 and 11), but the legal ramifications for a clinician who attempts to aid the victims should be clarified as well. In theory these victims should take upon themselves the responsibility to report that they have been beaten or raped. But if the woman is also a therapy client, her therapist may feel some responsibility to report as well. The most important guide to conduct in this respect is the clinician's own professional judgment, because there is presently *no* legal compulsion for a psychotherapist to report knowledge of battering or rape to a law enforcement or judicial agency. It appears that legislation protecting children from abuse and assault has far outdistanced legislation protecting adult women from the same sorts of crimes.

A key principle for a therapist to apply in deciding what to do about reporting is the Duty of Care that he or she owes to a client. If the client wishes her therapist to report the crime, that request should probably be granted. Even if the women who has been beaten or raped prefers to conceal the fact that she was assaulted, the clinician may decide that to make a report will eventually be in the client's best interest. That kind of decision may be the most difficult of a clinician's professional life. In making it, a therapist must weigh the knowledge that wife-beating can become an habitual pattern in a marriage and that a rapist who goes unpunished may rape again. This awareness may be counterweighed by the woman's current lack of emotional resources, as well as her vulnerability to renewed humiliation and prolonged psychological pain.

SPECIAL CHARACTERISTICS OF EMERGENCY WORK

Consent for Treatment

The concept of consent for treatment is an idea whose time has come. Even so, implementation has not yet caught up with conceptualization. There are few public agencies in which a thorough, formal consent procedure is conducted prior to the beginning of outpatient psychotherapy. A therapist in private practice who obtains formal consent for treatment before therapy begins is the rare clinician indeed. The reason is that a client, by seeking to enter therapy, has given a kind of implied consent for what is to follow—even though he or she may not have obtained any prior information about what therapy entails. By choosing treatment voluntarily, the client has activated a sort of quasi-legal contract with the clinician. For all subsequent legal purposes, that unwritten (and often largely unstated) form of convenant will suffice, especially because a client is entitled to certain common-law protections.

It is chiefly the inpatient setting, whether public or private, where definite strides have been made to implement consent procedures. In state after state, laws have been passed to grant more civil rights to inpatients, i.e., to shorten their mandatory length of stay in the hospital and to give them better access to legal means by which they can challenge their commitments and secure an early release. In short, involuntary patients have been accorded due process through liberalizing laws. In addition, most psychiatric hospitals have instituted elaborate procedures for informing people of their rights, and many have designated certain personnel to act as patients' advocates in disputes or complaints of unfair treatment, etc. These new developments in hospital care, while long overdue, will be seen by most clinicians as fitting and proper. As part of the larger-scale trend toward humanizing mental health services, heightened awareness of the informed consent issue will play a key role (see Everstine et al., 1980, pp. 831-833).

Civil Liberties in an Emergency

In some qualitative aspects, the work of a psychotherapist who answers emergency calls is unlike any other in the field of mental health. People who come forward in acute distress are often too anxious to make rational choices based upon logical processes. Some do not come forward at all, in the sense that a family member or a policeman will have brought a therapist to them. In their crisis state the clients of ETC are seldom obsessed with their personal or civil rights. They have little concern with the rules, duties, or legal requirements that govern mental health professionals. They are simply *inside* their problems. For that reason it is the clinician who must take initiative to make sure that rights are safeguarded while, at the same time, care is being given.

It is important to consider further the unique circumstances which characterize an emergency: There is no time for rumination or reflection. There is scant opportunity for conducting a discussion on personal freedom or privacy or the confidentiality of information. Even giving a "Miranda warning," such as a policeman reads to a suspect who has been apprehended, could seem hopelessly out of place in an urgent context such as this. A client seeks relief from distress. Or, if someone else has summoned the emergency team, that person wants something to be done at once. The exigencies of the moment cry out for action instead of platitudes, intervention before *politesse*.

When a person who is experiencing a crisis telephones a "hot line" or "suicide prevention" number, he or she can merely give a first name to the person who answers and thus keep a measure of control over the confidentiality of his or her statements. By contrast, when an emergency therapist arrives at the scene of a crisis, much confidentiality has already been breached, and once the clinician has met with family members in the living room or kitchen of their home, little privacy remains. As implied above, obtaining informed consent for treatment may be a luxury that neither client nor therapist can afford. The consent process, if it is to occur, may need to be deferred until a second visit is being planned or until the second visit begins. Suffice it to say that ETC routinely carries out an elaborate system of obtaining consent, contracting to provide services, obtaining a release for exchange of information, and determining whether or not a fee should be charged for follow-up visits—as befits the Center's role as a non-profit corporation receiving public funds. The relevant point in this context is that these procedures can seldom be completed during an initial visit. And the crass introduction of any of them during the course of a crisis situation may be the worst form of intrusion upon privacy.

There are times when a therapist can be too cautious, too careful, and too fearful of being sued for malpractice. There are times when the emotions of a person in crisis may be charged with a force as dangerous as a fallen power line, when the glass of fear is filled to overflowing and the nightmare will not end. Don't call a lawyer. Remember that as a clinician you have a Duty of Care, and if you do your best the common law will see you through.

REFERENCES

Addington v. Texas, 47 U.S.L.W. 4473 (1979), 3 MDLR 164.

California Department of Justice: Child abuse: The Problem of the Abused and Neglected Child. Sacramento: Crime Prevention Unit, Office of the Attorney General, Information Pamphlet No. 8, 1978.

Coyne, J. C. and Widiger, T. A. Toward a participatory model of psychotherapy. Professional Psychology, 9(4):700-710, 1978.

Everstine, L., Everstine, D. S., Heymann, G. M., True, R. H., Frey, D. H., Johnson, H. G., and Seiden, R. H. Privacy and confidentiality in psychotherapy. American Psychologist, 35:828-840, 1980.

Fraser, B. G. The court's role. In B. D. Schmitt (Ed.), The Child Protection Team Handbook. New York: Garland STPM Press, 207-219, 1978.

Garinger, G., Brant, R. T., and Brant, J. Protecting children and families from abuse. In G. P. Koocher (Ed.), Children's Rights and the Mental Health Profession. New York: John Wiley & Sons, 1976, pp. 171-179.

Kazan, S. Psychotherapy and the law: The duty to warn. American Psychologist, 36:914 (Comment), 1981.

Kempe, C. H., Silverman, F. N., Steele, B. S., Droegemuller, W., and Silver, H. K. The battered child syndrome. Journal of the American Medical Association, 181:17-24, 1962.

Kohlman, R. J. Malpractice liability for failing to report child abuse. The Western Journal of Medicine, 121(3):244-248, 1974.

McIntosh v. Milano, 403 A. 2d 500 (N. J. Super. Ct., 1979).

Megargee, E. I. The prediction of dangerous behavior. Criminal Justice and Behavior, 3:3-22, 1976.

Monahan, J. The prediction of violence. In D. Chappell and J. Monahan (Eds.), Violence and Criminal Justice. Lexington, KY: D.C. Heath, 1975.

Schmitt, B. D. Introduction. In B. D. Schmitt (Ed.), The Child Protection Team Handbook. New York: Garland STPM Press, 1-4, 1978a.

Schmitt, B. D. The physician's evaluation. In B. D. Schmitt (Ed.), The Child Protection Team Handbook. New York: Garland STPM Press, 39-62, 1978b.

Shah, S. A. Dangerousness: Conceptual, prediction and public policy issues. In J. R. Hays, T.

CLINICAL ETHICS AND LEGAL RESPONSIBILITIES

K. Roberts, and K. S. Solway, (Eds.), *Violence and the Violent Individual*. New York: SP Medical & Scientific Books, 1981.

Shea, T. E. Legal standard of care for psychiatrists and psychologists. *Western States University Law Review*, 6(1):71–99, 1978.

State of California Penal Code: Part 4, Title 1, Chapter 2, Article 2.5, Sections 1165–1172, 1174. Revised 1981.

Tarasoff v. Regents of the University of California: 17 Cal. 3d 425, 131 *Cal. Rptr.* 14, 551 P. 2d 334, 1976.

Thompson v. County of Alameda, 27 Cal. 3d 741, 167 *Cal. Rptr.* 70, 1980.

BIBLIOGRAPHY

1) *The Mental Disability Law Reporter*, published bi-monthly by the Mental Disability Legal Resources Center of the American Bar Association (1800 M Street, N.W.; Washington, D. C. 20036);

2) *The Mental Health Court Digest*, published monthly by the Juridical Digests Institute (1850 Broadway, New York, N.Y. 10023);

3) *Legal Aspects of Medical Practice*, published monthly by the American College of Legal Medicine;

4) The *Law Reporter* journal (or equivalent title) which is published in each state, in most cases by the State Bar Association;

5) The *Law Review* or *Law Journal* (published by virtually every law school) that is available in each state or locality;

6) The Ethics Committee (or equivalent) of each State Psychological Association, local chapter of the National Association of Social Workers, County Medical Society, etc.;

7) The Ethical Standards Review Committee (or equivalent) of your national professional association.

Index

253